BUTCH MARTIN
From the Dam to the World Stage

Del Gingrich

Canadian Cataloguing in Publication Data

Gingrich, Del
Butch Martin - From the Dam to the World Stage

Includes bibliographical references.
ISBN 978 0 981 3784 0 4

1st edition, 2014

Printed in Region of Waterloo by St. Jacobs Printery Ltd.

Editor: Susan Fish
Cover design by Ray Charbonneau
Layout by Tim Kohlmetz

Paper: Creator Silk Text White, 70 lb.,
        Stirling Dull Cover White, 12 pt.

Typeface: Avenir

Bindery: Express Bind Inc.

FLOYD "BUTCH" MARTIN

BRONZE MEDAL - VII WINTER OLYMPIC GAMES

SILVER MEDAL - VIII WINTER OLYMPIC GAMES

CAMBRIDGE SPORTS HALL OF FAME AS A GALT TERRIER - 1997

SILVER MEDAL - IIHF WORLD CHAMPIONSHIP - 1962

MEMBER OF CANADA'S ALL-OLYMPIC TEAM (AMATEUR)

CANADIAN OLD TIMERS HOCKEY HALL OF FAME - 1989

WATERLOO COUNTY HALL OF FAME - 1990

WATERLOO WALL OF FAME - 2007

CONTENTS

PROLOGUE

Before you open the pages of this wonderful tribute to my father, I'd like to pay homage to the other special man involved in the creation of this book, its author Del Gingrich. My name is Kelly Martin. My children, Paul and Kristie Martin, and I are Butch's immediate family. Yet we haven't been alive long enough to share in Dad's most memorable moments. When Del approached me with the concept of writing a book on Butch's life, a prayer was answered. Throughout my life I've been privileged to listen to stories told by family, friends, and complete strangers about the ways in which Dad's life has touched and affected others' lives. Now, thanks to Del, we have the opportunity to keep these stories alive forever. It gives me great pleasure to see this project come to life. I wish to thank Del and all those who took the time to contribute to this book. On behalf of Butch's family and friends, you have helped to make the Martin family dream become a reality. We hope you enjoy it as much as we have.

Kelly, Paul, and Kristie Martin

INTRODUCTION

If I were restricted to only one more book for my library, I wish I could choose the story of my father's life.

My father, Ozias Gingrich, was a humble, quiet man who briefly owned a farm, then worked at a feed mill for most of his adult life. His large family felt his support and care. In his own way he assured us that we were loved.

Like each of us, he had a unique story but it's one about which I know comparatively little and that my children have only hints about. My grandchildren will not likely know much more than his name.

I wish I could hand them each the story of Dad which would give them insights into their roots and some things about him that have shaped their lives.

Floyd "Butch" Martin is also a father and grandfather. Go to any library in Ontario and you'll find information about his life in an abundance of newspaper and magazine articles. Check websites about the Olympic Games, the World Hockey Championships, the Allan Cup and various Ontario Hockey Association teams and you'll see Butch's name, usually accompanied by a write-up. Talk to hockey people who've been around for a while and they'll tell you they saw him play hockey at a highly competitive level.

I have been given the opportunity to tell some of the story of my father's nephew, my cousin, Floyd "Butch" Martin. I feel greatly privileged and deeply honored to do so. I hope that by reading this account, his daughter Kelly and grandchildren, Paul and Kristie, will understand more completely why their father and grandfather has been so highly and widely acclaimed as an outstanding athlete and man.

I hope you will too.

Ab Martin, a friend since we were young children, was also an outstanding athlete. His career in hockey had some similarities to that of Butch. Ab has made Woolwich his home throughout his life. He and Butch were teammates in hockey and fastball, where each excelled. It's an honor to include Ab's story in this account.

When Phyllis Hoffman, Butch's niece, was in elementary school, she handed her teacher a story: "The Biography of Floyd (Butch) Martin." In it she said that Floyd was bored rather than excited at the first hockey game he attended. Phyllis earned an A for her project but neither schoolgirl Phyllis nor her uncle Butch could have imagined the fame he'd earn on hockey's international stage in the years ahead.

I'm grateful to Kelly Martin for her valuable contributions to this book, including personal anecdotes that could only be provided by a daughter's experience with a father she loves dearly. I'll let Kelly tell a bit of her story here:

No matter what it was, Butch missed nothing when it came to my son Paul and hockey. One day, Paul had a hockey practice at the Waterloo Recreation Centre. We took our usual place behind the top row of seats along the walking track. As I watched the walkers, I noticed an elderly gentleman plodding away with his wife. It seemed as though they were watching us. After a few more laps, changing lanes as they went, they began to get closer. He finally stopped. "Excuse me sir, he said to my dad. "Are you Butch Martin?" My father replied that he was. The man's eyes lit up as he explained that he and his wife had watched Dad play for years, and they had been members of the Dutchmen Booster Club. He recited stories of my dad's winning moves and selfless plays. According to him, my dad was the best hockey player Kitchener had produced. He said, "I'm sorry Butch. I hate to ask this.

Could I have your autograph?" A smile came over Butch's face and a tear came to my eyes. "My only problem is I didn't expect to meet my hero today, and I don't have a pen or paper." That was my cue. I rifled through my purse and immediately came up with both. The autograph was personalized and I watched the man as he returned to his wife. He was beaming like he was a young man again. I looked at my dad. His shoulders were back, and he too was a young man again.

Over the years Kelly and her twin children have proudly read many news reports and interviews that featured Butch.

I should also note that I have chosen to tell some of Butch's story using fictionalized characters. I think you will know when you get to that part of the story. Be assured that though the narrator may be fictional, the story is true.

How did Butch react to the suggestion of his story being published? "Yeah, we could do that," was his succinct reply.

Fans, friends, and acquaintances responded with enthusiasm to the idea—"It's about time!" "Thanks for doing this." "I've got a scrapbook filled with clippings about Butch." "Why don't you speak to Ab or Wayne or Neil or Gordie or Bill or Bush or Bill?" "Butch Martin, isn't he the guy who could have played in the National Hockey League?"

Larry Lynch, highly esteemed field manager of Canadian teams who've appeared in fifteen International Softball Congress World Tournaments offered his statement of support: "I am so happy someone is finally doing something on Butch Martin. He was a tremendous athlete. And while he has received some acknowledgement over the years, it seems to me a person of such talent should be known and remembered by all sports fans from our community."

Not many Canadian hockey players, at any level, have played more hockey games on the international stage than Butch. And few have done it with as little public recognition.

These pages also provide an opportunity for some of us to recognize Butch's contributions to our lives as teenagers and young adults. Butch and his brothers introduced us to participation in competitive sports. They also dramatically helped broaden and enrich our somewhat limited worldview. We've never forgotten those memorable initiations but we've neglected to say "Thank you." Hopefully this will be a start.

Butch was the one of the few of our small, closely knit community to dare to venture out into playing hockey beyond the local, frozen dam where unorganized shinny was the game of a frosty, winter day.

Butch and his older brothers, Elmer and Willard (Dick), introduced us teenaged rural and small-town boys to what it meant to be part of a hockey or softball team.

They also took a few of us, wide-eyed, to attend professional sporting events that we'd otherwise only dream about; like our first NHL games at Maple Leaf Gardens. We hustled up the stairs to claim a spot standing behind the end reds to watch the Leafs take on the Canadiens or the Rangers.

Then thanks to Butch and Dick, on October 8, 1956, we spent a splendid Thanksgiving Monday afternoon at Toronto's Varsity Stadium taking in our first Canadian Football League game where Coach Jim Trimble's Tiger-Cats defeated the home-town Argos 34-29.

For us, it was the end of a memorable day.

For Butch, as you will discover, 1956 had been a memorable year.

During part of his great career, in the 1950's, Butch was a member of the Kitchener-Waterloo Dutchmen Hockey Club, an OHA Senior A team. They played in an elite league, made up of some of the best amateur hockey players in Canada. Some Senior A graduates went on to enjoy successful NHL careers while other Senior A players were former NHL players who returned to play in the Senior A league, often for personal reasons. For most, the NHL lay just beyond their grasps: there were only six NHL teams in 1956, and only 105 players.

The Dutchmen had a large and enthusiastic following in Waterloo County, only second to the Toronto Maple Leafs. Their players had a major presence in the community. Hockey heroes in Kitchener (with names like Martin, Laufman, Hurley and Rope) were a part of us. We saw them on the streets, sat beside them at church, or met them while shopping with their families at local stores.

On winter Saturday nights, our little group of teenagers from the rural area of Woolwich Township faithfully gathered under the big clock at the North end of the Kitchener Auditorium, to watch Butch play.

Though we had little awareness of the fact, we were staying faithful to our non-conformist Mennonite tradition. Implicitly, in those days, we knew that we should remain on the periphery of many popular mainstream social functions; present, but not fully engaged. Our little isolated group, under the clock, symbolically, stood "appropriately" separate from the cheering crowd. None of our parents had seen a Dutchmen game. Their social activities were church-related events and Sunday afternoon visiting.

Our guy Butch, the one who came from our place, who grew up in a family with values like our families, had "Martin" sewn on the back of his sweater. As we grasped our first handfuls of buttered popcorn or licked the overflowing mustard from our hotdogs, we felt a freedom that was refreshing and embracing. Unlike our fathers, who grew up in even more restrictive families than ours, we were checking out what they described as "worldly things"—like watching Butch and the Dutchmen compete.

We loved the way Butch played hockey but we admired and idolized him for the steps he'd taken into a sports culture about which we knew little. Watching him play allowed us to dare to dream, to consider stepping into a world filled with opportunities beyond what we thought our simple, agrarian backgrounds would allow. He was our hero. For some of us, he was also our relative.

Butch really enjoyed playing hockey. Because of his excellence at playing the game, he came face to face with some very important, life-changing decisions.

On a blustery winter day in 1935, the Martin family answered a persistent knock on the side door of their Floradale home. When it was opened, the children were curious about the stranger who stood outside, a man who had a rather tired and worn appearance. The man had just stepped off the train that had transported him from Guernsey, Saskatchewan. He'd left his wife and four young sons behind, hoping to bring them east when he could pay their fare and had found a home for them. He'd reluctantly and sadly walked away from his once prosperous farm, like thousands of other hardworking Saskatchewan farmers of the depressing 1930s who were finally defeated by the devastation of the sandstorms that had blown their crops away.

The Saskatchewan farmers had looked with hope at what proved to be rainless clouds. They'd stared with unbelief, wiping away tears, as starving cattle finally succumbed. Their children, tired from the trudge, arrived home from school, looking like so many coal-miners. Their wives and mothers diligently and repeatedly cleared the sand from the furniture and beds.

Sand, an invasive, detested intruder, played havoc with young farm families, already struggling to provide the essentials of life. Wooden basement shelves, once bending from the weight of canned foods, were almost empty. Darkness had enveloped what was once sunshine. Hope was collapsing into despair.

Urgent action was required. Some beleaguered families made their way to British Columbia or the Peace River District in northern Alberta to begin homesteading. They begged for food at local farmhouses as they slowly but persistently made their way. Others, like this stranger, headed east.

The Martin children gathered around, and looked on as their visitor sat down to a welcome meal of homemade tomato soup, and summer sausage sandwiches on bread still warm from the oven. The Martin children's mother Blendina served food to this man who was much more than an acquaintance.

The desperate man, seeking refuge with the Martin family, was my father, Ozias. He'd walked away from his once prosperous Guernsey farm. Blendina was my father's sister. Dad had only a meagre ten dollars in his pocket, and a small satchel with extra clothing. He had decided that the best chance for his family was to come to Woolwich Township in Ontario where all his siblings resided. He'd left for the West as a young farmhand in his early twenties, supporting himself by working on farms along the way.

He and Blendina had been raised on an Old Order Mennonite farm about five minutes by car from where he now sat at a large, wooden kitchen table, enjoying his sister's comforting food. Reluctantly he began to unwrap the mysteries that seemed to envelop him.

Their conversation in the Martin home was in Pennsylvania German, the language of the Mennonite community.

Dad hoped beyond hope that Blendina and her husband Seranus could help him. They knew of the devastation in Saskatchewan. With eight children of their own, they clearly understood the urgency of helping out their close relatives in times of uncertainty and hardship.

My uncle gave my dad employment at his business, the S. S. Martin Sawmill. A small, unfurnished vacant house was located on the property. Seranus generously offered it as a home for my father and his family.

Some time later, with hope in her heart, my mother boarded a train from Guernsey with her four restless sons, my older brothers. They were accompanied by a large bag, brimming with sandwiches. She called the experience her honeymoon trip, a journey she hoped was a new beginning, a chance for a fresh start. On their arrival in Floradale, my mother and brothers were warmly embraced by relatives they had never met before but to whom they would be forever grateful. They settled into their small house, which was sparsely furnished but overflowing with love. My oldest sister was born in that house.

My two remaining brothers remember the long train ride and living in the house provided so generously by their aunt and uncle. To this day, they travel to Floradale, as I do, to look at the little house. It's a humble edifice to the love of a sister for her brother and his needy and growing young family.

More than seven decades later, on a 2009 winter Saturday afternoon, Butch entered the Elmira Memorial Arena with Paul, his grandson. Both were carrying their hockey equipment. The "old barn" of an arena, soon to be demolished, was abuzz with an enthusiastic group playing a spirited but friendly hockey game. Every player was a member of one of the many Mennonite communities in the township of Woolwich: there were Baumans, Brubachers, Clemmers, Webers, Hursts, Lichtis and Martins among them. Butch and Paul would play in the game that followed.

The arena's frosted walls were decorated with brightly colored pictures of hockey activities, created by children in the township's schools. Each had printed on it somewhere, the words "Woolwich is Hockeyville."

Former Toronto Maple Leaf, Steve "Stumpy" Thomas was on hand. So was Cassie Campbell, twice captain of Canada's national women's hockey team. This was all part of the Kraft Hockeyville Competition where, based on the greatest number of votes, a Canadian community would officially become Hockeyville for the year. Woolwich had made it to 2009's final five.

The entire township was swept up in the whirlwind of special hockey activities. The local library became "Hockeyville Reading Room" while the police headquarters was deemed to be "Hockeyville Penalty Box." The hub of activities took place in Elmira, inside an arena gasping its last breath.

Decades earlier an Ontario Minor Hockey executive had called Elmira "the biggest little hockey town on earth" because of Elmira's repeated Ontario minor hockey championships.

The Elmira (now Woolwich) Minor Hockey organization had some impressive graduates. Brothers Rod and Ric Seiling grew up across the street from the arena. Darryl Sittler's father was a milkman in St. Jacobs. The late Dan Snyder was an Elmira boy. Cam Stewart's home was a short distance away in Conestoga. Dennis Wideman, the youngest of three brothers, lived in rural Woolwich, just off New Jerusalem Road. Recently retired from hockey, Elmira's Jamie Wright brought home a gold medal in 1996 as a member of Canada's national Junior Team. All played in the NHL.

Butch could have been one of them.

But on that Saturday of the winter of 2009, he was doing something that he'd always enjoyed—playing hockey in his home community. He'd sat in the same place, put on his equipment, taped his stick and tightened the laces on his skates many, many times. Now, in his eighty-first year, it took a little longer.

At age twenty-two, he had sat there among his hometown buddies, preparing for a game that would bring a championship to Elmira. The place was packed that night.

The fun game in which Butch and his grandson participated had an interesting feature, something that could only happen in Woolwich Township. Even before the first puck was dropped, all present knew that the winner of the face-off would be a Martin; all goals scored, assists given and unlikely penalties called would be done so by Martins. Had there been a three-star selection, each would have had the Martin surname. Every participant had "Martin" sewn on the back of their sweaters. You get the picture. It was the "Martin Hour," one of the fun games in an uninterrupted twenty-four hours of hockey. It hadn't been a formidable task to find enough Martin folks in Woolwich to fill both players' benches to overflowing. They were a grand mixture of cousins, uncles and aunts, nephews and nieces. And, in at least one instance, a granddad and his grandson.

I didn't see Butch play that day. But reports on the game indicated there was a buzz among the fans when he took to the ice. Elmira businessman Ron Martin took part in the game because he knew that Butch, his former Elmira Polar King Old Timers teammate would be there.

The oldest man on the ice took it easy. He was enjoying himself. Yet, one suspected that with a little effort he could have deftly made his way through the opposition and picked a top corner. But then, amid his many accomplishments and honors, bringing purposeful attention to himself had never been that man's style, starting from the first time he held a hockey stick.

When my son was a child, he asked me if there was anybody famous in our family. I said, "Let me tell you about your cousin Butch."

I'VE ONLY JUST BEGUN

In 2014, Bonnie Lou Martin is the most celebrated person in the tiny village of Floradale. She is the always smiling and welcoming owner of Bonnie Lou's Lunch at the corner of Ruggle's Road and Floradale Road. In 2009 she bought the place from the Ruggle family. They'd been owners of Ruggle's General Store since the late 1800s. Bonnie Lou left some major features of the former store pretty well untouched. That enhanced its unique ambience and kept memories of the village's past alive.

On the last Tuesday of each month, folks start arriving early at Bonnie Lou's. That's the morning that Bonnie Lou and her staff serve their famous, one-of-a-kind head-cheese breakfast. Or as they say in rural Woolwich "Kopf Kase Frühstück."

Bonnie Lou also sells a thin booklet entitled "Floradale Then and Now." One of the brief stories in this booklet describes SS#5, the two-room school built for five thousand dollars in 1907. "Famous Graduates" listed in the booklet include Butch Martin and Cole Bowman.

If we imagined the village's boundaries to be modestly extended, we could include other famous residents.

Joyce and Graham Gladwell live nearby. In 2014, their Malcolm, then a resident of New York City, launched his newest bestseller book David and Goliath at Floradale Mennonite Church—the congregation of which the Seranus Martin family was a part.

Fifteen minutes away by horse and buggy, over on the Sixth Line of Peel, is a small school that Lloyd and Bonnie Lichti's daughter, Angela attended. In 2004 Angela was the starting shortstop on Canada's Women's Fastball Team. They competed for their country at the XXVIII Summer Olympic Games in Athens, Greece.

On a summer day in 1947, Joseph Ott, a tailor and then owner of Floradale General Store, made a morning coat for William Lyon Mackenzie King. When Mr. King became Canada's Prime Minister, he visited the small, rural village to meet his tailor and a group of wide-eyed school children.

When one enters Bonnie Lou's place, the dining experience includes flavorful ham and potato soup, and sumptuous fresh strawberry pie. But given the relics and memorabilia, it's also morphed into Floradale's unofficial museum.

In 1926, forty-five years after the construction of the West Montrose Kissing Bridge, Seranus and Blendina Martin lived on a farm, close to the village of West Montrose. One frightful night a tumultuous wind storm played havoc with the wooded area of their property. They hired the owner of a Floradale portable sawmill to clear the accumulation of fallen trees and branches.

The portable sawmill operation got Seranus' attention. After making some inquiries, he felt there could be a future for his family in the sawmill business. His offer to purchase the sawmill in Floradale was accepted by its owner, Daniel Bowman. Daniel's grandson Cole and Seranus' son Floyd would craft a relationship that lasted a lifetime.

The Martin family made a major decision to leave the farm. Seranus purchased and remodeled a former hotel, built in 1871. Its location was less than a minute's walk from Ruggle's General Store (now Bonnie Lou's Lunch). It became their new home. Seranus and Blendina needed a big house as they had a large family, eventually becoming parents of eight children: Elmer, Leah, Naomi, Willard, Lucinda, Valina, Viola and Floyd (who was born in their home in 1929).

When they were old enough to attend school, Floyd and his buddy

Cole walked along Floradale Road across the bridge over the local dam and to their school at the top of the hill just beyond the north edge of the village.

Mrs. Ziegler, their teacher, was pleased when the children in her junior room did well. She loved their imaginative stories, the overflowing joy with which they sang, and the smiles when she gave then praise.

But there was something really special about the grade four Bowman boy, Cole. Cole seemed to doodle a lot, even at times when he should have been paying attention to his times tables. The Valentine's card he creatively designed for her was simply wonderful! She had experienced a few gifted children at Floradale and it became increasingly obvious that she had such a child in her fourth grade class.

The Bowman family lived directly behind the Martin family's residence. In winter, after their teacher, or Mr. Lawson, from the senior room, dismissed the classes, the two chums raced home to put on their skates and head for the frozen dam, just across the street, and down an embankment from Floyd's home. Cole and Floyd loved to skate! On weekend afternoons the dam was the scene of spirited games of shinny, with a virtual multitude of participants.

Butch recalled, "Everyone came to the dam on weekends. It wasn't organized hockey. My brother was the best player on the team and I figured if I followed him and he got checked, I could pick up the puck and get a couple of goals."

But playing on the dam in a free and unrestricted kind of way also helped him to develop his skating and puck-handling skills. It was with his buddies on the dam that Butch also developed the skill and strength to persistently maintain possession of the puck, something with which he was identified throughout his career.

Floradale was a tiny, close-knit community and the shinny-playing kids got to know each other well. Their familiarity was such that they gave each other nicknames. Legend has it that because Floyd was the youngest of the Martin kids he'd be called "Babe." Elmer, Floyd's oldest brother, was a quiet boy but he felt he had to rescue his youngest brother and suggested, then insisted, "Babe" be changed to "Butch."

Willard, the middle of the three Martin boys, was also the recipient of a nickname. In the Pennsylvania German dialect, the language spoken in the homes of most of the shinny players, the word for thick is "dick" or "dicht." Willard was nick-named "Dick." As a big guy, the name seemed appropriate. Over the years, Butch and Dick played a lot of hockey together, in places far removed from the village's outdoor "rink."

In his senior years, Butch received a letter from a former Floradale resident relating how she clearly remembered seeing him playing hockey on the dam when he was still a child with no hint of the success he'd have in the game he loved.

Butch believes that if his older brother Elmer had gotten off the farm a few years earlier and had had the opportunity to join a team as a youngster, he too would have developed into an excellent hockey player. Speaking at Elmer's funeral, many decades later, Butch commented that throughout his hockey career, when he'd look into the stands during warm-up, Elmer was always there.

With eight active children, Blendina was a busy woman but she made room for a young, single man as a boarder. Cecil Capling was an enterprising young man. He built a garage across the street from Ruggle's General Store. The sign in front of his garage had printed on it the words: Red Indian Motor Oil. The logo on his gas pump was Marathon Blue. Once married, Cecil built a house next to the garage. He left Blendina's home and delectable cooking, but the Martin family had gained a friend.

Cecil Capling's garage became a meeting place. Elmer and Dick played cards there some evenings. On the occasional Saturday night they brought young Butch along to listen to the Leafs games on radio. Foster Hewitt's Hockey Night in Canada started at 9:00, about half-way through the second period. Young Butch never dreamed about playing in the NHL; he just loved playing hockey with his friends. Reliable sources had it, however, that he could identify an NHL player on a O-Pee-Chee hockey card as soon as it was laid on Cecil's well-worn, oil-stained work bench.

The garage, with new ownership and new logos on its signs remained in 2014: it became known as Floradale Garage. Sometimes the guys who worked in the garage crossed Floradale Road to partake of Bonnie Lou's delicious and satisfying offerings.

Starting at age six, Butch was the energetic and inquisitive stick-boy for the Floradale Indians Hockey Club. Elmer and Dick were members of the team. They played in the North Waterloo Rural independent Hockey League. The Indians' coach, Lorne Staulbaum, allowed Butch to skate with them during their warm-ups. Occasionally, he even tried to get a few pucks past Abbie Frey, the Indians' goalie.

The Indians played on natural ice in the Elmira Arena, an all-wooden structure purchased by Fred "Fritz" Rudow in 1929.

During the games Butch sat quietly and paid attention. Early on he recognized that it was tough for the other team to score if they couldn't get the puck away from you. He saw that the really good players, like his brother Elmer, passed the puck right onto the sticks of their teammates. Butch figured that maybe this game of hockey was a bit like school. You needed to skate, shoot and pass, but you also had to think.

One evening Butch received a gentle pat on his head as he was coming off the ice from the warm-up. The friendly touch was accompanied by a familiar sounding voice: "Young man, you might be training for the Toronto Maple Leafs in the future." Mr. Lawson, his teacher, had taken time from writing comments on report cards to attend a game.

During the rink's busy years, Ab Seiling, grandfather of Region of Waterloo Chair Ken Seiling, gathered the hopeful kids who were waiting to go into a game, and said to the owner, "I'll pay, Fritz. How much for the lot of them?"

Fritz had vacillated about opening the rink that 1947 season. It hadn't generated much income, and it was badly in need of repairs. That winter the roof of the rink collapsed, buckling due to a build-up of snow. It happened at 10:15 p.m., so fortunately no one was in the building.

At 7:30 the next morning, over coffee at downtown Elmira's Kares Café, the town's police chief, Harry Jarvis, told William Brown, the local tailor, and grocery store owner, Noah Brubacher, "It's the most fortunate affair this town has ever experienced in many a day." Elmira's hockey teams and the Floradale Indians had a problem: their home rink was flattened.

The Indians' road trips were to St. Jacobs, St. Clements, and Linwood, all with natural ice and outdoor rinks. St. Clements' rink was situated next to the Catholic Church. In a kindly, considerate gesture, the priest opened its doors so fans could warm up between periods of games. He commented in jest that they didn't have to be a Catholic to be allowed inside.

The Floradale Indians' name was revived and a new team formed in 1972. None of Seranus Martin's sons was a member. The team members came from within a ten-mile radius of the village, following the league's rules. The Indians were entered into the OHA Intermediate D division, and played for three seasons. On the night they won the grand championship, the guys got back to Floradale at 1:00 a.m. in the bitter cold of a February morning. The champs clung to the sides of the village fire truck as the chief drove them through the quiet, peaceful streets. Lights suddenly turned on in some villagers' homes. Rubbing their eyes, children curiously peeked through windows, roused from the calmness of their slumber. Their hockey team was back in town! And they were champions!

Elmira didn't have a minor hockey system in 1943, but they had a postmaster who was a respected and wise hockey enthusiast. Popular and personable O. W. Mike Weichel was a native of Elmira, and had been a very talented hockey and baseball player. He had been within reach of a professional career but while serving in the Canadian military in World War I, he had had one leg destroyed. Afterwards he devoted his time to the administrative side of sports. That included serving twenty years on the executive of the Ontario Minor Hockey

Association. His two sons, Ross and Earl, encouraged their dad to get a group of local boys together to form a team. Butch joined the team for the first time at age fourteen They competed against other centers in the juvenile category, a grouping with players at least two years older than Butch. Butch's brother Dick drove him to practices and games. He also was the referee for many of the Elmira team's games.

In future years Butch and Mike would find themselves in the same photographs of Elmira's championship hockey teams.

In a playoff series against the Preston team, Butch, and the Weichel brothers were uncharacteristically inept in finding scoring opportunities. Coach Weichel had no suggestions that were effective. Their own goalie was unusually busy. The situation was different from any other they'd faced. Their nemesis had a name—Barry Sullivan. The Elmira guys hadn't seen him previously because he'd been playing for his Junior A team. That unusual arrangement was allowed during those years. (If this had happened in 2014, it would have been like Kitchener Ranger Justin Bailey playing against the Woolwich Minor Midget team. One could predict the results.)

Transporting young hockey players to away games, in some situations, had significant financial repercussions during Butch's minor hockey years.

On February of 1943, Elmira's weekly newspaper, The Signet, carried the headline: "Gasoline Rationing Goes Into Effect on April 15." Until the end of March 1944, each owner of a passenger car would be issued forty coupons for the purchase of gasoline. That amounted to 2160 miles of driving. For some minor hockey teams it became an issue that could only be resolved by the goodwill of the community. Reportedly one Elmira team had an OMHA playoff series with Ilderton, a community close to London. Some generous Elmira car owners didn't have boys on the team, but allowed their cars to be driven and their gas to be used in order that the entire team could make the games. When funds were available, Elmira's Recreation Council, which sponsored the minor teams, paid five cents a mile to the drivers.

Butch was a very busy hockey player in his mid-teens. One season he played for a midget team, two teams in the juvenile age group and two teams in adult rural leagues. He says, "You might guess that I didn't make it to all the games."

Butch and a few of his Elmira hockey buddies took the next step in their hockey development. Together, with the help of older siblings who drove them, they made their way to Waterloo. The city's Junior B Raiters (later known as the Siskins) team was looking for players.

BREAKING AWAY
HOCKEY BEYOND THE DAM

In the fall of 1946, Butch skated out for the opening face-off with the Waterloo Raiters Junior B hockey team. His Elmira friend, Eugene Miller, immensely talented, had also made the team. It was a scheduled home game, but Waterloo, like many municipalities, didn't have an arena and artificial ice pads were rare commodities. For the 1946-47 season, the Raiters' home games were played in Preston.

Coach Leo Schmalz's team played twelve season games. Their record was one win, ten losses and a tie. Schmalz had a young team, so their eighth-place finish was something to build on for the next season. Their new home, the Waterloo Memorial Arena would open in February of 1947.

In the 1947-48 season, the team had new surroundings and a new name, the Waterloo Tiger Cubs. They ended the season with five more wins than the previous one. They scored sixty-one goals and allowed the same number. It was good for fifth place.

Dick and Elmer took in all the Waterloo Junior B games. They were astute observers and saw how their younger brother was developing as a hockey player—and he played like he loved the game! The Martin brothers' enthusiasm spilled over at home and Butch's sisters began taking an interest and attending some of his games.

There was talk in the Woolwich community about Seranus and Blendina's youngest child—"der jüngste"—and his hockey among some of his aunts and cousins who were invited to one of chatty Aunt Minerva's quiltings or among male relatives working with the threshing crew at Uncle Edwin's farm. Talk around the Martin family supper table, laden with their mother's platters of pork sausage, creamed potatoes and vanilla pie was often sports related but only after a silent prayer of thanksgiving.

Seranus didn't say a great deal, but he was a very good listener. He made the occasional inquiry about Butch and his hockey. Elmer and Dick filled him in on the details.

Seranus was one of hundreds of Martins in Woolwich Township. There were likely even a few dozen Martins whose first name was Seranus. So they were given nicknames like Brainy Seranus, Big Seranus, Henry's Seranus and Carpenter Seranus. Butch's dad was likely identified as Sawmill Seranus in some quarters but in his loving family, he was Pop.

Kelly Martin says: Pop didn't see Floyd play often. I was told a story of Dad playing for the Waterloo Raiters at a very young age. At the time, my uncle Elmer had taken the role of "father figure" to his brother during his hockey career, becoming a constant fixture in the stands. One day Elmer decided to bring Pop down to see his youngest son play. They sat at the top of the Waterloo Barn to have a good view of the entire game. When the buzzer went signaling the first period was over, Pop stood and said, "Well, he played a great game but I would like to go home." Elmer was very surprised and informed his father that two more periods remained to be played. Pop didn't wait to talk to Floyd after the game. He was found sitting, drinking coffee in his usual place at the table, when Floyd returned home. Pop stood, nodded, and said, "You did very well today, son." Then he shook Dad's hand. I now understand that was the Mennonite way. But that one handshake meant the world to my dad. I didn't get to know my grandfather, as he passed away after putting me to bed when I was ten months old. Pop had been very excited at the prospect of his youngest son having a child. He was heard to say that he was "gonna spoil that child." Time didn't allow for that. But I truly believe that his son became a great father because of the example he had had.

Unlike Pop Martin, there were those in the Mennonite community who felt Butch's playing for the Raiters was not what one of their young men should be doing. Competitive sports of any kind, some felt, were to be left to the world "out there." Social activities in the Mennonite way, for the most part, were held under the auspices of the church. Spending too much time engaged in "unproductive sports activities" would surely lead to gradually drifting away from biblical principles and from their Mennonite congregations. The fact that the sport was played in an urban area, and was run by non-Mennonite folks cast a further shadow. There would be many temptations for a young person and that could lead to "heaven knows what."

Given the agrarian nature of their work in the 1940s, there was little time available anyway for Mennonite youth to engage in "those" types of activities. The young people at Floradale Mennonite, like other Mennonite young people, gathered for activities like Literary Society meetings and singing for shut-ins. In the week following a wedding, they'd get together for a social, where crokinole games were played and where young men bid for the privilege of sharing lunch with the young woman who'd prepared it and brought it, decoratively wrapped for the special occasion.

On a frigid weekend afternoons, dressed in winter attire and relishing the experience with other Mennonite youth, they'd have skating parties on the frozen Floradale dam. Buttered popcorn, rice krispie squares, and hot chocolate awaited them at the Martin home just up the embankment, and across Ruggle's Road. Blendina, or "Mrs. Seranus" as her community knew her, was delighted to have the young people fill her home and have a good time in an environment that was far removed from the temptations of the "world."

For the Mennonite community, their church was a sacred place of worship. But it also was the hub of an assortment of social interactions. It was an inexpensive date on a Sunday evening; a concert hall for an acapella Mennonite College choir from Indiana or Virginia; and the scene of one's initial exposure to life in Africa or South America. Missionaries supported by local Mennonite churches returned on brief furloughs with picture slides of what poverty looked like, and the devastating effects of diseases brought on by malnutrition and the absence of treatment facilities and drugs. Such evenings became an inspiration for some Mennonite young people to serve in a variety of ways in voluntary service capacities abroad.

There were undoubtedly those in the community who felt such service was a more worthwhile activity to pursue than playing on a competitive hockey team. Such service was also considered a "higher calling."

Butch and his siblings were a part of that scenario. They were also part of lively, meaningful and pertinent discussions that often broke out over a game of Rook in someone's home after the Sunday evening service. Frequently the conversations related to activities in which Mennonite young people shouldn't take part: like attending movies, enjoying dancing, and participating in other "worldly" activities like competitive hockey.

On one such Sunday evening the Floradale Mennonite pastor was present, because the Rook game was in his home. He had teenaged children. Inevitably it happened: the question of Butch being a Raiter came up. While not involved in the Rook game, the pastor was listening. As the squares and warm apple cider were being served, he offered his thoughts in a gentle, non-confrontational, yet forthright manner.

In what was surely an unenlightened opinion, he questioned the morality of the game of hockey. After all, if you got a penalty, weren't you doing something wrong; something unacceptable? Lucinda, Butch's older sister, was a hockey fan. She'd seen her brother play at the Waterloo Arena. She replied to what she felt was an idiosyncratic take on the game. "Pastor," she said, as all eyes were on her. "It's all a part of the game. You have to understand, it's all a part of the game." Somewhere, her youngest brother Butch was smiling.

The church leader's opinion was reflective of so many within the Mennonite Church in the 1940s and '50s, and was given with no intended malice. Yet it puts into context the world in which Butch had grown up and from which some perceived he'd taken a step away by joining the Raiters. So the fact that Butch's Mennonite father had attended his game was very meaningful. Butch never doubted the support of his family.

GREAT EXPECTATIONS
BUTCH AS A JUNIOR

In 1946, when Butch skated for the Raiters, he was taking an unprecedented step for a Mennonite young man. It would also be his first step closer to two unexpected and major decisions he needed to face as a man in his early twenties.

Butch took another long hockey stride forward in 1947 when he joined the Guelph Biltmore Mad Hatters of the prestigious OHA Junior A League. It was a part of a hockey world that by today's standards was quite insulated. There were only six NHL teams with about one hundred players. The American Hockey League had the same number of teams. Attaining the level of Junior A was a highly regarded and coveted accomplishment. For some of the most talented of young men, this meant they were just one contract away from the National Hockey League, the fulfillment of every Canadian boy's dream.

The Biltmores were a new entry into a league with teams from St. Catharines, Windsor, Galt, Barrie, Oshawa, Stratford, and Toronto. The Marlies and St. Mikes were the Toronto-based teams and played their home games at Maple Leaf Gardens, usually in a Saturday afternoon double-header.

For the young, aspiring Guelph team a Saturday afternoon game at the Gardens was a prelude to the excitement of staying to watch the Leafs at night. The first-place Leafs of 1947-48 played a sixty game season and were led by stars like captain Ted Kennedy; prolific scorer

Syl Apps and bruising defenseman Bill Ezenicki.

Fantasy met delicious reality when the New York Rangers played in Toronto on a Saturday night after a Biltmore afternoon game at Maple Leaf Gardens.

Because every Biltmore player who graduated to the NHL would be a Ranger, the Rangers would own Butch's rights indefinitely. That's the way the system worked before the partial entry draft was instituted in 1963. During the 1947-48 season the farm team could see the Rangers' leading point-getter, Herbert O'Connor, in action. A young Fred Shero played nineteen games with New York that season. Freddie "The Fog" later became coach of the "Broad Street Bullies" Philadelphia Flyers teams.

Butch would personally "run into" 1947-48 Rangers tough defenseman Bill Juzda in 1961 in an Allan Cup Final series in Galt—but he could have been his Rangers teammate.

In Butch's two years in Guelph, he played against future Leaf captain George Armstrong. In the 1948-49 season, Armstrong, playing for the Stratford Kroehlers, led the league in scoring, and was named the league's Most Valuable Player. Tim Horton, for whom expectations were huge, was a Marlie. His record in the NHL notes, "He was the strongest man to ever lace up skates."

In Butch's final year in Guelph, the team won twenty games, lost twenty-six and tied two. That was good for seventh place. His teammate Lorne Ferguson went on to have a seven-year NHL career with Chicago and Detroit. Forward Glen Sonmor would spend nine years as head coach of the NHL's Minnesota North Stars in the 1970s and '80s.

Frank Bathgate played for the Biltmores during Butch's tenure. But the year after Butch left the team, Frank's brother Andy joined the club along with other future Ranger stars, Lou Fontinato, Dean Prentice, Harry Howell and "Bep" Guidolin. Their team won the J. Ross Robertson Cup in 1950, and with it the OHA Junior A championship. Two years later they took home the George Richardson Memorial

Trophy as Canadian Junior A champions.

Fans could purchase a Guelph Biltmore program for ten cents during the 1948-49 season. Right under the ad for Bob's Honi-Dipt Do-Nuts appeared Butch's picture, with these words: "Who at the end of last season turned in some real good efforts, is looking better every time out. Butch lives in Floradale (near Elmira) and drives to and from practices and games. He reported weighing 200 lbs and is 19 years old."

Bobby Bauer came on as coach in Butch's first year. Gifted Ken Laufman at age nineteen joined the Biltmores after Butch's departure. In 1951-52, he had fifty-four goals and eighty-six assists with the club, winning the Eddie Powers Memorial Trophy as top point-getter in the OHA Junior A League. Bauer and Laufman would connect with Butch four years later on a significantly larger stage.

Butch's team was called the Mad Hatters for a reason. They were owned by the Biltmore Hat Company, located in Guelph. It employed four hundred workers and made more than one million men's hats a year. In the 1940s and '50s, wearing an expensive hat was the sign of a professional man. It was a status symbol and perceived as a self-esteem booster. NHL players wore Biltmore hats, as did the Mad Hatters.

The policy of the company was that when a Guelph Junior A team member scored three goals, he could come to the factory and leave with the hat of his choice. There is a widely held belief that the term "hat trick" originated from this practice.

Biltmore Hats brought a lot of attention to Guelph. Harding Carpets and Rennie Industries, producers of men's shirts, also employed a substantial number of people. In 1874, the Ontario School of Agriculture and Experimental Farm opened, the first chapter in the story of the University of Guelph. The magnificent Church of Our Lady opened its doors in 1877. It was the largest building project in the history of the city. Guelph son John McCrae saw the slaughter at the Second Battle of Ypres in Belgium in 1915, and wrote the immortal poem "In Flanders Fields" shortly after the death of his best friend. The Guelph Elastic Hosiery Company invented the jock strap in 1920.

A contest was held to name the company's new invention. The winner received five dollars.

The Biltmores, like the Raiters, didn't have a home rink in Butch's first year. During that initial year in Guelph, home games were played in Galt Arena Gardens, a place to which Butch would return as captain of a Canadian Senior A championship team.

Guelph's second goalie was "a kid named Fisher." During games he sat in the crowd, in his street clothes, which was the practice in those days. He enjoyed engaging in conversations with the fans, especially those who were about his age--and most especially those who were attractive young women.

As Butch came out of the dressing room following a game against the first-place Windsor Spitfires, Fisher was waiting for him. Standing beside him were two attractive female fans who'd accepted his offer of a ride to their homes.

Butch drove his car to nearby Preston and dropped off Fisher and his new-found friend at her home. When he returned, he anticipated that his teammate would be waiting for him at the curb. But that wasn't the case. So Butch waited, while parked in front of the Preston home. Suddenly, Fisher came dashing towards the car, yelling at Butch to quickly open the door. Behind him was the girl's mother, flailing a broom in pursuit and screaming at the apparently unwelcome visitor to her home. Fisher said, "Heck, I don't even know what I did wrong!" Butch smiled, put the car in gear, and they were quickly on their way.

The Guelph Memorial Gardens was opened on November 11, 1948, out of what remained of a nineteenth century building that housed the Royal Winter Fair. When the Biltmores attracted a sell-out crowd, there were four thousand in the stands. The arena had an unusual shape, dictated by the train tracks behind the building. All emergency exits along its back side emptied directly onto the tracks so in emergency situations officials tried to get folks out of the building by the main front entrance. The Memorial Gardens closed as a hockey venue in March of 2001.

Bob Ertel, Mike Parsons, Kelly Bradley and Jamie Wright, all from Elmira, also played Junior A in Guelph.

The NHL New York Rangers were in a rebuilding mode during Butch's tenure with the Biltmores. The military draft, during World War II had left them with a struggling team. More often than they liked, they were being beaten by embarrassing scores. One game they suffered a 15-0 humiliation.

In his office in Madison Square Gardens, on 8th Avenue in Manhattan, Rangers' manager Frank Boucher was huddled with other members of his management team, including coach Lynn Patrick. They felt the team was slowly coming back. Rookie Emile Francis was a promising goalie. And Edgar Laprade, Fred Shero, and Allan Stanley were developing well, as expected.

They were trying to rebuild. Yet even by the 1948-49 season, their record was a miserable eighteen wins, thirty-one losses and eleven ties. Boucher knew that clearly his team had a long way to go. They were last in the six-team league and out of the playoffs.

François "Frank" Boucher's heart lay in a Ranger uniform and he was a proud man. During the Rangers' glory days, he had been part of a forward line with brothers Bun and Bill Cook, known as the "Bread Line." This line had helped the Rangers win their first three Stanley Cups. Knowledgeable hockey observers deemed the Bread Line as one of the greatest forward combinations of all time.

Boucher won the Lady Byng Trophy seven times. In his thirteen-year NHL playing career, he was only ever a Ranger. He coached the Rangers for ten years before taking the post of general manager, a position he held from 1946-55.

Joseph Lynn Patrick, Boucher's coach, had played ten years for the Rangers. He led the league with thirty-two goals in the 1941-42 season. He'd been appointed the Ranger's coach midway during the 1948-49 season.

In the winter of 1949, Butch's second with the Biltmores, the Rangers' scouts were increasingly impressed by his play. They felt his strength with the puck, good decision making, and rugged style would fit well into Madison Square Gardens with its smaller ice dimensions than most NHL arenas.

Boucher knew that Butch had committed to joining the Rangers at the next season's training camp. His signed A form was in the manager's filing cabinet.

Butch received correspondence from the manager in reference to the upcoming training camp in the early fall of 1949. He picked up the letters from the Seranus Martin mail box in Ruggle's General Store.

TERMS OF ENDEARMENT
BUTCH MAKES A LIFE-CHANGING DECISION

In between seasons with the Biltmores, Butch found opportunities to enjoy life at a slower pace. But he wanted to stay in shape. One way of doing that was to go roller skating at the Waterloo Memorial Arena, where he'd spent his last year as a Junior B player.

One summer evening, on returning to his Floradale home, Butch hurriedly parked his car beside his brother Elmer's, almost tumbled out, and with giant strides moved toward the aroma of hot coffee and warm cinnamon buns wafting through the side screen door of the Martin home.

His sister Valina was sweeping the linoleum-covered kitchen floor, the usual final task at the end of a busy day. Viola, the Martin family member closest to Butch's age, was singing, her deep alto voice filling the room with the strains of the well-known gospel song "Bringing in the Sheaves."

Neither sister had a chance to say a word. Their youngest brother, who was usually reluctant to tell them much, plunked himself down into Pop's creaky rocking chair, broke into the widest grin his sisters had ever witnessed, and blurted out, "I've just met the girl I'm going to marry! And her name is Ethleen Gerber. But they call her PeeWee."

Neither Valina nor Viola had ever heard of any girl named Ethleen. Her last name seemed to hint that she might be a Mennonite young woman, but certainly not from Woolwich Township. She'd have to be a

Brubacher, Bauman, Gingrich, Horst, or have some other familiar family name to be a member of a local Mennonite community. But if she were indeed a Mennonite girl, Pop and Blendina would be pleased. That is, if Butch would ever share his news with them.

PeeWee had been roller skating with a few of her Kitchener friends. She lived with her parents, Elmer J. Gerber and Vietta in the east-end ward of the city, just a few blocks from the J. M. Schneider Meat processing plant. She had a sister, Doreen and a brother, Stewart. Mr. Gerber aspired to leadership within the Mennonite community and preached at services that included his daughters singing duets.

When Butch rejoined the Biltmores for the 1948-49 season, spare goalie Mitchell was on his own with attractive girls who occasionally vied for his attention. Butch had obviously found a wonderful young woman who completely had his attention!

Butch's relationship with PeeWee brought a new layer to the growing complexities in his life. At twenty years of age his future held great promise.

By the end of 1949 there was a good chance he'd be skating on the ice at Madison Square Gardens. He'd likely be a New York Ranger. He'd be doing the thing he'd learned early on at Floradale Mennonite: "Be the best that you can be."

But Butch made a decision that astounded many people and had others asking questions. Still others deemed it as courageous and praiseworthy. The Kitchener-Waterloo Record and Elmira Signet carried the news of the decision that changed the direction of his life.

As his relationship with PeeWee had grown, so had the possibility that Butch might ask her to be his bride. But her father had strong opinions, it appeared, on many matters, including the men his daughters married. His Mennonite affiliation and his personality influenced his opinions.

Kelly picks up the story: Growing up, I had heard stories; "Butch could have played in the NHL." I remember when I was young there was a hockey game in Elmira to raise funds for the arena. Retired NHL players came to play the old timers from Elmira. My father was put on the NHL team. I asked my mom why that had happened. She replied, "That is where he should have played all along." And that was the end of that. I knew my dad had gone to the Olympics twice, and I'd held his silver and bronze medals. But I couldn't seem to understand the connection to the NHL. One day, while snooping through my parents' important papers (which I knew I shouldn't be doing), I found the answers that had changed his life, and mine, forever.

I found papers showing a contract between the New York Rangers and Floyd "Butch" Martin, signing him as a rookie. Wow, it really was true!!! Right behind those papers were legal documents showing that Floyd Butch Martin had broken that contract! I couldn't understand why that would have happened. To me it was every boy's dream to make it to the NHL. Why wouldn't my dad have gone?

Well, there was my proof. But what was I to do with it? I should never have been snooping around in those papers. Days went by, and one day while my mom and I were working in the kitchen, I tentatively asked, "Was dad really supposed to play in the NHL?"

"Yes, honey, he was that good." My mother was beaming.

"Why didn't he go?" I asked. A sadness came over her face and she wouldn't look at me. But she replied, "We don't talk about that, love." So we didn't any more that day.

Many years passed. The time came when my son started to play hockey. At one of Paul's first practices families were invited to watch. An older man came over to my dad and said he had watched Dad play with the Dutchmen many times. He smiled and said, "You should have played in the big leagues, Butch." Dad smiled, looked back at the ice, pointed to Paul, and said, "Maybe he'll be the one that gets to go."

I waited until Dad and I were alone again. Holding my breath, I asked the question I had withheld for years: "Dad what happened with the New York Rangers?"

"Not much," was his reply. My dad has always been a man of few words. But that day I decided to push the boundaries.

"I'm a grown woman, Dad. Did you really break your contract with the Rangers?"

He didn't take his eyes off the ice. "Yes," he replied. "Why?" He turned and looked at me. "Your mother's father, Elmer, said playing hockey was not an honorable career and that therefore he wouldn't give me permission to marry his daughter."

I was stunned. But back then in the Mennonite community, a father's word was law. I'd read bits and pieces of a newspaper story that told of my dad taking flack for not playing hockey on Sundays due to his Mennonite heritage. So I understood what Elmer's words had meant to Dad.

"Do you ever regret it?" I asked.

Dad said, "I wouldn't have you.........or them." He was looking at Kristie giving Paul his water bottle at the boards on the far side of the ice. "Now would I?" And with that, my father hugged me, making that moment that much more memorable for me.

Rookies preparing for training camp were usually overflowing with enthusiasm, grateful for the opportunity given to them and hoping to make a positive impression.

There was no preliminary "How's the weather in New York?" inquiry. Butch simply requested that Boucher allow him to rescind the contract he had signed, briefly filling him in on the details.

Boucher was called "Gentleman Frank" for a reason. His seven Lady Byng trophies attested to that. But the manner by which he related to people was a further example. There was no acrimony in his response to Butch's unusual and unexpected request, nor in the conversation that followed. He inquired about Butch's plans for the next hockey season. He had one request. Could he check back with Butch during the next season to see how things were going? And by the way, he'd be welcome in New York if he changed his mind.

Boucher and the Rangers wanted to be there should Butch decide to pursue a professional career, so Butch would continue to be property of the Rangers.

Butch's decision was a watershed moment in his life. Needless to say it received lots of attention in Waterloo County and beyond. From the time of his decision to turn down an NHL contract to the 2014 Winter Olympic Games, most media references to Butch's career included a statement similar to this: "Martin turned down a professional career because of his Mennonite beliefs."

But that often-repeated statement has been unfortunately a misrepresentation of the depth and complexities of Butch's decision. It was one of the most important decisions of his life and it brought him many rewards, including the marriage to the woman he loved, a wonderful daughter, and eventually two beloved grandchildren. Representing Canada at international hockey events wasn't possible for NHL players when Butch was playing. Turning down the NHL meant he had the opportunity of going to the Olympics on multiple occasions.

Had he decided to join the New York Rangers, being a Mennonite would not have been a deterrent to him on a personal level. Yet such a decision would have received a mixed reaction in the Floradale Mennonite congregation where Butch attended. There is plenty of evidence to suggest that the church's leaders, in the 1940s and 1950s, if they'd been consulted, would not have approved.

His situation in the context of the Mennonite faith was unique because Butch was the first Mennonite young man anywhere who'd been in the position of becoming a professional hockey player.

Nevertheless, the history of the Floradale Mennonite congregation presents a mini-study of the gradual shift in modern Mennonites' attitudes about participation in high-level sports.

Zenas Buehler, about ten years younger than Butch, grew up a short distance from Floradale Mennonite and still remained a member by 2014. When he started his hockey career as a goalie in Elmira's Minor League system, the attitude in the congregation seemed less strident.

However, Zenas' father Edwin received a few visits from Floradale Mennonite's deacon, concerned about his son's sports involvement.

Zenas went on to be a stand-out goalie with Butch's former Waterloo Junior B team. Later, Butch helped him contact someone who could assist him in getting to Holland to play goal for the country's team. He also provided encouragement.

Butch and Zenas worked for a lot of years together at the sawmill. When it came time to sell the business, the Martin family approached Zenas who became the new owner. The two men eventually played for the same hockey team.

Butch and Zenas were the first to venture into organized hockey from Floradale Mennonite. They set a precedent for others to follow from this rural congregation, an unlikely hotbed of hockey. These men followed, from the early 1980s to 2014:

Roger Buehler: Waterloo Siskins, Junior B

Don Bauman: Elmira Sugar Kings, Junior B

Rodney Bauman: Ottawa 67s, Junior A

Dale Wideman: Elmira Sugar Kings, Junior B

Darren Wideman: Elmira Sugar Kings, Junior B

Dennis Wideman; St. Louis, Boston, Washington, Florida, and Calgary, NHL

Evan Buehler: Waterloo Siskins, Junior B.

Towards the end of the 2013-14 hockey season, Floradale Pastor Fred Redekop attended a Sunday evening Junior B game in Elmira, wearing the championship jacket of his son's hockey team. That was not an unusual occurrence for a Mennonite pastor. He was a living metaphor for the change in attitudes towards competitive hockey and other sports since Butch was a Waterloo Raiter.

A few other Woolwich Township Mennonite young adults took brave and unusual steps for their times in ways other than sports. They were part of slow change within the Woolwich Township Mennonite community in appreciating the value of education that stretched beyond high school and into the professional world.

Willard Martin (no relation to Butch) grew up in an Old Order Mennonite family in Wellesley Township. He'd attended school only to the end of eighth grade. In the early 1960s, as a young adult he took a giant step in leaving his job as a hired man on a local chicken farm to begin studies as an adult student at Goshen College, Indiana. Willard became a highly respected professor of German at Pennsylvania State University. His was a most unusual and admirable educational journey. Martin never forgot his Old Order Mennonite roots, and returns regularly to the farming area of Woolwich. In 2014, as a senior citizen, Willard continued teaching courses at Penn State, one of them about the Mennonite community. (Willard Martin was also a graduate of the Elmira Gems hockey team in the Elmira District Church League!)

Before moving on to Rideau Hall as Governor-General, the Right Honorable David Johnston owned and lived on the Wellesley Township farm where Willard Martin grew up.

Emerson Gingrich was the only child in a Woolwich Township Mennonite farm family that attended Elmira Mennonite Church. He went to a small rural school a short distance from the farm. In the 1960s, this motivated, highly intelligent young man continued assisting his father on the farm while excelling in high school correspondence courses on his own. Eventually Emerson graduated as a medical doctor and enjoyed a long and successful career in medicine. In 2014, also as a senior citizen, Dr. Gingrich continued a medical practice in Calgary, Alberta.

The stories of Martin and Gingrich are unusual and remarkable in the context of their rather sheltered communities and church affiliations. A decade earlier Butch had been a trail blazer for Mennonite youth desiring to excel as athletes. All played important roles in the community for those Mennonite youth looking for ways that allowed them to join mainstream society. They were important steps forward.

But Butch was a Mennonite in the spotlight—on the international, public stage. He would have benefitted significantly if he'd been starting his career in the community many decades later.

In an editorial on February 17, 2014, Dick Brenner, editor/publisher of the Canadian Mennonite wrote:

> *"What seemed so important decades ago now seems less important or approached differently. We no longer live mostly in small, rural communities, where it was easier to define and implement our unique religious values. There was little dissent or challenge to what church leaders imposed. Today younger generations have moved to urban centers which, in most of Canada, are highly multicultural. We encounter, every day, persons who are not like us, who do not share our cultural heritage. Most of us are no longer agrarian in our workplaces. We have successful businesses; occupy some of the leading centers of higher learning; have our own high schools and universities; are generally more educated than our forebears; are successful in the arenas of law, finance, art and literature as poets and writers; and in growing numbers have influence on government officials. All of this is bound to change our worldview, our perceptions of where we fit into society in which we have been integrated and are now intertwined, how we view both ourselves and our neighbors. No longer the 'quiet in the land' we struggle to be "in this world, but not of it."*

Brenner's description is of today's Mennonite community from which present-day Mennonite NHL players James Reimer and Nick Spaling have their roots.

Reimer is from a Mennonite community in Winnipeg, but Spaling's home church is Community Mennonite Fellowship in Drayton, Ontario, a comparatively short drive from Floradale. In 2014 he was a member of the NHL's Pittsburgh Penguins.

Spaling's former pastor at Community Mennonite, was Willard Metzger, who became in 2014 the Executive Director of Mennonite Church Canada. In reference to Mennonite participation in professional sports, Metzger said, "We want to give an alternative view to the many Mennonite stereotypes that exist in society and in the media. In a sense we are speaking to the public and ourselves at the same time. Our own Mennonite young people need to know that they can pursue their dreams and hold tight to their faith at the same time."In 2014, Metzger continued his long running weekly summaries of church league games, in an Elmira newspaper.

Mennonite church leaders during the time of Butch's early twenties had an opinion that was diametrically opposed to that of Metzger's.

Butch's chosen situation meant that he could continue playing hockey. He also continued to be employed where he had been since age fourteen; at S. S. Martin and Sons in Floradale. He'd continue to show up for work at 7:00 a.m. and end his work day at 5:00 p.m. Following supper, he'd collect his hockey equipment and make his way to a practice or game. In later years Butch said, "I know what work is. Hockey was never work."

During the summer months Butch and Dick played hardball (baseball) for Elmira's Read Brothers Fertilizer team. Butch was the catcher. Dick played first base. You could flag down the Elmira Service Cab for a ride to a game from anywhere in the town for thirty-five cents.

Before the Blue Jays arrived in Toronto, Butch, his brothers, his friends, and eventually his wife made many trips to see the Detroit Tigers in Tiger Stadium, becoming ardent fans of stars like Al Kaline, Lou Whitaker, and Alan Trammell.

Butch was co-owner and operator of S .S. Martin and Sons. Pop, and brothers Elmer and Dick were his partners. Their business was essentially a sawmill. They also sold wood for heating, coal, and coal oil.

When a farmer let them know that he had a woodlot for sale, Elmer would go into the area and identify the trees that he determined would make good lumber. In most cases the trees were hardwood maples. The logging operation took place in the winter. Butch's job was to assist in loading logs on to a big, flat-bed truck-with the aid of chains, hooks and either a team of horses or a small bulldozer. It was freezing out there in the bush, and the work was physically demanding.

When warmer weather arrived, Butch was employed as the sawyer, sawing the logs into lumber at the mill. The S. S. Martin sawmill business, with the co-operation of father and three sons was a successful one.

The Martins also pressed apples, producing cider and apple butter for local farmers from the bushels of apples they brought in from their orchards.

S. S. Martin also engaged in cooking and canning fairly large quantities of meat for the Mennonite Central Committee. The canned meat was sent to people in needy countries. The Martin's meat canning operation was the precursor of the 2014 large MCC mobile meat canning operation that traveled to thirty-six locations in the United States and Canada. A small, permanent staff and thousands of volunteers have canned over one million pounds of meat. The mobile operation carries out its work annually.

A MAN FOR ONE SEASON
BUTCH AS A DUTCHMEN

After turning down the New York Rangers, it was Butch's decision to join the Kitchener-Waterloo Flying Dutchmen Hockey Club for the 1949-50 season, in the OHA Senior A League. It made sense. He'd be close to his family and home in Floradale. The caliber of play would be just a step away from that played in the NHL. A growing number of nieces, nephews and cousins would have the opportunity to see him play. His financial sacrifice would be minimal. With his wages from the sawmill and his stipend from the Dutchmen, Butch earned more than he would have if he'd played in the America Hockey League. Even NHL salaries weren't substantially greater than some regular 8:00-5:00 employees.

Butch also fit into the Dutchmen's plans. They were looking for younger players, just into their careers, to balance their veterans.

During 1907, the Berlin Dutchmen had been in the Ontario Professional Hockey League. Three years later, after winning the league championship, they were allowed to challenge for the Stanley Cup. They lost to the Montreal Wanderers by a 7-3 score. In 1926 they became the Kitchener Dutchmen and members of the Canadian Hockey League. The Kitchener-Waterloo Flying Dutchmen were formed in 1947, and joined the Ontario Hockey Association Senior A League.

Walter "Punch" Scherer was coach of the 1949-50 Flying Dutchmen during Butch's first season. A native of New Hamburg, Scherer had played at a high level including in the Senior A League. He had a fifty-year career in hockey. It was an unexpected surprise to have Butch join his team.

Once more, Butch had joined a team without a home rink. So when the Toronto Marlboros, Hamilton Tigers, or Owen Sound Mercurys were the visiting team, they'd travel to Galt or Waterloo to play the Dutchmen at "home." That meant some nights Butch was back playing in the Waterloo Memorial Arena, the site of his home games during his second year of Junior B and where he'd met PeeWee at summer roller skating.

It wasn't until October 8, 1951 that the Kitchener Memorial Auditorium was officially opened. Eight thousand fans attended the first game, an exhibition match between the Montreal Canadiens and the K-W Old Timers. Rocket Richard, Doug Harvey, Dickie Moore and Bernie Geoffrion were in the line-up for the Canadiens. That season the Canadiens lost to the Detroit Red Wings in the 1952 Stanley Cup Final Series 4-0.

Summaries of Flying Dutchmen games appeared in Kitchener-Waterloo Record at four cents a copy. Its circulation was 24,475. One of the paper's headlines on November 29, 1950, was: "Fever of Sunday Sport Hits Strait Old Ontario." The province's municipalities were allowed to put the question of Sunday sports to a vote. A simple majority would decide. But any Sunday sports could only take place between 1:30 p.m. and 6:00 p.m. Horse racing would not be permitted at any time on Sundays.

On December 5, 1950, the citizens of Kitchener turned down Sunday sports by an almost two-to-one margin.

On January 3, 1950, the citizens of Toronto were already on record as favoring commercial sports on Sunday. A Toronto columnist wrote, "Attending a ball game on Sunday afternoon isn't nearly as bad as gathering at a friend's home to gossip and expose the faults of neighbors."

Prior to the Toronto vote, a bowling tournament between teams from Toronto and Buffalo couldn't be completed because the final game would run a half-hour past midnight on a Saturday night.

The Dutchmen's #4, Butch Martin, became a favorite with Waterloo County fans, not only as a hockey player but also as a person. People from all walks of life felt comfortable in approaching Butch. There was no such thing as a quick stop for coffee for Butch. He'd have too many stories to share, too many people to greet, too many inquiries about families, and too many hockey games to rehash.

Clearly Butch enjoyed people and their stories. When he talked about a holiday trip, or a game in which he'd participated, he related stories about the people he'd met: the humorous incidents with teammates, the antics of a trainer, or the clever one-liner of a fan disagreeing with a referee's call.

Butch may have scored a hat trick during a Dutchmen game on a Tuesday night. But on Wednesday morning he'd stop beside the cart of Elmira's street cleaner and invite the simple, disheveled man to join him on a delivery to a S. S. Martin customer.

His Dutchmen teammate Jack Shewchuk played parts of six seasons with the Boston Bruins. Waterloo County native Bobby Bauer, Butch's coach with the Biltmore Mad Hatters and former Boston Bruin star, joined the Flying Dutchmen in 1949 as a player after regaining his amateur status. He and Butch would experience some major hockey victories and disappointments over the next ten years. Dick Behling and Aug Herchenratter were other Waterloo County residents on the team.

The Flying Dutchmen had twenty wins, nineteen losses and three ties in the 1949-50 regular season. They won their first playoff series and went on to meet the powerful Toronto Marlboros in the league championship seven game series. The Marlies lost only eight times during the season. Joe Primeau, coach of the team was a former Leaf. Harold Ballard, soon to be owner of the Leafs, was the president and general manager of the senior team.

The unlucky Dutchmen were quickly down three games to none in their series with the team from the big city. But with a vociferous and exuberant crowd behind them, they responded by winning the next two games. The much anticipated sixth game, played at Maple Leaf Gardens, drew 11, 547 fans.

Kitchener and Toronto hockey fans had generated an acrimonious relationship. It was a case of a small city in rural Ontario taking on the enemy: the glitzy, slick, and well-heeled mega-city. A Kitchener reporter wrote, "Toronto has a million dollar organization which will stop at nothing to buy a hockey title, no matter how small." Some questioned whether the Marlies were really professionals playing on an amateur team.

Butch had met the Marlies' top scorer, George Armstrong, in his Guelph days. Armstrong was the best Toronto player, followed closely by another future Leaf, Danny Lewicki. The Dutchmen were limping along, with injuries to several key players as they prepared for the important game at the Gardens. Team leader Bobby Bauer had sustained an injury that kept him out of the game.

The Marlies took a two goal lead, the second goal scored by Lewicki. At 14:10 of the third period, Butch electrified the Dutchmen fans by scoring short-handed. It would be his last goal in Senior A competition for six years.

In the end, his team was one goal short. Armstrong led the Marlies to the Allan Cup that year, with a championship series win over the Calgary Stampeders. He would go on to be a Leaf for twenty-one seasons, eleven of them as captain. Ironically, hockey experts described him as a clumsy skater with a less than average shot.

Ballard coached his only game ever in the championship series as Primeau was attending his father's funeral.

In the previous year the Senior A Marlies forward Lewicki had had his NHL rights purchased by the Leafs for $35,000. That meant he could only play for a team in the Leaf organization. They ordered him to report to the Toronto farm team. He refused. NHL president Clarence

Campbell told him he was suspended. That made the young star's decision to join the Marlies easy.

His case was taken up by the Canadian Parliament, and resulted in the abolishment of the "C" form which allowed professional team to dictate for what team a graduating junior would be playing. The "C" form was similar to the "A" form that Butch had signed that tied him to the New York Rangers. The Lewicki incident was a major break in tradition and practice. It was the precursor to the NHL introducing the partial entry draft in 1963.

The impressive Marlies ended Butch's involvement as an active hockey player, with no certainty as to what his future might bring in the game he loved to play.

Butch's between-seasons activities returned to the familiar: playing ball, going to the family cottage at Chesley Lake, attending Tigers games, and finding himself being increasingly enamored by the game of golf. Elmer, Dick, and Butch spent many Saturday mornings playing eighteen holes or more at the Fergus and Listowel courses.

TO BE OR NOT TO BE
LEAVING THE DUTCHMEN

But the most important occurrence for Butch during the off-season was his marriage to Ethleen "PeeWee" Gerber on June 23, 1950 at Kitchener's First Mennonite Church. John Hess, pastor of the church, was in charge of the ceremonies.

Butch and PeeWee had many conversations with Pastor Hess, a gentle, amiable and highly respected church and community leader. A few years later, during his time as pastor of Warden Avenue Mennonite Church in the Toronto Borough of Scarborough, Hess was honored to be chosen as Citizen of the Year.

Hess was raised in Lancaster Pennsylvania. His wife Ruth grew up in Waterloo County. They met at a Mennonite college. Hess was personable, likable and caring. Young people particularly were drawn to him. In his later years of ministry he worked with women prisoners in Kingston. His life was one of service.

The discussion of sports participation generally, but especially on Sundays, was part of the conversations the pastor had with Butch and PeeWee. It was but one of the many concerns that Mennonite leaders, in particular, had with recreation of any kind.

This became evident in a survey of 350 Mennonite leaders, parents and young people that was undertaken by the Mennonite Conference of Ontario's Sports Committee. Pastor John F. Garber reported on this survey to delegates at an annual conference. The results, while varied, presented a good overview of where the constituents stood in regard to their opinions regarding recreational activities, especially participation in sports.

Some Mennonite pastors saw the need for such activities only at school. One commented, "The situation is not good" in regard to amateur sports participation. Some felt that sports were negatively affecting attendance at Wednesday night prayer meetings, thus contributing to a perceived spiritual decline.

Seventy-five percent of Mennonite youth surveyed participated very little in sports. Generally the youth felt there was really nothing wrong with participation as long as games were played in a "decent" way.

The report spoke further to the issue. "To give a Christian testimony, one must not be guilty of anger, jealousy, fighting, rowdiness, boisterousness and an ungodly attitude." Respected Mennonite leader Paul Martin stated, "There is a need for proper leadership as this is no small problem, because our traditional attitude has been that a spiritual person will have no time for recreation."

This was a time when church leaders were seldom, if ever, questioned about their decisions so they were in positions with considerable influence and power.

Butch's brother Dick approached three Mennonite bishops in the area, hoping to get their support in starting a church softball league. He reported that it was a major undertaking and said, "It wasn't an easy job. These guys were tough!"

At First Mennonite in Kitchener, Hess led a congregation that was generally a bit more liberal than those in the more rural areas of Waterloo County. But he was a leader within the Mennonite Conference of Ontario and generally accepted the teachings and traditions inherent therein.

The question of Sunday sports was timely in that the Dutchmen's schedule included some Sunday games. Competitive sports on Sundays had not yet been embraced by Ontario municipalities other than Toronto and Windsor so the question was more widely spread than simply within the confines of Mennonite teachings. There seemed to be an informal public sentiment that the Sabbath should be "a day of rest."

With the assistance of his sincere and caring pastor, Butch made a decision about the matter based on biblical principles in the context of the Mennonite Church and the larger local community that had turned down Sunday sports: he would not play on Sundays.

In late September 1950, the Kitchener-Waterloo Record reported on the first Dutchmen practice of the season. It noted that although Butch wasn't in attendance, he had been given permission to miss the workout by General Manager Punch Scherer.

On Sunday October 1, the Dutchmen defeated the Hamilton Tigers 2-1 but the coach was nevertheless concerned about his shaky defense. That may have had a connection with #4 once again not being in the lineup. Butch's absence from the Dutchmen roster gave no hint as to the real reason for him not being there.

The public found out about Butch's stance before the season began. Many were shocked or at least surprised, not unlike the public's response to Butch's decision to turn down the NHL.

Reverend John H. Hess was quoted in a report in the October 12, 1950 edition of the Elmira Signet. The following is a summary of his comments:

> "The Dutchmen were recently informed of a clearcut decision made by Floyd Martin, their very able defenseman on last year's team that he is retiring from the team. Last year, Butch was signed by the New York Rangers professional team. But he begged to be released from his contract. The Rangers complied and loaned Butch to the Dutchmen for one season, hoping his convictions would vanish. But before this season began, Butch informed Rangers manager, Frank Boucher, that his decision sticks. Boucher respected his decision. Butch also told the Dutchmen, that after a year spent with the club, he

was retiring from the team. The Dutchies coach, Bobby Bauer, accepted the decision."

The piece went on to explain the reason for the most recent decision was mainly because of Butch's desire to not play hockey on Sundays.

In 2013, pastor Hess's widow, Ruth said she didn't know all the details of her husband's conversations with Butch. She said, "I know that John was pretty tough on Butch in regards to his Sunday hockey playing,"

Butch said, "I have great respect for Manager Bobby Bauer and other officials of the Dutchmen. If I ever play senior hockey again, it will be for the Dutchmen." His words were prophetic.

Within a relatively short time, Butch had made three major decisions: the decision to cancel a contract to play professional hockey; the decision to marry Ethleen Gerber, the woman he loved; and the decision to retire from the Dutchmen. In retrospect, that seemed a lot to ask of a young man in his early twenties.

In many places in Waterloo County, Butch's decision to leave the Dutchmen was well received and publicly supported.

Kitchener resident Irvin Erb had played junior hockey and made a tremendous contribution to hockey in Waterloo County. He was also the owner of a successful insurance company. Shortly after Butch's decision was made public, the highly respected Erb was the guest speaker at a Kitchener Lions Club Dinner. Erb attended a non-Mennonite church. He said, "I am indeed sorry to see steps being made to legalize money sport in the city of Kitchener on the Sabbath. In recent years amateur sport has become a professional business. Fortunately, some players like Butch Martin bear testimony to the Christian principles of life that make them people to be respected."

The Elmira Polar Kings, an Intermediate B team, was looking for local players to bolster their roster going into their second season, 1950-51. The fledgling Kings played in the recently opened Elmira Memorial Arena. Unexpectedly, Butch, a very talented local player seemed to be without a hockey team.

O. W. Mike Weichel, president of the club, inquired about Butch's availability. Butch responded, "I'm sorry, but at least for the present, the answer is no."

The Kings wisely became affiliated with the Dutchmen. That meant that a Kings' player could play a limited number of games with the Dutchmen without hurting his status with the Kings. Butch also remained the property of the New York Rangers, who placed him on their voluntary retirement list.

For the first time since his brother Elmer first laced his skates so he could play hockey on the dam, Butch didn't have a hockey team lined up for an upcoming season. He stepped away from the game. Given his experiences of the previous few years he needed time away to think about his future in hockey.

During the 1950-51 hockey season Butch never played a competitive game.

Butch and local house-painter, long-time Elmira minor hockey supporter, Norval Leslie, joined up to take over an Elmira juvenile team. Butch was the coach. It got him onto the ice during practices and gave him a taste for coaching, a path he thought he might pursue in the future.

During a juvenile league game in Preston, the home team was down 5-0 at the end of the second period. Leslie believed that hockey should be fun, a time for young people to make connections. The score really wasn't that important. So at the end of the second period he suggested that Butch play for Preston, the opposition. All parties willingly agreed. But when the final whistle blew, the Elmira boys went home with a 6-5 loss, thanks to the very talented "over-ager" on the Preston team.

By 1950, the town of Elmira had a population of less than three thousand. Among them were two sets of triplets: Corrina, Molly and Barbara Carbet; and Judith, Susan and Patricia Duench. The enrollment at the town's high school was just over 250. Principal H. B. Disbrow said, "Discipline is tight and expected and supported by parents." At the school's Friday night Teen Town Dances, the girls wore crinoline slips, black gored skirts, and saddle shoes on sale at Brubacher's Shoe Store for $4.95, downtown on Arthur Street.

On December 4, 1950, Elmira officially opened its new $130,000 arena. J. G. Taggart, Federal Deputy Minister of Agriculture, assisted by Elmira mayor C.J. Gibson did the honors. It was an unforgettable occasion for "Canada's Biggest Little Hockey Town."

More than 1600 Elmira residents witnessed three exhibition hockey games and a demonstration by the Elmira Veterans Bugle Band. The adoring crowd rose as one for the national anthem, as William Brown, the Arthur Street tailor, led the Elmira Musical Society Band. It was a proud moment for the small, rural, community of Elmira. Fritz Rudow's collapsed rink was never rebuilt, but its site was replaced by the town's first beer store.

In the spring of 1951, the Elmira Polar Kings, with local "boys" Forester, Trapp, Bowman, Vines and Sherk giving it their best for their hometown fans, ended their first season in the new Elmira Memorial Arena.

Leslie Dunbar, owner of the south-end Great West Felt Company, donated $25,000 to give the Kings a sound financial footing. They were called the "Polar Kings" because that was the name of a popular winter boot made by Great West Company. The Company had been in town since 1910. It employed sixty men and women and gained a national reputation for the high quality of its products. Come 1934, Great West Felt had a team in the Waterloo County Rural Industrial Hockey League. Harry Jarvis, a team member, became the town's police chief.

Things were good! Just across from the arena, facing Ernst Street, a new $40,000 outdoor swimming pool had opened a few months earlier. Local businessman and entrepreneur Ab Seiling had made a considerable sized donation to the swimming pool fund.

The local folks were responding better than expected to the town's "Final Drive"—a $15,000 fundraiser to install artificial ice in the new home of the Polar Kings. On September 21, a Giant Bingo was held at the arena. More than $1500 in prize money was ready for the Bingo players. Profits from the night's games went towards the $6300 still required to meet the goal.

Elmira really needed artificial ice! In spring, the town's bantam team had to go to Waterloo to win its OMHA championship game against Sundridge as Elmira's natural ice had melted. "Let's Not Let This Happen Again!" screamed the headlines on page three of the Signet, right beside the advertisement for Selrite Stores, where a kid could spend his five-cent allowance in a minute at the candy counter buying black jaw breakers and Double Bubble chewing gum.

BACK TO THE FUTURE
ELMIRA POLAR KINGS

As early as June of 1951, after their team's first season, Polar Kings fans inquired about the upcoming season. In the previous season they'd done okay, but not as well as the dreaded Bridgeport Vets, led by the aggressive, pugilistic, tough guy, Wally Kullman.

An advertisement about a 1951-52 pre-season game with Bridgeport said, "You can bet your bottom dollar the Polar Kings will be out to knock the Vets off their high and mighty horse."

The 1951-52 season promised to be a really exciting one. A few of the "rink-rats" at the Arena were on duty during the Polar Kings pre-season practices. They'd seen all the players perform in games, except for one new arrival.

A rumor began, as many rumors did, in the local hotel, the Steddick, just up the street from Roy Aberle's Cities Service gas station. Elmira resident Eddie Cather had dropped by for an after-work beer. He needed to cool down. It was sweltering inside the Link Belt Factory up on Church Street where he was the janitor.

Al Conner pulled up a wooden stool and joined him. Like Eddie, he was an ardent Polar Kings fan. The Department of Highways crew with whom he worked loved the guy. They said that Al had such a booming voice that he could stand outside the Steddick and, after a few beers, utter a howl so loudly that he could be heard four blocks away, up by Doc McQuibbon's house next to the high school.

The "boys" at the Link Belt had heard that Butch Martin might be joining the Polar Kings for the upcoming season. Eddie had seen Butch working out by himself at the arena a few times. But neither was a guarantee that he'd signed a contract. Maybe he had other plans.

Al figured that the head guys on the Polar King executive had enough influence and persuasive powers to attract Butch to join the team. They were respected by Butch and the town thought highly of them.

After all, Bill Becker, the King's coach had played Senior A hockey in Chatham. Doc Gibson, the town's mayor, and local dentist was the team's manager. Doc Wyatt, a local physician, was on the executive. And there was O. W. Mike Weichel, the town's congenial postmaster and OMHA member who knew his hockey. With businessman Ab Seiling on board as well, Butch could see that the Kings were a well-run outfit.

Suddenly Eddie plunked his head with the bottom of the palm of his hand. Heck, Butch's brother Dick was on the team, and so was his Floradale school chum, Cole Bowman. Butch might just be comfortable playing in Elmira with his friends. The thought of it made Eddie happy, really happy. Butch as a Polar King! That would be like the Rocket joining the Leafs! He gave Ed, the server a wave and showed him four fingers. Eddie bought the next round for Al and the two guys from the Naugatuk Chemical plant who had joined them.

Arlie Davis had made a successful career in the newspaper business for a reason. He had connections in Elmira and area. Few things of importance escaped his awareness. His idea of reportage was to beat someone else to the story. In Elmira, it meant getting the facts published in his Elmira Signet newspaper before the rumor mill had escalated to the point that the dark clouds of gossip blocked out the sunshine of the facts.

Arlie knew that Butch was going to join the Polar Kings for the 1951-52 season. Doc Gibson had told him. The "rink rats" finally recognized the newcomer at the team's practices. Arlie was preparing a report about Butch's signing that would appear in the next edition of the Signet. The layout was done, and he was ready to send things to the printer. But, with a bit of adjustment he was able to squeeze the "Butch story" onto the front page. It was a big news item and deserved better than to be hidden in the back pages with Arlie's "I See By The Signet" column.

Butch was quoted in Arlie's story: "I haven't changed my mind about playing professional hockey. I just want to play as an amateur for my old hometown. Hockey is not the most important thing in my life."

Elmira hockey fans were in a tizzy after they'd read Arlie's announcement. The first exhibition game of the season, as advertised in the Signet, was against the hated Bridgeport Vets, and Wally Kullman, the Polar King's nemesis.

On the night of the game, about 1500 fans crowded into the new Elmira Arena, with its seating capacity of 900. Each paid fifty cents admission. When Butch skated onto the ice with his teammates, the place exploded with the sounds of cheering.

Arlie Davis wrote, "Butch was greeted with a tremendous ovation." It wasn't Madison Square Gardens. And the Bridgeport Vets weren't the Montreal Canadiens. But Butch could feel the love!

At the end of the second period of the Bridgeport game, Eddie Cathor made his way unsteadily over the boards and onto the ice. A little wobbly, and with arms flailing like a broken windmill, he sashayed his way along the blue line. In his own idiosyncratic way he was leading the fans in a cheer. They clapped. They jabbed each other playfully. They yelled recklessly, and followed the lead of their "official" cheerleader.

Harry Jarvis, Elmira's sole police constable adjusted his holster, rubbed his forehead, and smiled. He'd seen the act before. And he'd see it again—at every Polar Kings home game of the season: no additional admission charge required.

Likable and friendly Al Conner had been at the Steddick with Eddie earlier in the Friday evening and had accompanied him to the arena for the Bridgeport game. Once each period, when play was a little slow, and the fans were quiet, Al cupped his hands in front of his mouth and let out a howl as loud as a blaring trumpet sound. Al was the second act of the long-running Cantor-Conner "theatrical" production.

The surprising news of Butch's return to hockey made its way to the land of the Dutchmen.

Len Taylor was a sports reporter and columnist with The Kitchener-Waterloo Record. He'd watched Butch's work with the 1949-50 Dutchmen.

His columns during that time indicated that he thought highly of #4. When Butch retired from the Dutchmen, Taylor paid attention. Many people were bewildered by Butch's decision to turn his back on "every Canadian boy's dream." Taylor saw it as more of a personal moral ideology that Butch was following, and the choice as to whether or not to play professional hockey was the choice that fitted into that ideology.

Taylor commented in The Record after hearing of Butch's return to playing hockey with the Polar Kings. His column headline was, "Back in Hockey—Butch Martin Decides Playing Hockey Morally Right." He praised the former Dutchmen for taking the positive step of returning to the game, rather than criticizing it from a distance.

Taylor concluded, "This is no argument that hockey is perfect but it is proof that the imperfections in hockey, like the cracks in more noble undertakings in our civilization, stem more from the misuse of the idea than faults in the basic structure."

Harvey Vines, Don Sherk, Floyd Foster, Doug Schwindt and smooth-skating Eugene Miller knew what Butch meant to their Polar Kings team. With his brother Dick, and school chum Cole Bowman on defense, Butch must have had the feeling, some nights, of being back on the frozen ice of the Floradale dam.

Butch was the heart and soul of the Polar Kings in the 1951-52 season. Frequently he scored more than a goal each game. In an exhibition game against Listowel, he scored six goals. The Polar Kings' best player was also a captain. No player was able to give the consistent effort or high level of performance as their leader.

Against a very competitive Georgetown team, Butch scored a hat trick, as well as assisting on two others. In a 9-2 victory over Walkerton, he scored five times and assisted three times.

The Elmira fans were very supportive. Five hundred of them bought Booster Club memberships at $2.50 each. It guaranteed them the same reserved seat for each league and playoff game. They also regularly purchased tickets for $1.50 each to travel by bus to away games.

But some fans called the season "troubled." Too often on games away from home, the Polar Kings had a meager ten players—or less. That's when coach Bill Becker played Butch as a forward on one shift and defense on the next: then repeated the assignment. On occasion, Butch played almost a complete game.

Midway through the season, manager Doc Gibson coaxed Elmira's fire chief, the affable Harry Soehner, out of retirement. The Kings needed some help in goal. Soehner hadn't played hockey since the 1933-34 season when he had been the goalie for the Elmira Polar Bears in the North Waterloo Heritage Rural League, but he knew most of the Polar King players. He didn't need much persuasion.

Butch's Polar Kings of 1951-52 reached the finals of their league where they met a really good Georgetown Raiders team. The winner of the series would enter the OHA Intermediate B play downs.

Playoff fever gripped Elmira. In one series game, Butch received a ten-minute misconduct penalty for "taking out" the referee on a play behind the Georgetown net. In the deciding game of the series, over four hundred Kings fans showed up at the Georgetown arena.

Coach Bill Becker met with Butch and his schooldays chum Cole Bowman in the dressing room before the final game in Georgetown. Becker explained that the key to winning was to shut down the Raiders' Junior Beaumont. He'd scored a lot of goals in the series skating in from the left wing. Becker was relying on his two top defensemen to do the job. They didn't disappoint, although each played a complete game in the process. Bowman scored an empty net goal and the Kings were jubilantly off to the OHA play-downs.

In the first round of the playoffs, the Kings easily defeated the Durham Huskies in a three-game series. The series wasn't completed after Durham forfeited, following a 13-4 defeat. Butch scored four goals in that game.

In a round-robin quarter final series, the Polar Kings played against Milverton and Point Edward. The two top teams, Milverton and Elmira went on to the OHA semi-finals. Gord Trapp, former Polar King and a friend of many Kings players, was a defenseman with the Milverton club. The Polar Kings defeated Trapp's team and had arrived in a place they'd never been to previously. Neither had their fans.

The Polar Kings were on their way to the OHA Intermediate B Championship Series. And they were heading north to Bracebridge, soon to become Santa's "home town." Fans in both towns were in for the hockey series of their lives.

Bracebridge was a beautiful town in the picturesque Muskoka area of Ontario. A huge waterfall at the foot of the town was its centerpiece, providing hydro-power for the community. In 1955, Santa's Village opened. Its location seemed appropriate: at forty-five degrees north latitude, it was exactly halfway between the equator and the North Pole.

Bracebridge was named after early nineteenth century American author Washington Irving's book, Bracebridge Hall, published in 1822. The story centered on an English Manor, its inhabitants, and the tales they told. The Ontario postmaster in charge of naming towns, for reasons known only to him, adopted the name Bracebridge for the future home of Santa.

By 1952, Bracebridge had maintained its strong hockey tradition. Among its hockey graduates would be NHL players Roger Crozier and Kris King. But undeniably, the town's hockey hero was Irvine Wallace "Ace" Bailey, born in Bracebridge on July 3, 1903. Bailey was a Toronto Maple Leaf from 1926-33. He led them to the Stanley Cup in 1932. A year later, his career ended abruptly when he hit his head on the ice and fractured his skull, following a hit from behind by Eddie Shore of the Boston Bruins. He never played hockey again.

An all-star benefit game was held at Maple Leaf Gardens on February 14, 1934. Over $20,000 was raised for Bailey and his family. Before the game began, Shore and Bailey shook hands and embraced at centre ice. It was the league's first all-star game. Thirteen years later, all-star games became an annual occurrence. Bailey's #6 banner hangs above the ice at Toronto's Air Canada Centre in the middle of other great Leafs so honored.

Bailey's #6 jersey was the first ever to be retired by an NHL team. He and Bill Barilko's #5 are the only two permanently retired by the Leafs. However, at Bailey's request, Leaf forward, Ron Ellis wore #6 throughout his career.

By the time the championship series began, maple syrup season was over in Woolwich Township. Farmers were in the fields with manure spreaders. The winter ice at the Floradale dam had long since disappeared.

But in the glorious spring of 1952, the Bracebridge Bears and the Elmira Polar Kings were playing for the OHA Intermediate B Hockey Championship. The games provided arguably the most dramatic, exciting, and unusual hockey series in the history of Canada's game in either town.

The first, tension-filled game in Elmira ended in a 5-5 tie. It was an indication of what was to follow. The Bracebridge fans weren't sure if they should be alarmed or amused by an Elmira fan who seemed to be doing a dance on the ice, and another whose howl gave them goosebumps.

With five minutes to go in the second game in Bracebridge, the Kings were leading 4-1. They lost 5-4. Butch's buddy, Cole Bowman said of the Bears, "They could really tear your heart out in the last few minutes of play. They had established a reputation as a come-from-behind team."

Eddie Cantor's bar stool didn't have a reserved sign on it. But if he was at the Steddick, it's where he sat. His favorite happy hour place became the unofficial headquarters for Elmira's enthusiastic fans. Following home games, a few of the Polar Kings dropped by for spare ribs and mashed potatoes. Business was never so good. Even the annual always popular Elmira Fall Fair, which attracted up to twenty thousand people, didn't bring in as many thirsty citizens,

The hotel's management had to hire Esther, one of the young tellers at the Royal Bank to come in about eight o'clock in the evening to answer the never-ending phone calls during games in Bracebridge. Schultsie, the King's trainer, would call Ed from a phone booth outside the Bracebridge arena at the end of each period, with the score. Esther had the answer to the question she knew every caller would ask.

On the way to Bracebridge, one late afternoon of a game day, Schultsie startled everyone on the bus when he shouted, "Stop the bus! We forgot the skates! Stop the bus!" Contact was made to someone in Elmira, who, breaking some speed limits, got the skates to the bus in time for the start of the game.

In 1952, the OHA didn't have teams go to overtime to break a tie in playoff games. After seven games in the Elmira-Bracebridge series, each team had won three games and they had tied one. The OHA determined that there would be a total goals two-game home-and-home series to decide the winner. The first of the two games was scheduled for beautiful Bracebridge on a Friday night.

Elmira fans were determined to show their support. The Link Belt and Naugatuck Chemical parking lots were empty shortly after the bells rang to signal the end of the final shifts of the work week. It was late afternoon on the last Friday in April. If they didn't stop for supper, the men (and a few women) could make the three-hour ride to Bracebridge in time for the 8:00 p.m. game start. Bracebridge was a small town, but they had enough hotel rooms for the Elmira folks who wanted to stay for the weekend.

The game was worth the drive to Bracebridge. It was as exciting and close as each of the previous seven. The Polar Kings managed a hard-fought, nail-biting, 5-4 victory. But they were only up one goal in the two-game total goals series. No one was celebrating yet. However, coach Bill Becker and manager Doc Gibson felt their team was in a good position to win it all at home.

Bracebridge and Elmira were safe, friendly towns. Car doors were seldom locked. Neighbors sat on their front porches and invited passersby to join them. If you didn't know the person you passed on the street, he was either new in town or was visiting.

Polar Kings and Bears fans treated each other like well-connected neighbors. The hockey games became social gatherings where you found out the names of children and the interests of their parents. And when the siren howled to signal the end of a game, if you didn't know, you really couldn't tell which team won or lost by the reactions of the fans.

The early May Monday in Elmira was the start of a record-setting day. That evening, the absolute last game of the championship series would be played at Elmira Memorial Arena. No sports fan had ever heard of a seven-game hockey series going to nine games.

Children on Elmira's sidewalks were skipping double-dutch and roller skating before the school day began. A caravan of horses and buggies were taking Old Order Mennonite families to a funeral at the Elmira Meetinghouse up on Church Street, a scene that made Elmira unique, and piqued the curiosity of the Bracebridge visitors.

Clarence Brubacher from the Brubacher Grocery Store, Dave Dreisinger from his funeral home business, and Lefty Weichel from his family's hardware store, were in an animated conversation on the corner of Arthur and Mill streets, in front of Harold Blair's Drug store. The topic of conversation was about the Polar Kings' goalkeepers. Would it be the local favorite Soehner, or the equally talented Hillis from Hespeler in goal for the final game?

Polar Kings' team manager Doc Gibson cancelled all dental appointments scheduled after 4:00 p.m. at his downtown upstairs office.

By 3:30 in the afternoon, the lineup outside the Elmira Memorial Arena stretched from Ernst Street to South Street, the length of the building. Arena manager Jack Sumner unlocked the doors three hours later.

Cole Bowman, Butch's friend and Polar King teammate, remembers the day: "It was a beautiful morning in Elmira and everyone was in good spirits. Shopkeepers were sweeping their section of sidewalk. I went to Kares Cafe and Candy Store for a coffee with a colleague. Up on Snyder Avenue, people were lining up outside the arena, hoping to get tickets to the game. The guys at the railway station at the south end of town were expecting a train from Bracebridge loaded with fans. I dropped into Jack Cameron's Barbershop for a shave. "

Jack said, "Anyway, I've got a good-sized bet on you guys tonight. And if you don't come through, the next shave will be a real dandy."

Cole went to pay, but Jack held up his hands. He said, "Forget it, this one's for good luck."

Cole thought about his teammates, the small-town guys like himself, guys the team could count on. He thought of Butch's brother, Dick, back on defense—"a big, good-natured player, over six feet fall, and 230 pounds of muscle."

He thought of his Floradale school chum. "Then, of course on right wing was Butch Martin. Here was our hope. The coach knew it and every man on the team knew it. He was an outstanding playmaker. Together with his knowledge of the game, that made Butch Martin the great player he was. I breathed a sigh of relief. After all, with a man of that caliber, we had a good chance, providing we worked hard."

Polar Kings' coach, Biil Becker, came to Cole's mind. "Bill Becker became a great coach. He was a credit the team and to the town. Nothing upset him. There is nothing we players wouldn't have done for him."

By game time at 8:00 p.m. there were more people packed into the arena than there were residents of the town. Unbelievable as it may sound, there were teenaged boys sitting on the rafters extending over the ice surface. Usually there was adequate space for one row of fans behind the seating area. At the final game there were three, and sometimes four rows packed together. The fire chief didn't say a thing about fire regulations: he was playing goal for the Polar Kings.

By the start of the game, Elmira's streets were as quiet as a fly landing on Blendina Martin's feather duster. The Steddick had a family of four in for supper, enjoying smoked pork sausage and creamed potatoes. Ed, the server, cleaned the bar counter. Then he cleaned it again. He swept the floor. For an antsy guy, the quiet seemed cruel and punishing.

Finally, he plopped down on a wooden bar stool and browsed through Arlie Davis' "I See By The Signet" column. It noted that once again Elmira hoped to be Canada's only weedless town. Two springs back, about fifty percent of lawns had been sprayed with 2-4-D. The others hadn't needed it. Boulevards and the grass at the downtown Gore Park, and other public spaces were sprayed. The spraying was going to happen again this spring, right after the hockey season.

Cole's strength was his remarkable skating ability. From his defense position he'd take off with the puck and see what developed. Sometime, during the season he scored on such a solo rush. But in the championship round he played a little more cautiously. What he needed to do, and did well, was hustle back to his defensive position to help break up a potential two-on-one, or other scoring threat. Amazingly, but not surprisingly, the Floradale school buddies were on the ice for the entire game.

The jovial and party-like atmosphere at the final game was enhanced by the presence of the Elmira Musical Society town band, squished into the stairway easing up to the crowded snack bar.

Elmira minor hockey star Abner Martin wiped his supper plate with his bread and left the kitchen table. He'd eat his share of vanilla pie after the game. Bill McLean hired him to sell bags of peanuts in the shell at ten cents a bag at the game. Business was great! By the time the teams skated out for warm up, Ab had sold a hundred pounds of peanuts.

McLean owned Bill's Grill where Hampton Street and Streeter Lane met. He'd advertised a pre-game special: a generous supply of fish and chips for thirty cents. He promised patrons that they'd be squeezing lemon on their battered cod within four minutes of placing their order. There were only a few places to sit in Bill's place. It didn't matter. That evening kids and their parents grabbed the thin cardboard food containers and rushed to their homes. If you didn't know why, you'd never seen a Polar Kings game.

Abner Martin, with no more peanuts to sell, stood quietly on his own at the top of the wooden arena stairs. "In the future," he said, "I'll be a Polar King."

Between the game in Bracebridge and the final game in Elmira, Polar Kings forward Doug Schwindt had other things than hockey on his mind. The attractive young woman who had been in the stands at the Friday night game in Bracebridge was now Mrs. Schwindt. She and her Polar King husband were celebrating their third day of marriage.

The Kings and the Bears went through their warm-up skate and drills in similar fashion—totally focused, occasionally chatting, getting energy from the packed house who couldn't stop cheering, and keeping their shots on goalies low. The days of goalie masks had not yet arrived and shooting a puck close to his head was a perfect recipe for a very upset goalkeeper going into the most important game of the season.

Elmira's band played a more spirited version than usual of "God Save the Queen." Fans stood tall, removed their hats and joined the band with their vocal rendition of the anthem.

The referee blew his whistle, checked with the goal judges, waved the centermen into the face-off circle and dropped the puck. The magic of the evening began to unfold.

The town's minor teams had brought home championship after championship and had received good local support. But the final Kings-Bears game was an event the likes of which Elmira folks had never experienced. It was new territory and felt as much like a giant, happy, noisy, party as it did a sporting event.

The days of watching NHL hockey on CBC television didn't arrive until October of 1952, five months after Elmira's big hockey night. If you wanted to catch the emotions and hear the sounds of a hockey game, you needed to go to the rink and be a part of it.

Bracebridge scored a goal and Elmira tied it up. Elmira scored the next goal and Bracebridge tied it up. This quid pro quo style of game played havoc with the fans' emotions. Each goal brought a short-lived feeling of exhilaration or letdown, depending on which team scored.

Going into the third period, you couldn't have predicted a winner. With increasing tension, there seemed to be an unsettled quietness throughout the crowd, ready to be disrupted with a roar when the red light behind the goal signaled that your team had scored.

The blue haze of smoke settling over the ice seemed to expand as fans lit up their Lucky Strikes more frequently.

Every shift, every pass, every shot on goal or save by a goalie could make the difference of winning or losing. One giveaway could mean a goal. The stigma of a selfish penalty might last a career. The Kings needed one goal to clinch the title: just one goal!

Late in the final period, with the score tied 5-5, a Kings forward quickly broke to the center of the ice, in his team's zone and yelled "Mike!" Winger Mike Forester, a home-town guy, took a quick look to his left and directed the puck in the direction of the sound-a voice he'd often heard in previous games. But he was taking a big chance in his own zone. Then he looked. A teammate was skating furiously into the Bracebridge end with the puck on his stick on a breakaway. Mike didn't see the light flash, but he heard the crowd. Doug Schwindt had scored! His Polar Kings were champs!

Somewhere in the crowd, a new bride hugged Mrs. Marion Forester.

The Elmira Musical Society Band led the parade around the perimeter of the ice. Some of the crowd, including Bracebridge fans, many arm in arm, exuberantly joined in.

Harry Soehner doffed his goal equipment and hustled to the fire station. By the time his teammates were leaving the dressing-room, Harry was ready to lead the parade through the now lively streets of the town as custodian of the fire engine. Butch, Dick, Cole and their teammates climbed aboard. Elmira fans, joined by their friends from Bracebridge joined in the parade,

Eddie Cantor hurried to the Steddick. As he ordered a beer for himself and another for Al who hadn't yet arrived, he saw the place get so crowded that folks were lining up outside on Arthur Street as far as Frankie McCormick's Service Station. Eddie felt like a king; a real king! He never stopped smiling. His Kings were champs and he didn't have to report to work the next day until the afternoon shift! Butch had made the difference.

Arlie Davis's next Signet carried a front page picture of Butch and PeeWee waving from the fire engine. It wasn't the New York Rangers, and it wasn't the Stanley Cup. But neither were the NHL Rangers in a parade along Broadway celebrating a championship.

It was a night to remember. Butch had done what he'd announced he'd do—"play with my hometown friends." He was now able to add, "And win a championship."

THE ARTIST
COLE BOWMAN

Cole Bowman the other "famous graduate" from Floradale School had a story with some similarities to Butch's. His grandfather, Daniel, was an old Order Mennonite. Pop Martin, Butch's dad, had purchased the sawmill from Daniel, turning it into S. S. Martin and Sons.

Cole, like Butch, played hockey, as a teenager with and against players at least a few years older than he. His teammates included Butch's brothers, Elmer and Willard. Cole went on to join the Kitchener Greenshirts Junior A team. They lost to Toronto in a league final series. His defense partner was Frank Udvari. By 1952, Udvari had reached the NHL as a referee. At the end of his career, about fourteen years, later, he'd earned the reputation as the NHL's top on-ice official.

During a Greenshirts game against the Paris Maroons, Harold "Hap" Day, then coach of the Leafs, and his manager Harold Ballard were in the stands, watching and evaluating. They invited Cole to the following season's Leafs training camp.

But World War II came. Cole was drafted and never made it to the camp.

Nevertheless, Cole made it as a professional when he played for a Canadian Services team, the Infantry A-19. His team, along with air force and navy teams, had NHL players on their rosters. An opposing centerman that Cole had to shut down at his defense position was Punch Imlach, who went on to coach the Toronto Maple Leafs to four

Stanley Cups.

Cole had to make a major decision after his time in the armed services. He was told by the Leafs that he could play professionally for St. Louis in the American Hockey League. He also thought he could return to Waterloo County to pursue a career as an artist.

In the end, Cole, the artist and Cole the hockey player found space for each other.

Cole returned to Elmira. He played on Intermediate hockey teams as a Bridgeport Vet, a Palmerston Flyer and the champion Polar Kings. He became player-coach of the Exeter Mohawks. Cole even had a season as coach of a team in the Elmira Mennonite Church League.

Cole was a wonderful skater. I'm sure he could have been an accomplished figure skater. When combined with his competitive spirit and desire to win, he was fun to watch. As was the case with his Floradale buddy Butch, he simply loved to play hockey. He enjoyed himself on the ice.

Cole's skating ability and competitive spirit stayed with him into his later years. He joined a group of seniors for pick-up games at the Kitchener Auditorium. When Cole got the puck, he automatically did what he'd always done: skate fast, stick-handle, and more often than not get a shot on goal. But the "old guys" couldn't keep up with him and that concerned them. So they gathered 'round and reminded Cole that this was no longer the Polar Kings, but rather a bunch of old-timers out to have a bit of exercise.

Golf became a passion for Cole, as hockey had been. And as with hockey, his competitiveness and aspirations to go far beyond "good" never left him. Those qualities were a part of Cole's persona. He was always far beyond "good." In fact he was outstanding in whatever he undertook.

Cole's renown came as an artist. He was called "a majestic realist, capturing on canvas the seasonal beauty of Ontario landscapes." Coincidentally some of his work showed brilliant scenes from the

Muskoka area of Ontario, home of the Bracebridge Bears. But he also created numerous paintings with Mennonite themes. His marvelous oil paintings have been hung in hundreds of homes in Canada, and internationally. He donated one to Floradale Public School "where it all began."

In 2014, Cole's son Terry had scrapbooks filled with notes of praise and appreciation from people with his father's paintings hanging in their homes, or whom he'd taught. Cole received Christmas greetings from around the world.

Cole said, "Although I have been successful as an artist, I never felt I deserved the fame that people have awarded me. My most honest critic will be time. Simplicity, in my mind, is the key of good design in painting."

Flora McCrea Eaton, Lady Eaton, wife of Toronto department store president and heir Sir John Craig Eaton, arranged to have Cole's paintings shown in Eaton Stores across Canada. Later, a similar arrangement was made with the Simpson-Sears chain.

For ten years Cole displayed his paintings four times a year in Ottawa. Some of them were purchased by the Dutch ambassador to Canada to be hung in the Dutch Embassy.

Group of Seven painters A. Y. Jackson, and Arthur Lismer went to Cole's Ottawa shows. Amid words of praise for his work, they added a few helpful tips from their experiences.

Susannah Shantz, a Woolwich Township Old Order Mennonite teacher, took art lessons from Cole. In a community that had been reluctant to become involved with the arts, it was a major step. When she married Milton Bauman, Susannah and her husband moved to a home just across Ruggle's Road from the former Seranus Martin home, and a short distance from the dam.

For years, Elmira jeweler, Aden Bauman, shared a space with Cole and his studio. The Bauman and Bowman relationship grew into a close friendship. Cole had a keen sense of humor and was a wonderful storyteller; his friend Aden was an appreciative audience. Aden was deeply moved when Cole presented him with an oil painting depicting the personable jeweler working at his watch repair bench.

Many aspiring artists from Waterloo County and beyond got their start and encouragement from Cole, in his Elmira studio. The heartfelt cards of appreciation he received from many of them brought tears to his eyes.

On October 27, 2003, Cole died. He was in his seventy-ninth year. Butch lost a lifelong friend. Canada lost a gifted artist.

THE BEST YEARS OF OUR LIVES

Butch spent some summer weeks at beautiful Chesley Lake Mennonite Camp, as a counselor at a boys camp. One summer he met Carl Buschert, a young adolescent camper from Kitchener. Carl's parents' once-happy relationship was deteriorating. Butch made a promise that should the need arise, Carl could live with he and his wife. Unfortunately, that time came. With the assistance of pastor John Hess, who knew all the families involved, Carl was welcomed into Butch and PeeWee's home in Floradale.

For the next twelve years, Butch and PeeWee, as well as the Seranus Martin family provided a comfortable home to "Bush" who became a part of the Martin family and was hired on as an employee at the sawmill.

Pop was asked by a customer who the new young guy was piling lumber in the yard at the sawmill. Pop proudly replied, "Why, that boy is my adopted son." In 2014, more than sixty years later, Carl's voice wavered when he recalled the incident. In many ways Carl became a son, fully accepted into the Martin family. And Butch was like a brother.

When Carl was putting for par on the golf course, Butch was holding the flag. When Butch played first base for Elmira's softball team, Carl was beside him at second. When Butch was finding their seats at Detroit's Tiger Stadium, Carl was at the lunch counter, buying his first hot dog and Pepsi.

Butch was honored to be inducted into the Old Timers Hockey Hall of Fame; Carl nominated him. When Carl was looking for a new car, Butch was the salesman he approached for advice and from whom he made the purchase.

Brothers Butch, Dick and Elmer unselfishly gave of their time to introduce us Mennonite adolescent boys to organized hockey. Most of us were used to playing shinny—on an outdoor rink at little Yatton school; on a sheet of ice inside at Martin's Tile Yard in Wallenstein; at the Floradale dam, or on frozen farm ponds.

Our initial visit to Waterloo Memorial Arena, as a put-together hockey team, was worthy of inclusion in a comedy act. Some of us wore regular winter mitts as hockey gloves. Others of us had no equipment, other than skates and a hockey stick. Few had regular hockey pants. When we played the game we carried on like we were on a frozen pond, with boards. Icing and off-sides were new concepts.

In some ways we were the hockey version of Richard Wagamese's Ragged Company.

With the Martin brothers' help and understanding, we'd opened a window into a part of society that few of us had previously experienced. After more than sixty years, we remember it vividly.

That game may have lapsed from Butch's memory but some of the members of that team still meet monthly for breakfast. In 2014, all had reached our seventy-fifth birthday and beyond. Occasionally one of us drags out the picture of the hockey group, with arms around each other's shoulders, smiling: not because we'd won anything important, but because we knew we were a part of something very special in our lives.

Butch had a great deal to do with that.

After games, we stopped most frequently at the iconic Harmony Lunch, the first restaurant some had ever entered. Our naiveté knew no bounds. When a waitress asked what we'd like on our burgers, one of our group replied, "Well........I guess, ham." It seemed like a reasonable request for something called a hamburger. We needed thirty-two cents to buy a burger and a bottled soft drink—more than the weekly allowance for most of us. Butch and Dick looked after the shortfall.

Some years later, Butch donated the "Butch Martin Trophy" which became the annual award to the top scorer in the Elmira and District Church Hockey League. Their games were played at the Elmira Arena. On the occasion of the league's twentieth anniversary, Butch and Dick played with Elmira Mennonite's team in an exhibition game that Carl Buschert had arranged.

Elmira Gems, Elmira Mennonite Church's team in the church league at a later time, had a forward line made up of Graham Snyder and his sons Dan and Jake.

After an outstanding Junior A career, Dan entered the NHL as an Atlanta Thrasher. On October 5, 2003, he died as a result of a single vehicle accident in a car driven by Dan's teammate, Dany Heatley, in Atlanta. Dan's untimely death had a huge impact on the entire hockey community. His funeral was held at Elmira Mennonite Church, a ten-minute drive from Floradale Mennonite, Butch's home church.

As the driver of the car, Heatley faced serious criminal charges that seemed certain to result in his incarceration. It was a high profile case and carried by media releases across North America.

Dan's parents, Elmira residents, Graham and LuAnn, responded in a manner that one could fairly describe as counter-cultural. They forgave Heatley and petitioned the judge to show leniency towards him when he stood trial.

Twenty-five years earlier, Butch had made counter-cultural decision that gained much publicity. The two situations are entirely different on many levels. However, they are both examples of the strength of convictions that have their roots in the belief systems of the times and the very similar Woolwich Township communities in which most family members grew up.

One hockey season, members of the Elmira Gems, then evolving into maturing young men, were in a playoff series with Stirling Avenue Mennonite of Kitchener. As the series progressed so did the competitive juices.

Buschert, our player-coach, noticed some unfamiliar players on the Stirling team; guys whose skills were superior to most Church League players. They were playing for OHA teams from the area and hadn't played during the season for Stirling. Coach Bush rightly felt that the opposition was taking unfair advantage which encroached on the spirit of fairness that the league promoted.

One game remained, the one that would decide the winner.

Butch and Ab Martin, both playing at high competitive levels, responded positively to Bush's invitation to be Gems for one game. Needless to say, it was no contest. In previous games, the Stirling team had played a tough physical game. Lloyd "Striker" Martin, brother of Willy, a member of the Gems team, hollered, "Why don't you try to hit our two new guys?" The rest of us smiled. Our two protectors were close by.

Butch and the Polar Kings graduated to the OHA Intermediate A League for the 1952-53 season. Their season ended one series short of reaching an OHA championship.

On January 12, 1953, the Canadian Amateur Hockey Association President, W.B. George announced that Canada would not be sending a team to the IIHF World hockey Championships. The tournament was played in Basel and Zurich, Switzerland. He said, "Every year we spend ten thousand dollars to send a Canadian team to Europe to play exhibition games. All the games are played to packed houses that only enrich European hockey coffers. In return we are subjective to constant, unnecessary abuse over our Canadian style of play."

The 1953 tournament was the first IIHF championship that included only European teams. Sweden went undefeated to win their first World Championship. The Soviets were expected to make their first appearance in international competition, but withdrew. Some nations suspected it was a serious injury to star player Vsevolod Bobrov that was responsible for the decision not to take part. Czechoslovakia withdrew partway through the tournament and returned home. The action was in respect for their leader Klement Gottwald who succumbed to pneumonia nine days after the death of Soviet dictator, Joseph Stalin.

Concerned about finances, the CAHA was looking for a Senior A team to look after their own expenses to the 1954 IIHF Championship in Stockholm, Sweden. None volunteered. The best available team, under the circumstances, was the East York Lyndhursts, a Toronto Senior B team. They were named after and sponsored by a local car dealership. The East York team had been runners-up in the 1953-54 OHA Senior B championship series.

The Lyndhursts' management was looking to strengthen their team for the World Championships. They invited Butch to join them. He thought about it carefully. But in the end his decision was to stay with the Kings for the entire 1953-54 season. He said, "I was playing at home, with a group of players with whom I was comfortable. I didn't even recognize the names of any of the Lyndhurst players."

There were many doubts about the Lyndhursts' ability to represent Canada in a competitive manner. The Canadian press ridiculed them, and thought they would be an embarrassment. But they won their first six tournament games.

The Soviet Union made its first international appearance, and Canada's team met them in the final game. On March 17, before 16,000 fans, the Soviets completely dominated Canada and earned the gold medal with a 7-2 final score. It was an improbable and impressive victory. Canada's Lyndhursts earned silver. The United States again wasn't represented.

Vsevolod Bobrov was named the tournament's top player. He and Nikolai Pushkov, the Soviet goalie, were on a course to meet Butch two years later.

Butch and the Polar Kings won the OHA Intermediate A championship in the 1953-54 season. They easily defeated the Aylmer Trojans in the final series. Ab Martin, then a member of Elmira's championship juvenile team was called up by the Kings for the final game. In an 11-1 romp, he scored one goal. Ab's dream of being a King, even for a day, had arrived. But there were many exciting days ahead in hockey for Nelson Martin's youngest son.

During the next two seasons, 1954-55 and 1955-56, Butch and the Polar Kings were in the OHA Senior B league. They had some success, but didn't return to the glory days of 1952 when they had beaten Bracebridge in the unprecedented nine-game series.

In the 1954-55 season, while Butch was playing for the Polar Kings, his former team, the Dutchmen were on their way to winning the Allan Cup. Their success was unprecedented for the team and the city of Kitchener.

The Allan Cup was originally awarded annually to the national Senior AAA amateur men's hockey champions of Canada. Later it was changed to Senior A. Colonel Sir Montagu Allan of Ravenscrag, Montreal first donated the Cup in 1909. By 2014 it retained an important place in Canadian Ice Hockey, although the interest in Senior A hockey had dimmed.

Historically, the final series which would determine the recipient of the Allan Cup was played in either eastern or western Canada, in the home community of one of the teams represented. Since its inception, the Cup has been won by a team from every province and the Yukon.

During the years of the Senior A League in which the Dutchmen participated, winning the Allan Cup was a really big deal. In the 1954-1955 season, the glory of winning the cup was considerably enhanced by the knowledge that its winner would represent Canada in the following year's World Championship as part of the VII Winter Olympic Games in Cortina d'Ampezzo, Italy.

The Kitchener-Waterloo Dutchmen earned that privilege by winning the 1955 Allan Cup, defeating the Fort William Beavers four games to one. The championship series was hosted by the Dutchmen.

WOOLWICH IS HOCKEYVILLE
BUTCH - 80 + Grandson PAUL - 19
The "All Martin" Game

The Martin Family

Front Row: Lucinda, Seranus, Blendina, Valina
Middle Row: Lena, Viola, Naomi
Back Row: Elmer, Willard (Dick), Floyd (Butch)

The youngest Martin Children - Viola and Butch

Floradale School Students - 1939
Butch is second from left in the first row.
Cole Bowman is fourth from left in back row.

Floradale Indians Hockey Club

Butch is seated in front.

First Row (from left):   Cecil Capling, Cole Bowman, Ab Frey, (unidentified player), Emmanuel Bowman

Middle Row (from left): Henry Gatey, Goodie Hilker, Howard Bauman, Owen Bowman, Edgar Dahmer, ( ) Kinzie

Back Row (from left):   Jack Soehner, Elmer Weelan, Dick Martin, Bill Hilker, Coach Lorne Stahlbaum

At the Floradale Dam
Butch is on the left. Vern Gingrich is to the right of Butch. Gord
Gingrich is on the far right. Both are brothers of this book's author.

Waterloo Raiters

1945-46 Ontario Hockey Association Junior 'B' Club

Back Row - (left to right) Clayt Voisin (Trainer), Jerry Lorentz, Grant Uhrig, Roy Schafer, Butch Martin, John Dooley, Harry Weaver, Leo Schmalz (Coach)
Front Row - (left to right) Carl Kreutzweiser, Bun Martin, Don Mitchell, John Fisher, Orval Hahn, Howard Zeigler, Durwood Garner.
Front - Lorne Winkler (Mascot)

Courtesy of Waterloo Library

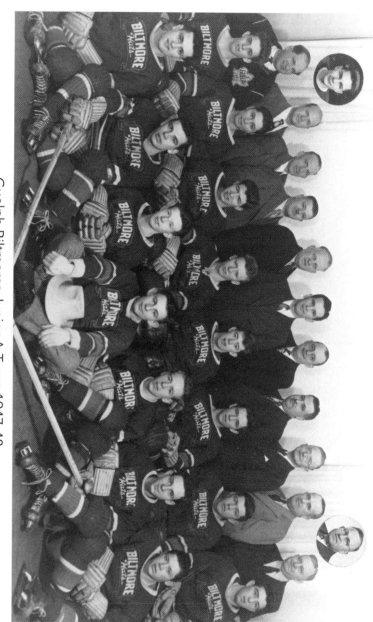

Guelph Biltmores Junior A Team 1947-48

Middle Row (left to right): G. Sonmor, F. Bathgate, N. Gordon, R. Plumb, J Beasley, L. Ferguson, Butch Martin, E. Bolan

Front Row (left to right): L. Thomson, G. Millar, J. Flynn, A. Dudlick (stick boy) S. McLellan, R. Ewing, L. Speck

Courtesy of Guelph Civic Museum

Newlyweds

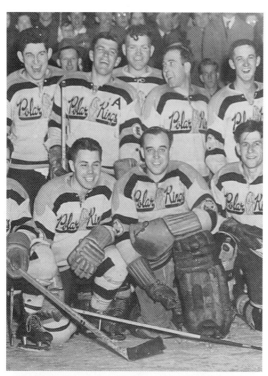

Jubilant Polar Kings:
Intermediate B
Champions 1952

Back Row (from left):
Eugene Miller, Butch
Martin, Dick Martin, Cole
Bowman, Harvey Vines

Front Row (from left):
Doug Blake, Don Sherk,
(   ) Hillis, Ed Symonds

Celebrating OHA Intermediate A Championship as an Elmira Polar King
Peewee is with Butch in the vehicle. Harvey Vines in on the right and
Gord Trapp is the driver. Both were team mates of Butch with the
Polar Kings

FROM RUSSIA WITH LOVE
THE VII WINTER OLYMPIC GAMES

In 1956 the winners of the Winter Olympic Hockey competition would also be declared World Champions. The European team with the best record at the Games would be European Champions, also considered a prestigious honor.

A new concept for developing a national hockey team in Switzerland was in the news in 1955. The best players in the country were selected. They went to a training camp together in Geneva and got to know each other. That was important because there was a mix of Italian, French and German speaking players. Their coaches were Canadians and their sticks were made in Canada. For Canada, such an idea was not yet on the table.

The legendary Bobby Bauer was coach of the Allan Cup-winning Dutchmen. He consented to coach the team at the Winter Games. Bauer wanted to assemble the best team possible. But he'd be losing a few really good players, re-instated professionals. Olympic rules clearly stated that no one who'd participated in professional sport of any kind would be allowed to be an Olympian.

Bauer needed some really strong amateur replacements: guys with great skills and equally great character. As Canada's team, they would be the representatives of their country. Canada and the world would be watching.

Bauer was a member of a Waterloo family of eleven. The six brothers in the family all served in the Canadian armed forces. He and two lifelong friends, Milt Schmidt and Woody Dumart were members of the Kitchener Greenshirts Junior A hockey team. They had signed contracts together and joined the Boston Bruins as a forward line.

The three Waterloo County friends helped the Bruins dominate the NHL in the 1930s and early 1940s. A minor league coach had dubbed them the Sauerkraut Line because of their German-Kitchener heritage. That got changed to the Kraut Line, described by hockey historians as one of the best lines ever in the NHL. Bauer was awarded the Lady Byng Trophy on three occasions. All members of the Kraut line were inducted into the Hockey Hall of Fame, Bauer posthumously in 1996.

Bauer clearly understood Butch's rationale for the important, tough decisions he made about his involvement in competitive hockey. His brother had faced a few such choices

David Bauer was an outstanding player with the St. Michael's Majors Junior A team. The year the Majors won the Memorial Cup, David had left in mid-season to enlist in the military. Bobby said, "David was a terrific hockey player. He could have made it to the NHL easily, had he wanted to pursue a professional career." David chose to enter the seminary of the Basilican Fathers to become a priest. Father David Bauer returned to St. Mikes as a teacher and coach of the Majors. In 1964, following up on his brainchild, he took a team of university students from across Canada to the Winter Olympic Games in Innsbruck, Austria. He was later inducted into the Hockey Hall of Fame as a builder.

Bobby Bauer had coached Butch as a junior in Guelph and played twenty-three games beside him with the 1949-50 Dutchmen team. He invited Butch to join his former team, the Dutchmen, for the Winter Olympic Games of 1956.

Butch found Bauer to be a very knowledgeable hockey person, a calming presence, a gentleman, and a man of character. Butch played on the same team with some of the Dutchmen players. And while the Dutchmen would be Canada's team, it would also be identified with Waterloo County, where the Martin family and relatives resided, where

Butch was employed, and where he had many dear friends. "Count me in," said Butch.

But he was a Polar King. He'd won two Ontario championships with his hometown buddies. There was a realistic chance that the Kings could be in the hunt for the Ontario Senior B championship with the arrival of the spring of 1956. And five years earlier he'd made headlines in the press, announcing that he was retiring from the Dutchmen because of ethical concerns that included playing competitive hockey on Sundays.

In the end, the Dutchmen, Polar Kings, and Butch came to compromise. He'd stay a King for the season but he'd be loaned to the Dutchmen for the duration of their Olympic experience. He'd play a few pre-Olympic games with the Dutchmen. Butch's assignment was to play right defense. He was twenty-seven years old. At the conclusion of the Olympics he'd return to the Polar Kings.

There were approximately fifty thousand people residing in Kitchener in 1956. A year earlier they had rejoiced with the rest of the world when the Salk vaccine arrived, putting a stop to the recurring terror and crippling effects of polio.

Around the same time, nine thousand Kitchener students took part in a drill based on the scenario of a bombing attack from enemy aircrafts on their way to strike Niagara Falls.

It was the era of poodle skirts, sock hops, drive in theaters and soda fountains. A new Chevy Corvette cost $3631. Gas was twenty-five cents a gallon. Harmony Lunch's famous hamburgers sold for fifteen cents.

On the world stage, the Cold War began after the allied victory in World War II. The Soviet Union made its Olympic debut at the 1952 Summer Games in Helsinki, Finland. Their athletes would make their Winter Games debut in 1956 at Cortina, Italy. Butch and the Dutchmen would meet their hockey team.

Stalin's successor, Soviet general secretary Nikita Khrushchev's well publicized aim was to use international sports competitions, like the

Olympics, to demonstrate the superiority of Communism, strengthen political ties with other Communist countries, and project the Soviet Union as a peace-loving nation actively engaged in the world.

Fortunately there was no international political upheaval to disturb the 1956 Winter Games. However, by the time the 1956 Summer Olympic Games opened, seven countries had boycotted, because of the Soviet's participation. Their actions were a response to the Suez Crisis, and the Soviet invasion of Hungary to suppress its revolution.

In a November 1955 league game against Chatham Maroons, the Dutchmen's Ken Laufman had four goals and six assists. He was the leading scorer in the Senior A League. With an enviable scoring record he was seen as a key member of the Cortina-bound Dutchmen. His success would have a lot to do with their success. Butch thought very highly of him.

Butch left the Polar Kings in a hunt for first place when he joined the Dutchmen.

The hockey Dutchmen were in need of funds to cover their Olympic costs. A new set of hockey pants, for example, was about five hundred dollars. The CAHA paid the travel expenses for up to a party of twenty. The minimum cost per person was estimated at seven hundred dollars

Kitchener travel agent Clare Miller waited to get permission to start booking for an additional charter plane for Dutchmen fans. The cost was estimated at $550 return fare between Toronto's Malton Airport and Milan, Italy.

Kitchener resident and future Polar King goalie Ron Kilby played exhibition games against the Soviet National team. Kilby played for Harringay, England in the games, although his home team was London's Wembley. After a 5-4 exhibition loss to the Soviets, Kilby warned the Dutchmen of the strength of the Soviet team. Gene Miller, the resident of Elmira who once played for the Polar Kings, also spent some time with the Harringay team.

London's Evening Standard newspaper had this message: "I don't know how good they are but I hope the Dutchmen are heeding the red light. They must train like iron-men. The Russian steam-roller is now jet propelled."

Some observers felt that although the Soviets trained year round, they lacked the key factors of the flair and instincts for the game. They described their approach as mechanical.

Jack Adams, general manager of the Detroit Red Wings, predicted that the United States team was strong enough to earn a medal in the 1956 Olympic Hockey competition. He was impressed with the American coach, John Mariucci, and star player John Mayasich.

Responses to requests for financial support for the Dutchmen were varied. Windsor Bulldogs had a special Dutchmen Fund Raising night. On January 23, 1956, the CAHA called for all Senior A teams across Canada to raise their admission for that day's home games by ten cents per ticket as a contribution to the Dutchmen's cause. But too many teams balked at the idea to have it come to fruition.

CKCO, Kitchener's television station, sponsored a fundraising telethon. Donation boxes were set out at the Dutchmen home games at the Auditorium.

During the afternoon of January 13, 1956, a Saturday, the Kitchener Police Department led a Dutchmen parade from the Kitchener Auditorium. The float with the team on board travelled down Borden Avenue and followed King Street through downtown Kitchener and Waterloo. The parade was organized by the Kitchener Chamber of Commerce.

The Dutchmen lost six consecutive games before a game against Windsor Bulldogs on the eve of their departure. But that evening, before a packed house at the Auditorium, the Dutchmen convincingly defeated the Bulldogs.

Representatives from the Elmira Polar Kings team were on hand to present Butch, with a gift of luggage.

Some hockey writers expressed concern about the possible fatigue of the Dutchmen. They had played forty-three league games in sixty-five days. Bauer was concerned that the heavy schedule left precious little time for team practices. Others felt that the Dutchmen's greatest concern could be the different climate conditions, as all their games would be played outside.

Bauer's assessment was, "We have built our attack on speed, strong skating, and accurate passing. There is no question about the Soviet's stick-handling abilities. But their team is too mechanical, and they are unable to maneuver with dexterity."

He also credited Butch for his fine two-way play and suggested that he would be quite a help to Canada's team.

An Olympic Committee member said, "Canada's K-W Dutchmen are such prohibitive favorites for the Olympic title, that most of the pre-tournament speculation concerns the runner-up spot."

The optimism was realistic. In spite of losing a lot of talent with the absence of their former pros, they had plenty of strength remaining. For example, Denis Joseph Germain Stanislaus Brodeur, one of their goalies, had the best record in the Senior A league the previous year.

Denis was the father of Olympic gold medal winner Martin Brodeur. By 2014 the two were the only father and son goalkeeper duos to win medals in Olympic history.

When Martin played for Canada's team at Salt Lake City, he honored his father by etching "Salt Lake 2002" and "Cortina 1956" on the chin protector of his mask. Denis Brodeur became one of Canada's most successful sports photographers. He was one of only two photographers to capture the iconic image of Paul Henderson celebrating scoring the winning goal of the 1972 Canada-Soviet summit series.

Forwards Jim Logan, Paul Knox, captain Jack McKenzie, Don Rope, Gerry Théberge and Ken Laufman were proven competitors with the Dutchmen. Tiny Elmira was well-represented. Keith Woodall, Brodeur's goalie companion, was born in the town. McKenzie and Rope were married to women who had begun their teaching careers at Elmira

District High School. Also, the Dutchmen's hard-hitting, hard-shooting defenseman Byrle Klinck had played his minor hockey for Elmira teams. He went on to star for the Kitchener Greenshirts Junior A team before an excellent career in the OHA Senior A and B leagues. Klinck said, "I couldn't believe I made the Olympic team, I was surprised and honored."

Of Butch, his hometown friend, he said, "He was always a gentleman. But he was rough, tough, and solid as a hockey player. On the ice, he always had your back. Butch was a very supportive teammate."

The Dutchmen played hockey at a high level. But they earned their livings from their day-to-day employment. There was a service station attendant, a lithographer, a carpenter, a bricklayer, a sawmill worker, a real estate broker, a branch manager of a finance company, a men's wear salesman, two high school teachers, and three college students. Len Taylor, Kitchener-Waterloo Record sports columnist wrote, "With two teachers and three college students, they should be able to talk the Russians out of a couple of goals."

In the cold, morning darkness of January 15, 1956, Butch and PeeWee locked the front door of their Floradale home, double-checked Butch's luggage and necessary identification, and made their way through Elmira to the Kitchener Auditorium parking lot.

More than two thousand family members, relatives, friends and committed fans were already in a party mood. They carried homemade banners. Small children sat smiling and waving on their parents' shoulders. Three Lishman buses were taken from their usual Elmira to Kitchener run. Decorated with large Go! Dutchmen Go! banners, they lined up to lead the growing cavalcade of cars that was winding around the headquarters.

The Dutchmen supporters were led by a strong group of Blue Line fans. They often gathered at an unofficial downtown hangout located beneath the H. Boehmer Company at Ontario and Charles Streets.

The Reverend Finlay Gordon Stewart of St. Andrews Presbyterian Church, and the Reverend H. B. Smith of St. Anne's Roman Catholic

Church, raised their arms for silence. They led a brief service, concluding with the words, "We urge the players to show themselves not only as fine hockey players, but Christian gentlemen."

Their exhortations echoed the words of Record sports columnist Len Taylor: "The players take their responsibility seriously. I know there will not be any disciplinary problems to worry about, and few on the score of bad manners and loud talking."

Ontario Premier Leslie Frost said, "The people of Canada and Ontario are pulling for this great team and wish for them the greatest success."

PeeWee Martin seemed to sum up the feeling of the wives of the Dutchmen. They'd be remaining home but their thoughts and hopes would be with their husbands. PeeWee said, "We don't care what medals they bring back. We just hope they all come back in one piece!"

The following day she returned to her job at the switchboard at Naugatuck Chemicals in Elmira.

The Dutchmen were carrying on a strong tradition of Canadian hockey presence internationally. In 1924, the first Winter Olympic Games (the International Winter Sports Week), was held in Chamonix, France. After games against Switzerland, Czechoslovakia, Sweden, Great Britain and the United States, Canada earned a gold medal by outscoring the opposition a total of 110-2.

Forward Harry (Moose) Watson scored thirty-seven goals in Chamonix. In 2014 it remained the record of a single Olympics. Watson had lucrative offers to play in the NHL but said, "I put the love of the game before money."

In 1949 the unheralded Edmonton Mercurys were the Western Intermediate champions. They were a controversial choice to represent Canada at the 1950 World Ice Hockey Championships in London, England. Their coach, Jimmy Graham said, "We're not as good as a senior team. But from all accounts, you don't need a senior team to win over there." The Mercurys won the gold medal with a 5-0 record. The Soviets had not yet entered into international tournament.

Czechoslovakia, embroiled in espionage charges with their national team, labeled as "state traitors" were also absent.

In retrospect, the 1950 results likely left Canadians with an unrealistic view of what was forthcoming from European hockey teams.

S. S. Martin and Sons would shut down the sawmill operation for a month early in 1956, which was their usual practice. They'd get their apple press in order to produce apple sauce and apple butter for the folks who brought in apples from their trees and orchards. They'd all pitch in, put in a few more hours than usual, and check out the news from Cortina d'Ampezzo in the evening, in The Kitchener-Waterloo Record.

During Butch's absence from his home area, another Martin was making his mark at the Kitchener Auditorium, where Butch had boarded the bus on the first leg of his Olympic journey.

Abner Martin—the "other Martin"—no longer sold peanuts at Elmira Polar Kings games. He'd joined the Kitchener Canucks of the prestigious OHA Junior A League. Ab was more than holding his own with and against players whose careers would take them to the Hockey Hall of Fame.

In a game report in November of 1955, the headlines in The Record stated; "Abner, the banker from the up-country hockey hot-bed was just about the busiest Canuck on the ice last night as the Canucks joisted with St. Kitts."

Ab played against the future NHL great Frank Mahovlich when he was with St. Mikes. When the Toronto Marlboros visited Kitchener, Ab lined up against his one-time room-mate Bob Pulford and rugged defenseman Bob Baun; both future Leafs. The Record reported: "Ab Martin barged unceremoniously into the Dukes left and right. He was in a big measure responsible for keeping the visiting team scoreless in the final twenty minutes."

By December 1955, Ab and the Canucks were on top of the Junior A League. But he was closely watching the happenings in Cortina. Ab and Butch, both from the same Mennonite community, led the way for other Mennonite youth to follow their athletic dreams.

Amid the early morning goings-on at the Kitchener Auditorium, a large green and white banner held high by two minor hockey players spelled out "Defeat does not rest lightly on the shoulders of a Dutchman." Those words were similar to the one's Conn Smythe wrote in the dressing room of his Toronto Maple Leaf team.

At 7:45 a.m. units from the Kitchener Police Department made their way in front of the first Lishman coach. The cavalcade of three buses, each with a "Go! Dutchmen Go!" banner flapping in the wind, were about to lead an amazing one-hundred and twenty-five vehicles, overflowing with hollering fans, to Toronto's Malton Airport.

Car horns bellowed, fans yelled and a lone cowbell ringer joined in a cacophony of sound. A few tears were shed and warm embraces given.

By 1956, traveling by air to Europe, or taking commercial flights anywhere were uncommon occurrences for families from Waterloo County.

Their beloved Dutchies were more than great hockey players. They were husbands, fathers and brothers. Most had never been away from loved ones for an extended period. Their families had concerns about safety and injuries. The war was over, but ten years later, Europe was still rebuilding from its ravages. But compared to 2014, the concerns about security were minor. Nevertheless, their prayers were more about safety than about winning.

The clamorous entourage drove along highway 7 through Acton and Georgetown. Children on their way to class waved and blew kisses. Folks at the local coffee shop stepped onto the street to see what all the commotion was about. It was the invasion of Canada's team!

Malton's Trans Canadian Airlines terminal had never seen anything like the scene that erupted in the parking lot and made its way inside. Without apology or inquiry, the space was suddenly packed with green and white. The Dutchie faithful shook hands, slapped each other on the back, and marched and danced to the strains of the Branch 50 Canadian Legion Pipe Band.

Resplendent in identical grey flannel trousers, blue blazers, station wagon coats, and red toques, the Dutchmen made their way up the steps to the Trans Canadian aircraft awaiting them. Legion Pipe Band were their guard of honor. Butch had never seen the inside of an airplane. He wasn't alone.

The flight landed at Montreal's Dorval Airport, the Canadian headquarters of Trans Canadian Airways. Montreal Mayor Drapeau hosted the Dutchmen at a noon luncheon at Ruby Fay's Restaurant. Then the plane stopped at Gander, Newfoundland before crossing the Atlantic Ocean.

Butch's comments about his first trans-Atlantic flight were, "Yeah, we were excited. I was. Like a lot of us, it was the first big airplane ride I had. We were on that plane a long time because it didn't go as fast as the jets go now. But the whole thing was exciting."

The Dutchmen landed at Scotland's Glasgow Prestwick Airport, thirty-two miles from the centre of Glasgow. The airport had only two runways. A three-mile bus ride took them to the west coast, seaside village of Troon. The Royal Troon Golf Course was considered one of the best in Scotland. The village, steeped in history and ancient architecture, was home for the Dutchmen during their stay in Scotland.

The Dutchmen's first test in Europe was in Paisley, Scotland, that country's hot spot for hockey. It was a hockey oasis in a country where little boys dreamed of playing on a national soccer team that would compete for the World Cup of soccer.

In 2013, Paisley had grown to a population of approximately 74,000. Its location is in the west central lowlands. Because of its industrial roots, Paisley became a target for the German Luftwaffe bombing in World War I. But it grew into a major player in the textile industry. Historically, if you were a sports hero in Paisley, you were a soccer player. But, thanks to a "Canadian invasion" hockey was making a statement.

The backbone of Scotland's hockey system came from the large influx of players from Canada, especially in the years between 1946 and 1955. In 1946 alone, seventy Canadian youth made their way to Scotland to pursue their hockey dreams, playing in the newly reformed Scottish Ice Hockey League.

Transplanted Canadian coach, Keith Kewley was crucial to the success of the program. The coach was born in Stratford, Ontario. He played with a few hometown teams, but began a successful coaching career at twenty-two years of age. Ironically, Kewley grew up in Kitchener where he attended Victoria Public School.

When the Dutchmen played the Paisley Pirates in Glasgow, Kewley was behind the Pirates bench. Reports on the game suggested that there were at least thirteen Canadians on the Paisley team. Pirate forward Ted Lacey was a former Waterloo Siskin. Harold Schooley, described as "last of the old-time dipsy doodlers, and as colorful off the ice as on," was a Pirate. He'd been a Polar King nemesis. Butch had competed against Schooley.

The Dutchmen beat the Pirates 6-5 but Kewley warned them to be wary of the Czechoslovakian team at the Games. The Czechs had beaten his team 6-2.

Bauer and his players filed the advice and boarded the plane for their flight to Prague, Czechoslovakia, a beautiful city, steeped in history, with some of Europe's most striking architecture.

First they stopped briefly in Amsterdam, the Dutch City with canals, narrow buildings, fabulous chocolate, world-renowned museums, and come spring, it seemed, as many cyclists as tulips.

When the Dutchmen landed in Prague, a city with a population of one million, they were mobbed by hundreds of school children, seeking autographs, and yelling "Canada! Canada!"

Prague had always been known as one of the cultural centers of Europe. But reputably, the country of which it was the capital, more than any other European country, had profound and continuous adulation for their athletes, simply because they were athletes.

The Czech leadership, not unlike that of the Soviets, was using sporting events to demonstrate the strength of their spirit, and the correctness of the path they were following. In the 1940s their national hockey team had earned its reputation as the best in Europe.

In the 1950s, during the early years of the rule of the Communist Party of Czechoslovakia, some 100,000 of its citizens were jailed for political crimes. Under the rule of Antonin Novotny, First Secretary of the Czechoslovakian Communist Party, thousands died as a result of torture in prison. Hundreds more were executed on political charges.

In 1949, the Czech National hockey team had won the World Championship. But the government prevented them from defending the title at the 1950 World Championship Tournament in London, England.

As they were about to board the plane, all were handcuffed by the national state security police and taken to jail. The police had heard reports that some players were planning to defect. But from all indications, none had such plans. All were charged with treason. It appeared that their fate was predetermined by authorities who ruled the totalitarian regime.

In the end, twelve members of the team were sent to jail, with sentences from eight months to ten years. It would be twenty-three years before the country's national hockey team would win another World Championship Gold Medal.

The Czechoslovakian people loved the Dutchmen, who were even invited to a high school dance. The team members were guests at an official reception at a six-course dinner. They joined the Czech players, their opponents in two exhibition games, in a lively sing-song. Prague Mayor Adolph Svoboda invited them back to the city after the conclusion of the Games.

Butch and the Dutchmen played two games against the Czechoslovakian B team. The games were played in an outdoor arena, located on a small island in the famed Moldau River. Each game attracted a capacity 14,000 fans.

In the 1950s hockey players wore skate guards to protect the blades as they made their way from the dressing room to the ice. Byrle Klinck was so excited about the occasion that he forgot to take the guards off as he went out for warm up. For decades he delighted in recounting the stumble that followed.

In reference to Butch and his defense partner Howie Lee, a Prague newspaper reported, "They were impregnable in front of the net. The two defensemen threw up a wall that held off all attackers. This allowed their forwards freedom to counter-attack."

At the conclusion of the second game, the Czech crowd stood for more than five minutes clapping and yelling "Canada! Canada!" The Dutchmen won both games by scores of 10-1.

As they left the rink, Czechoslovakians rushed up to Butch and others. They said, "Canada must win in Cortina." They viewed a Canadian win as vital for the cause of democracy. The country was communist, but it seemed they preferred to live under their pre-communist system. They felt that ninety percent of them were worse off in the present totalitarian system. Some felt that the Czechs wouldn't be allowed to beat the Soviets at the Games. So the Canadians had to do it. Some also preferred that the Dutchmen defeat their own country's team. Should the Czechs win that match-up, their leaders, in the people's opinion, would say that the communist system was superior.

The people on the streets of Prague treated the Dutchmen's visit as a national holiday. One was reported to have said, "People went to work smiling for the first time in many months."

Dutchie forward Don Rope said the experience of meeting the Czech people was like experiencing "a loss of innocence" for the Canadian players. These people were advertised as enemies of the West. The outpouring of goodwill toward the Canadians was unexpected—but welcomed.

Bauer was pleased with how his team handled themselves. But there was a concern. Center Laufman sustained what was considered a mild concussion during the second game. He was a key component of the Dutchmen's offense. Laufman's health was of major concern. Goman thought of leaving him in Prague for rest and recuperation. But he stayed with the club.

Years before this, when I was in eighth grade at Elmira Public School, our teacher was Harold Dunk, a hockey enthusiast. On a Monday morning he told us he'd been to Toronto to see a Junior A game. He had words of praise for a player he'd seen that Sunday who wasn't flashy, wasn't a great skater, but showed a lot of heart, worked hard, and could score. His name was Kenny Laufman. In eighth grade that didn't mean much. But in the years since, the name Laufman had been a name I saw frequently in hockey reports, most often associated with Butch.

The Swiss Airlines took the team to, Zurich, Switzerland and on to Innsbruck, Austria. From there they travelled by bus through the Alps on the Brenner Pass, considered one of the most important transit routes between northern and southern Europe. The stunning beauty of Cortina, d' Ampezzo, Italy awaited them

Italy (then officially the Italian Republic) was a country with a rich history and a reputation for its food, wine, elegance, ancient architecture, and steeped in the arts; it was not well-known for its hockey prowess. But by 1956, the Italians had won two World Cup soccer championships.

Until 1954, Canada had ruled in international hockey. They'd lost only two significant games: one to the United States in the 1933 World Championships, and one to Great Britain in the 1936 Olympics. Italy joined the International Ice Hockey Federation in 1923.

Beautiful Cortina d'Ampezzo is located in an alpine valley in the southern Dolomite Mountain Range, in the Veneto region of northern Italy. The town is like a huge amphitheater, completely surrounded by the majestic mountains. In 1956, Cortina's population was less than seven thousand. The Dutchmen were taken aback by its beauty.

A tourist magazine's description was telling. "The valley has lofty castles of stone; gigantic towers; colossal pyramids; dizzy blood-red precipices; forest of pinnacles and needles; weird festoons dangling over the abyss; twisted turrets held up by Heaven knows what; juggling, roaring waterfalls and rusty torrents; forests of fir and larch; brilliant flowers and emerald meadows." The area's beauty and class attracted a jetset crowd and European aristocracy.

It also had the coldest recorded winter temperatures in Italy.

Bobby Bauer's team arrived in Cortina d'Ampezzo on a weekend. A spontaneous snow-ball fight broke out! The Canadian and American hockey teams were "taking on" the Germans. Dutchie Don Rope yelled, "For every snowball you throw, we'll put five pucks in your goal."

Cortina's first bid for the 1944 Winter Games had been successful and preparations had been underway, but the outbreak of World War II called a halt to everything. Once the war was over, they continued the planning and renewed their application for the 1952 Games, only to be beaten out by Oslo, Norway. Undeterred, they tried a third time with success, beating out Montreal, Colorado Springs and Lake Placid.

Italian count Alberto Bonacossa, an accomplished alpine skier, figure skater and a member of the International Olympic Committee (IOC) since 1925, tenaciously and masterfully headed up all three bids. Unfortunately, he died in January of 1953, three years before the event for which he'd worked tirelessly.

At the time it was awarded the Games, Cortina d'Ampezzo was a small town, and its pre-Olympic infrastructure was sure to be overwhelmed by the crowds expected. There was no ice stadium or speed skating rink. The ski runs, ski jump and bobsled run were in poor condition. New roads and rail lines had to be built and it needed expanded sewer and water capacity.

But to the surprise of many, the beautiful town was ready for the Games.

The focal point of the Games was the Ice Stadium, or Stadio

Olimpico del Ghiaccio built in Maron, to the north of the town. It was an eight-minute walk from the center. Normally it held about 8,000 spectators but with temporary seating installed for the Games, the capacity extended beyond 12,000. Most of the eight venues were within comfortable walking distances from each other.

Unlike other Olympic hosts, Cortina didn't build an Athletes Village. Instead, the 821 participants from thirty-two nations lived in local hotels and homes. The Dutchmen's headquarters and place of lodging was the Albergo Concordia. The arrangement gave the team some privacy but it isolated them almost entirely from interactions with Olympic athletes from other countries who were also in their own hotels and homes. Forty-four hotels served as accommodations for the Olympic athletes.

The impressive Stadio Olimpico del Ghiacio where the hockey was played, was in a horseshoe shape. In order to save space, the spectator stands were as close to the ice as possible, rising almost vertically and on four levels. They were paneled over with Siberian cedar.

When the players looked up from the ice level, they were met with the spectacular open view of a dark sky, most often with bright stars shining through. The extraordinary view through the far end, the open part of the horseshoe, with no stands for spectators, framed a scene usually saved for postcards. It was the sight of the majestic Dolomites' stunning beauty. And it came with the price of admission! Floodlights illuminated the artificial ice pad.

Tournament games were played as early as 8:00 a.m. and as late at 10:30 p.m., when the temperature plummeted to minus 26 degrees Celsius. Butch put it succinctly: "It was really cold!"

Hockey tournament tickets were at a premium. About 220,000 tickets were eventually sold, making up almost half of the total ticket sales for all of the events.

Canada was a hit. Mayor Frederick Dreger of Kitchener mailed 1500 additional pictures to team manager Goman. There were lineups for autographs and pictures.

Canada's team was among ten nations competing in the hockey venue. The teams were split into three pools. Each nation began by playing each other one time in their pool, in a round-robin format. The top two teams from each pool advanced to the final rounds, with the remaining teams playing in a consolation group for seventh through tenth places.

Manager Ernie Goman and Coach Bauer felt confident they'd get out of their division, their opposition being Germany, Austria, and Italy. But they clearly understood that the Italian team, playing in a stadium in their own country, before their fellow countrymen, would be given a tremendous lift.

There were other concerns, such as the chemistry on the team. Five familiar, high performing players had been replaced with five newcomers whose efforts were impeccable, but who realistically had less to offer. Would fatigue be a factor? The team had to squeeze in extra games in their schedule before they left home. What effect would the distractions, the pomp and ceremony, the spotlight, and the media have? Could the team remain focused on the task? Would the pressure of representing Canada from Atlantic to Pacific take its toll? They were no longer "the Dutchmen." Now they were "Canada."

In an interview during the Games, Bauer said, "I've played for the Stanley Cup. But that pressure is nothing compared to what we're experiencing here."

Perhaps the most pressing concern, however, was the condition of Laufman. How would his head injury affect his play?

In a brief interview with the Italian press, Goman spoke clearly and with emotion: "We didn't come here to lose!"

Neither Butch, nor any of his teammates had multi-million dollar contracts. None had an agent. They were guys with regular jobs, living in small communities, who'd done some special things as amateur hockey players. They'd made arrangements to get time off from work to participate in what would be for most a once-in-a-lifetime experience. It was their Stanley Cup. They needed to trust each other, play the role assigned to the best of their ability, and make it a team endeavor.

During the team's absence, young boys at 7:00 a.m. practices at Waterloo County arenas would pretend they were Laufman, Martin, or Brodeur. The Reverend Finlay Gordon Stewart would say a public prayer for "our boys in Italy" before his Sunday morning sermons at St. Andrews Presbyterian Church on Queen Street. Sharing time in Mrs. Fretz's grade one class at Suddaby School became a contest: every child was certain they had at least one uncle playing for Canada.

Pop Martin seldom made an inquiry. But he tended to be taking a little longer than usual leafing through the sports section of the Record, before he nodded off in his rocking chair with the paper scattered at his feet.

Workers coming off shifts at Elmira's Naugatuk Chemical Plant would drop by the switchboard office. They usually had the same question: "PeeWee, how's Butch doing?" She would swivel around in her squeaky chair, give them her smile and two thumbs up. PeeWee would be in charge of the plant's switchboard for forty-five years.

The magnitude and magic of the Olympic experience had left its mark on Canada's team earlier in the day of January 26, at the Opening Ceremonies in the Ice Stadium. A total of thirty-seven Canadian athletes were there to compete in seven sports.

Canadian pairs figure skaters Frances Dafoe and Norris Bowden were highly touted. Quebec's Lucille Wheeler was twelve when she'd won the Canadian Junior Ski Championship. Her parents paid her way for two winters of training in Kitzbühel, Austria in preparation for Cortina.

Iran was there for the first time, with three competitors; Germany, seventy-five; and the United States, seventy-four. But it was the Soviet Union's delegation of sixty-seven that caused the most stir in the crowd. Many learned forward to take a closer look. This was the first Winter Olympic Games for the Soviets. What kind of success would they have?

From the presidential box, Mr. Giovanni Gronchi, President of the

Italian Republic, declared the Games open. Giuliana Chenal-Minuzzo delivered the Olympic oath, the first female to do so. The Olympic hymn, officially recognized as such at the IOC congress in Paris in 1955 was played for the first time. After tripping over a television cable, speed skater Guido Caroli regained his balance, and lit the cauldron with the Olympic flame.

Canada and Germany prepared to face off in their first game. Canada had practice sessions, but this was their first meaningful game in a week. Folks in Waterloo County and across Canada were waiting.

Germany had been Winter Olympic participants since 1924. In the 1956 Winter Games, the hockey players from Germany joined to form the United Team of Germany.

The Canadians came out strong, although a little tentatively at first against the Germans. Speedy winger Gerry Théberge gave them an early lead which they never relinquished. The German game brought no surprises. The Canadians won 4-0.

But Bauer and Goman were upset with what they thought was sloppy officiating. It was an opinion shared by other countries. After their game in Paisley, Scotland, Keith Kewley had given them a heads up about that possibility. While Canada was pleased with their start, they couldn't have imagined the enthusiasm back home.

The Kitchener-Waterloo Record opened a special Olympic telephone service. During the German game, they received almost eight hundred calls in four hours. A staff of five answered ten phones.

At the J. M. Schneider meat plant on Courtland Avenue, each score was announced over the public address system. Record staff pasted photos of the action in their windows. When informed that the score was 4-0 for Canada, one caller asked, "Yes, but what about the Dutchmen?"

In a Kitchener Court Room, Traffic Sergeant, Wilfred Henrich announced, "Court now stands adjourned for five minutes. The score is 2-0 for the Dutchmen. Théberge scored both goals." Even the guy who'd just been ordered to pay a fine broke out in a grin.

Inside the busy Elmira Post Office, postal worker Viola Martin sat down over a coffee and muffin. She needed a break from all the inquiries. Few had to do with Elmira's postal service. News about her brother Butch had taken priority over purchasing stamps and checking for mail.

In the Senior A league, the Dutchmen were known as a fast-skating and skilled team. But as the Olympic Games progressed the European press described their play as "beasts on ice" and brutally physical. In the Canadian's opinion, the on-ice officials were significantly influenced by the media's portrayal.

Austria's national team was up next. They'd won a bronze medal at the 1947 IIHF World Championships. It was their only international hockey medal. The national team hadn't competed in the 1952 Olympic Games.

The world knew Austria through Vienna and the classical composers, Beethoven, Mozart and Brahms. The famous Vienna Choir Boys performed in the Kitchener Auditorium, home of the Dutchmen. In November of 1959 the Broadway production of "The Sound of Music" opened, starring Mary Martin. Canada knew Austria through its music.

The Record's report of the game against Austria, stated, "Canada had 76 shots on Austrian goalie Alfred Puelsand and hit a goal post 8 times, in a 23-0 win." Yet the day before, Austria had tied Italy 2-2.

Bauer received criticism from some quarters regarding what was, by European standards, unnecessary rough play. And it may have appeared that his team was trying to embarrass their opponents. One sportscaster said, "It's no credit to Canada." Bauer reminded the critics that if you're an athlete, there's no reason to let up.

The critics may have forgotten the 47-0 Canadian win over Denmark in the 1949 IIHF World Tournament in Stockholm, Sweden.

J. F. (Bunny) Ahearne, president of the International Ice Hockey Federation, was fielding complaints from many teams. Their concerns lay with the competency of the on-ice officials, accented by their poor skating abilities.

In response, the president floated the idea of putting the referees in a type of cage above the ice. A spotlight would follow each referee as he headed upwards to the cage. Penalties would be called by the referees, and the reason for the penalty announced over a loudspeaker placed in the cage. A few linesmen would be on the ice to handle face-offs and get between potential combatants.

The plan went no further.

With two wins, the Canadians felt good. But in a round-robin format, strange things could happen. When they skated out for their game against Italy, the place erupted. But that was because the Italian team made their way to the ice at the same time. The Canadians were "strangers in a foreign land." And they faced a national team in front of their animated, passionate, and loud home crowd.

The cheers of "Ura! Ura! Segnare un gol! Segnare un gol!" overwhelmed the valiant efforts at noise from the small crowd of Dutchmen supporters. It was like a few Italians cheering for their country's team in a game against England in Manchester United's Old Trafford Stadium.

The play on the ice was aggressive, fueled by the crowd that turned a little bitter and angry. Referees Hans Unger of Germany and Tolle Johannsen of Norway were clearly influenced by the atmosphere. A few times the game threatened to get out of hand. The Canadians got called for penalties. They had no idea what the infractions were and there was no official with whom to discuss the matter, as none spoke English. A few times it looked like the Canadians would leave the ice. In a very hostile environment, and being at the mercy of the inefficient referees, Canada defeated Italy by a 3-1 score.

Bauer commented that the referee made sure it was a tough game, but also suggested that it might have done his team good to work through adversity. He said, "Goodwill is diminished when the referee is influenced by a partisan crowd and practically incites players to lose their tempers. The referees had an uncharitable attitude towards the Canadians."

The best of the Italian team were Guiliano Ferraris and Ernesto Avitti. Their coach was a transplanted Canadian, Billy Cupola. He'd played in Canada, and at one time was a right-winger with the Dutchmen. Cupola felt that the Italians were playing way over their heads, emotionally charged by their fans.

At a RCAF base in Germany, the community was talking about D-Day—Dutchmen Day. Children purchased autograph books and pens. Newspaper clippings describing the progress of Canada's Dutchmen's games in Cortina were taped on walls of messes and barrack blocks. After the Winter Games, Canada's team was planning to visit the base and play an exhibition game. The kids found the waiting onerous.

With the win over Italy, Canada remained undefeated in the round-robin round. But it was the next round where medals would be won. They'd meet Czechoslovakia, United States, Germany, Sweden, and the Soviet Union. The team with the most points at the end of the medal round would win gold, the second silver and the third bronze. Canada remained the favorite. Many experts said they'd win easily.

The Soviets were the unknown factors. But the year previously, at the IIHF World Championships, a club team, the Penticton Vs had convincingly defeated them 5-0. There was an undercurrent of resentment against the Soviets in Cortina. The issue for most was about the supposed amateur status of the Soviet players, although they had been given jobs by the state, and were paid by the state.

Canada'a first medal round game was against Czechoslovakia. They'd defeated a Czech team twice. But that was the B team. This Czech team was obviously a superior group of players. Their national A team was led by leading scorer, Vlastimil Bubnik. He was tied with Canada's Harry Watson and Russia's Valeri Kharlamov for the all-time Olympic scoring lead. (He was finally surpassed by Finland's Teemu Selanne in the 2010 Winter Olympics.) Czech player, Karel Gut, went on to coach the Czechoslovakian National Team. His team won the

World Championships in 1976 and 1977.

Canada defeated the Czechs 6-3 but needed two third-period goals, rallying from an early one goal deficit. The Czechs scored a short-handed goal with Bubnik in the penalty box. It was a very good game. The officiating received accolades.

Twenty-four hours later the Canadians faced the Americans. Each had a perfect record. The American media felt good about their team.

The United States team's coach, John Mariucci, had played five seasons for the Chicago Black Hawks. He had assembled an Olympic team of young, college players, many from Minnesota. They were led by forward John Mayasich of the University of Minnesota. The coach had high praise for his forward. "John brought college hockey to a new plateau. He was the Wayne Gretzky of his time. And today, if he were playing pro hockey, he would simply be a bigger, stronger, back-checking Gretzky."

Mariucci figured they'd need outstanding goal-tending from Minnesota's former high-school sensation, goalie Willard Ikola if the team was to have any success.

Canada's hockey team was inspired by the outstanding performance of an attractive, freckle-faced nineteen year-old woman from St. Jovite, Quebec. They were cheering with the rest of the Canadians at the ski hill as downhill skier Lucille Wheeler became the first Canadian in Olympic history to win a medal in skiing. As she entered the dining room for dinner at the Concord Hotel, the Canadians jumped to their feet and gave her a loud reception. Lucille had won a bronze medal for Canada!

In spite of many distractions in downtown Cortina, including a sighting of Italian film star Sophia Loren, the Canadians remained focused on their goal of a gold medal.

They knew little about the Americans but it was clear that with an undefeated record they would be primed for the game. A large crowd filled the Stadio Olimpico, paying from $2.50 to six dollars a ticket.

The shock came two minutes into the game. Mayasich, the best of the Americans, lifted a flip shot from outside the blue line in a high arc toward the Canadian goal. Goalie Brodeur misjudged the puck and it landed on his shoulder and into the net. Some called it one of the most important goals of the Games.

The territorial edge by far belonged to Canada but they were up against a hot goaltender in Ikola. Mayasich scored a second goal before the first period ended, and the Americans were up by two.

Determined and aggressive, the Canadians hit goal posts and missed scoring chances in the second period. The young American goalie continued his outstanding play. On at least three occasions, Butch and his team mates were about to raise their sticks to signal a goal, only to have Ikola make a great save. Nevertheless, captain Jack McKenzie scored and his team was in the game. By the end of the second period Canada had outshot the Americans 30-11, but were down one goal.

Bauer had his team on the attack for the majority of the remainder of the game. The American goalie was sensational! Exhibiting his star status, Mayasich completed his hat trick in the final period. The final American goal was scored by Wendell Anderson, the future governor of Minnesota.

The Americans had been outshot 40-29. When the final siren sounded, they mobbed their young goalie. At the end of the tournament Ikola was selected as the best goalkeeper by the directorate. He'd been the reason they'd accomplished the improbable in beating Canada 4-1.

In a post-game conversation with Bauer, United States coach Mariucci confided, "We could play you twenty games; win the first, and lose the next nineteen."

One hockey nation was ecstatic; the other was shocked and disappointed. This wasn't supposed to happen. It was like being slammed by a 2x4 from S. S. Martin Sawmill.

The Kitchener-Waterloo Record published a picture of Butch and four team mates as they sat after the game in the silent dressing room.

Classy captain Jack McKenzie sat beside Butch, using the sleeve of his Canada hockey sweater to wipe away his tears.

The scene was a metaphor for what happened in Canada. When the Dutchmen lost an important playoff game at the Kitchener Auditorium, its effect was felt in homes of Waterloo County hockey fans. But when, as Canada's team, they lost on the world stage, a family in St. John's Newfoundland was disappointed; a young child's joy in Saskatoon was replaced by gloom. And critics across the nation sat at their typewriters as they prepared to unload.

For Bauer, there were no words he could say that seemed appropriate. The tears being wiped away by some of his players was sufficient. But the pressure on his team had just been turned up significantly. It was a quiet evening at the Concordia Hotel.

The Record reported: "Dutchies' tears flow after the game."

One news headline called it, "The greatest upset in Olympic history." Hockey fans in the United States were shocked and exuberant. Canadians were stunned. Some were angry.

The next day, in his broadcast for CBC Radio, reporter Thom Benson began his report with a solemnity that some listeners felt appropriate:

"Today, in this small mountain village, there was a funeral. The bells of the ancient church told the passing of a procession. The mourners chanted prayers as they trudged up the steep hills behind the coffin bearers. Those who were left were saying their farewell to a robust and lively friend. The cortege wound its way through narrow and twisted streets up past the Concordia Hotel. Inside that building, there was a similar ceremony where the inhabitants mourned the passing of an era. In the hotel was housed the Kitchener-Waterloo hockey team and all those other Canadians who aspired to Olympic heights in the field of amateur competition. There was no joy there, no happy words, no jubilation, for last night Canadian amateur hockey suffered a blow to its prestige from which it may never recover. The Kitchener-Waterloo team was beaten fairly and squarely by a

team which would never make the junior finals in Canada. If you think saying that is easy, then you are greatly mistaken."

W. A. (Billy) Hewitt, registrar treasurer of the Canadian Amateur Hockey Association, said, "The U. S. team should have been taken seriously." Canadian hockey officials were already conferring about changing the practice of sending the Allan Cup winners to represent Canada. One put out the idea of picking an all-star team from across the country, and getting them together early to prepare.

Benson, Hewitt and others may have struck a chord with some Canadians. But they'd never met the loyal Waterloo County fans of the Kitchener-Waterloo Dutchmen! The team received a telegram, forty-five feet in length, with the signatures of almost 1500 people. It was the largest telegram ever sent from Canada, and took two hours to transmit.

Two days later Canada met Germany's national team. The Germans made their displeasure with the officiating known after their earlier games, threatening at one point to withdraw from the hockey tournament.

In the outdoor rink, in minus 20 C weather, with the face-off at 10:00 a.m., our Canadians took fifty shots at German goalie, Ulrich Janzen. They shut out the Germans 10-0. Laufman looked more comfortable, seemingly recovering slowly from the injury he had sustained in the second exhibition game in Czechoslovakia.

After the game, Goman and Bauer moved their team to a small hotel in the village of San Vito. They planned to stay there for the remainder of the tournament. Located seven miles from downtown Cortina, it provided freedom from the many distractions. It was important to stay focused.

Sweden was their next opponent.

Sweden had never defeated a Canadian hockey team at the international level. The country's biggest star by far was Sven Olof Gunnar Johansson, more informally known as Tumba. In 1999 he was voted the best Swedish Hockey Player of All Time, outranking Swedish NHL stars Peter Forsberg and Mats Sundin. The Swedish star was the first European to be invited to an NHL training camp when the Boston Bruins did that in 1957.

Canada defeated Sweden 6-2, but was criticized for missing many scoring chances, shooting erratically and overall ineffective play. But Butch and all of Canada had hope! Winning the gold medal was still a possibility. They found themselves in an unusual and unexpected place, cheering for the Soviets when they played the Americans. The Soviets shut out the Americans 4-0 and Waterloo County residents knew there was still a chance for their guys to bring home a gold medal.

And for the first time in the history of the Olympic Games, Canada would meet the Soviets.

A Cortina newspaper reported a breach in security, the only one of the Games. A cameraman, filming "White Vertigo," a documentary of the Games, was caught hiding in a refreshment van which had brought supplies for the bar at the Ice Stadium.

The last game of the championship was planned so that the Soviets met the Canadians. In a perfect scenario for the organizers, the game would have been for the gold medal. They partly got their wish. The gold medal belonged to the Soviets if they won the game. Gold would be presented to the Canadians if they defeated the Soviets by at least three goals.

Bauer said, "It's a big task, but we'll be in there fighting." Butch and his teammates had to play the game of their lives. Support from Waterloo County remained solid. A single telegram could be sent at a cost to the sender of $2.40. Many arrived.

Back home at S. S. Martin Sawmill, the guys at the apple press talked hockey more than usual. And how they wished they could be in the crowd for that final game! It would be awesome!

Bauer knew that the Soviets had spied on his team during their practices. He repaid the visit. He said, "The Soviet coach seemed to know who I was. Because when I waved at him he waved back. But his wave slowed down while passing his nose."

Butch said, "The Soviet team of 1956 was a rag-tag group." Not everyone had a stick, and some of the sticks had been repaired. All players wore flimsy bicycle helmets and generally their equipment was second rate. But their players had trained together for eight months leading up to the Olympic Games.

The undisputed leader and captain of the Soviet team was Vsevolod Bobrov. In the league in which he played, he'd scored ninety-one goals in fifty-seven games. He was also a star football player, and the captain of his country's national team. A sports columnist wrote: "Had Bobrov played in the NHL, he would have ranked with the likes of Lafleur or Bossy." Some referred to him as the "Russian Rocket" comparing him to the great Rocket Richard.

The Sverdlovsk air disaster of January 5, 1950 had claimed the lives of ten members of the Soviet National hockey team. Vsevolod Bobrov and two others had been permitted to travel by train. For years the crash remained a secret. Reportedly the Soviet media helped suppress the story. Some suggest that Stalin's son wanted to save his seventy year old father from hearing about it.

Bobrov shared the starring hockey role with rugged Nikolai "Soly" Sologubov, a stalwart on defense. He'd finish the tournament voted by the directorate as the best defenseman. Butch knew a bit about the Soviet goalie, Nikolai Pushkov. But there was nothing in his hockey history that hinted that he was anything but a good goalie in the Soviet league. The goalie had helped the Soviets in their 7-2 win over East York Lyndhursts in the 1954 World Championships.

There was great news for Canada from the figure skating competition. Frances Dafoe and Norris Bowden had won silver in the pairs events. The figure skating events, like hockey, took place in an outdoor facility.

On the afternoon of February 4, the second last day of the Games, the Ice Stadium in downtown Cortina was sold out, with the largest crowd of the Games. Fans in the very top row of the fourth level were completely in the open.

Fiat cars, the official cars of the tournament, transported VIPs from the downtown hotels. Olivetti was the official typewriter. Mr. Ovaltine, dressed in yellow, poured out hot and comforting drinks for anyone who asked. The "brave" among them tried Grappa, consisting of thirty-five to sixty-five percent alcohol by volume. One swallow, they said, would have steam coming out of your ears.

Arkady Ivanovich Chernyshev was the distinguished Soviet coach. He was one of the founders of the well-known Russian Hockey School. Chernyshev and Anatoli Tarasov were partners in leading the Soviets to many championships. They complemented each other: Chernyshev's reputation was that of a diplomatic, rational man, while Tarasov was known as explosive and emotional. Chernyshev coached the Soviets to four Olympic gold medals, and eleven world championships.

Bauer's strategy became clear early on in the game. His team would focus on Bobrov and attempt to shut him down with physical play. In the first period Butch and the other defensemen "flattened" Bobrov three times and kept him scoreless. The Soviet star spent the entire second period on the players' bench. He returned for the third but was basically ineffective.

Canada played one of their best games of the tournament, allowing only nine shots, but they had no good fortune, hitting the cross-bar or goal posts five times. The Soviets got their first shot on Elmira-born goalie Woodall at 16:20 of the first period.

The Soviets demanded that the ice not be resurfaced at the end of the second period. Goman and a Soviet official had words but the ice was resurfaced.

In the end, Bobrov wasn't needed. His teammates, Krylov and Kuzin scored. Goalie Pushkin was outstanding. The Soviets as a whole broke up a Canadian attack after attack. They were impeccable on defense, led by their twenty-year-old star, Sologubov.

In their first visit to the Winter Olympic Games, Bobrov's team won a gold medal. It would not be their last. They'd made a tremendous improvement since their 5-0 defeat at the hands of Canada's Penticton Vs one year earlier.

The Americans were winners of the silver medal and Canada the bronze.

Coach Bauer said, "We were amazed by the precision of their offensive movements. Russia has emerged as a world power of hockey." Indeed, it was the Soviet's coming out party, and the start of their dominance in international competition for the next thirty years. Their skills and creativity shone bright against attempts by teams to physically intimidate them.

Len Taylor, the Record sports columnist, wrote, "The mechanical men of Moscow altered the balance of world hockey power in sixty dramatic minutes on Saturday night."

Following the game Goman and Bauer visited the Soviet dressing room, presenting them with a Canadian pennant. The Soviets responded with an invitation to visit Moscow.

The next school day little Ingrid Doernhoefer sat on the special wooden chair facing her classmates at Suddaby School and broke the news. It was a teachable moment for Mrs. Fretz. She patiently explained how important it was to try your best. That's all coach Bauer had asked of his hockey players. And that was all she asked of them.

International Olympic Committee President Avery Brundage presented captain Jack MacKenzie with a bronze medal, as his teammates and fellow Canadians cheered. MacKenzie was selected as the best forward at the tournament. Each player also received an official Olympic diploma. The diplomas were delivered first to Canada's diplomatic representative in Rome, then on to the Canadian Olympic Committee, and finally to the recipients.

An injured Laufman played in the tournament, but in the opinion of Butch he clearly wasn't playing like himself and had he been healthy, it would have made a considerable difference.

1956 was a significant turning point for our Canadian approach to international hockey participation. It became a time to reflect and regroup. Months later, a Dutchmen player said, "We weren't prepared for the magnitude of the event and never got back on track."

The CAHA was looking towards a new approach, one that would put Canada back on top. In England something similar was happening in football. In 1953 Hungary's National Football Team had come into Wembley Stadium and had beaten England 6-3. It was England's first ever loss on native soil. The result brought England to its most important time in its national game and influenced greatly the future development of the sport. Yet as far back as 1945, the Moscow Dynamo football club had defeated the highly regarded Arsenal side and other top teams. There was a warning that was given too little attention.

There were many critics of the CAHA who strongly suggested that its members, like England had in football, had missed the warning signs of the growth and improvement of hockey internationally.

What was said to the English people, many Canadians concurred, could also have been said to Canadians: "The outcome may not necessarily prove anything conclusively; maybe no more than it points the way to how things may develop in the second half of the century. English football can be proud of its past, but it must awake to a new future."

At their first Winter Olympic Games, Soviet athletes dominated, earning fifteen medals. Second was Austria with eleven. Canada took home three.

Back on the streets of Kitchener, Waterloo, Elmira and Floradale, there were no words of criticism. There was no blame cast or pointing of fingers. Some comments were about the cramped schedule their team had to play before they left for the Games. Others suggested that it was time to send Canada's best hockey players—the professionals. "They should send over the Montreal Canadiens and really wallop those Russians!" said one Kitchener resident, only partially in jest.

Kitchener was proud of their Dutchmen and they got busy planning a warm homecoming.

Ontario Premier Leslie Frost rose in the Ontario Legislature and said, "The gauge is not victory but the way the game is played, the spirit of sportsmanship and good heartedness. They have demonstrated to those people behind the Iron Curtain, the principles of good sportsmanship."

Their sportsmanship and spirit of goodwill as outstanding ambassadors for their home community and all of Canada seemed to be the prominent way the Dutchmen were remembered at the 1956 Winter Olympic Games.

On Sunday, February 5 the closing ceremonies were held at the Stadio Olimpico Del Ghiaccio, where twelve thousand spectators watched an exhibition of figure skating that included Canada's Dafoe and Bowden. Avery Brundage, chairman of the International Olympic Committee, declared the Olympics closed, and a fireworks display ended the Games.

The Dutchmen bade farewell to the stunning beauty of Cortina d'Ampezzo but took with them the ugly feeling of not attaining the goal for which they'd arrived. Bauer suggested that his team might have made more fans by losing than they would have by winning.

Months later, in an assessment of the team's performance, a Record sports columnist wrote, "In 1956 the forwards going to Europe were spearheaded by a standout centre in Ken Laufman. But you will recall that he was only a shadow of himself due to a head injury suffered in the final exhibition game in Prague." It took a year before he began to regain the touch that had escaped him.

The cost of the Cortina Games was eight million dollars.

For the Canadians at the RCAF base in Zweibrechen, Germany, D-Day arrived. The Dutchmen, their hockey heroes, were there to play the RCAF Flyers, a team made up of jet pilots and ground staff. 1500 jammed into the arena to see the home team lose 15-5.

The Dutchmen went on to Baden-Baden, in the southern German

State of Baden-Wuerttemberg, surrounded by the gigantic nature park that is the Black Forest. They played two games against the RCAF Flyers at the air force base in Bad Solingen winning 15-4 and 15-5. Bobby Bauer, Milt Schmidt, and Woody Dumart, the famous Bruins' Kraut Line had all proudly served in the RCAF.

The team flew from London to Dorval Airport on the island of Montreal on their way home.

On their return to Toronto's Malton Airport, over seven hundred cheering fans were on hand to greet them. One sign assured the Dutchmen that their fans were still proud of them. A team member told the crowd that he hadn't been sure they'd be welcome back.

As the parade of buses and cars made its way through Acton, homemade signs with the words "We Still Love you Dutchies" hung from store windows.

On their arrival in Kitchener, the Dutchmen were honored at a civic reception and paraded by a fire truck that followed a police motorcycle contingent. More than twenty-thousand adoring fans waved and yelled. It was an exuberant crowd! Four bands entertained, led by 54th Light Anti-craft Regiment Pipe Band. School hockey teams dressed in team sweaters and clutching green and white ribbons lined the streets. All children in Kitchener schools were dismissed early so they could join in the excitement of this major moment in their city's history. A small group of fans and family from Floradale shouted, "Good to see you Butch! Welcome home!"

Prime Minister Louis St. Laurent sent a message thanking the team for a magnificent job in representing Canada.

The Dutchmen were Waterloo County heroes, still highly respected and loved. They'd returned gloriously home with a bronze Olympic medal! In the long history of the city's sports accomplishment this moment was its crowning glory. It was believed that the Olympic medal was the city's first.

Mrs. Fretz and her restless Suddaby School grade 1 class were gathering excitedly on the curb at Frederick and King, a few minutes' walk from their now vacant classroom.

Coach Bauer observed, "To get a reception like this makes us proud to be Canadian."

Elmira and Woolwich didn't forget their hockey heroes. At a special night in their honor, over one-thousand people showed up in the Elmira arena to applaud Butch, Klinck and Woodall. Each received a silver tea set. Reeve Lloyd Ziegler of Woolwich Township presented Butch with a "token" from the Township.

Butch's former Polar King buddies Cole Bauman and Gene Miller returned and joined in an exhibition game between the K-W Old Timers and the Polar Kings. And, by special request, the dapperly dressed Little German Band made their way from New Dundee to entertain the fans in Waterloo County style.

Butch returned with PeeWee to their home in Floradale, and in a relatively few days got back to work on the truck hauling logs for S. S. Martin and Sons.

In 1956, Lester B. Pearson was Canada's Secretary of State for External Affairs in the Liberal Cabinet of Prime Minister Louis St. Laurent. Following the 1956 Winter Olympics, Pearson received an official letter from G. B. Summers, Charge d'Affaires at the Canadian Consulate in Prague. Summers expressed high praise and appreciation for the overwhelming success of the Dutchmen's visit to Prague. He was proud of their on-ice and off-ice behavior, friendly attitude, and their keen interest in the Czech people. It was his opinion that the Dutchmen were outstanding ambassadors for Canada.

The Elmira Polar Kings welcomed back their captain for their OHA Senior B playoff run. But events didn't turn out in the manner they'd hoped. In the quarterfinal series, in the final, and deciding game against Woodstock Athletics, the Kings had a 4-1 lead after two periods. Woodstock brought along a supply of oxygen, advised of its potential benefit. Whatever the cause, the Woodstock team definitely got a second wind as they scored four unanswered goals with eleven minutes to go in the game. They won 5-4, ending the season for the Kings.

The Dutchmen team got back to league play and the Senior A playoffs on their return from the Olympic Games. Goman invited Butch to rejoin them following the Kings' defeat. After discussions with the Polar King management, Butch consented. He joined the Dutchmen in the second game of the league championship series against the Chatham Maroons. His addition was seen as a major help. But the surprising Maroons went undefeated in the series to claim their first OHA Senior A Championship. Many felt that the Dutchmen were ripe for the picking after their emotional ride at the Olympic Games.

A Kitchener sports columnist wrote, "Butch Martin was the most solid defenseman for the losing side. Whatever the situation, wherever the game, Butch seemed to play at a consistently high level." Those words would fittingly follow Butch for the rest of his career.

Butch also received praise for being one of the key factors in holding the opposition to a meager twelve goals at the winter games. The Dutchmen scored fifty-three times

In the official report of the hockey competition, Walter A, Brown, President of the IIHF wrote, "The hockey tournament of the Seventh Olympic Games at Cortina d'Ampezzo was the finest in history; the competition beyond compare." With the exception of 1952, Brown had seen every tournament since 1928.

On the international scene, the Cold War (a term coined by English writer, George Orwell) showed indications of heating up. There were ramifications for international hockey as politics and sports became increasingly intertwined.

The Suez Crisis of October 29 - November 7, 1956 was seen by Nikita Khrushchev, First Secretary of the Central Communist Party of the Soviet Union, as a personal victory. He seemed emboldened by the knowledge that the threat of nuclear war was an effective way to do business internationally

On November 18, 1956, while addressing Western ambassadors at the Polish Embassy in Moscow, Khrushchev said, "Whether you like it or not, history is on our side. We will dig you in." The repeated comment in much of the United States was "We will bury you." Subsequent speeches on the same theme by the Soviet leader were taken by some Americans as a nuclear threat.

Canada's Lester B. Pearson was the recipient of the 1957 Nobel Prize for Peace for organizing the United Nations Emergency Force to resolve the Suez Crisis. The award's presenters said he saved the world.

Pearson was Canada's Prime Minister from 1963 to 1968. He had more than a passing interest in the Dutchmen and hockey. He'd been a member to the University of Oxford's hockey team.

Butch stayed with the Dutchmen for the next four seasons. Bauer stayed on as coach for two of them. During the 1956-57 season Butch totaled thirty scoring points. The team had a record of thirty wins, eighteen losses and four ties. Bauer resigned as coach of the Dutchmen and became the team's president.

Sadly, on November 22 of the 1956-57 Dutchmen season, Butch's mother Blendina died. Her funeral was held at Floradale Mennonite Church, presided over by Pastor Rufus Jutzi. Blendina left behind her husband Seranus, eight children, and eight grandchildren.

Canada boycotted the IIHF World Championships in 1957. The action was taken as a protest in response to the Soviet invasion of Hungary. The Soviet's action came as a result of the Hungarian Revolution.

The 1957 IIHF Tournament was held in Moscow, with no Canadian team in attendance. In the gold medal game, an estimated 55,000 fans watched the Soviet team and Sweden play to a 4-4 tie. Based on the tournament's scoring formula, the championship was awarded to Sweden. This game was seen as the point in time when hockey was brought to the masses in the Soviet Union.

Bill Durnan, legendary Montreal Canadiens goalie from 1943 to

1950, was appointed the Dutchmen's coach, and was in charge of the training camp for the 1957-58 season. His record had been remarkable: he was an NHL all-star six times; the Vezina Trophy winner six times; and had six straight shut-outs in 1949.

Durnan was an anomaly among NHL goalies. He was ambidextrous so he wore an identical glove on either hand; one that served as both a blocker and a trapper. It also allowed him to quickly change his stick to either hand and to repeatedly take away what looked like sure scoring chances.

In the 1957-58 season, the coach led the Dutchmen to forty-two wins. Butch had forty-eight scoring points. The Dutchmen lost to the Belleville McFarlands in the Eastern Canada Allan Cup finals.

Butch had a career high sixty-nine points in scoring in the 1958-59 season, but the Dutchmen won only thirty-three times. They lost to the Vernon Canadiens in the Allan Cup play downs.

Some of the world's greatest hockey players skated for small centers across Canada. At times the Dutchmen were the very best and always among the top teams in the nation. They would frequently beat American League teams in exhibition matches. The Kitchener Auditorium was often sold out. During one playoff run they had thirteen straight standing-room-only sell-outs.

Following 1958-59 season, the coach and Goman evaluated the make-up of the team and the players' individual performances as was their usual routine. Their intentions were to strengthen the team to improve their standing in the Senior A League during the 1959-60 season. Nothing other than that was on the radar for the Dutchmen and their fans.

BUTCH MARTIN AND THE
FLIN FLON KID
THE VIII WINTER OLYMPIC GAMES

The Dutchmen weren't Allan Cup winners in 1959, so didn't expect to represent Canada at the 1960 Winter Olympics in Squaw Valley, California. But the Whitby Dunlops, who had won the Cup, declined the invitation to represent Canada because of the great financial burden. The opportunity was presented to a surprised Dutchmen organization.

The team and their community took up the challenge. A fundraising committee got to work. They needed $17,000 to cover expenses incurred from travel, doctors, trainers, uniforms, extra baggage and insurance. A car raffle brought in $12,000. CKCO Television, the Kitchener station, had another telethon fundraiser. Donation boxes were again placed at home games at the Auditorium. There was tremendous support from the community, reliving the great experience of only four years previously.

The team received donations from unexpected sources. Conn Smythe of the Toronto Maple Leafs chipped in with two thousand dollars.

But the dark shadow of the Cold War was taking on a new meaning in the United States. On February 16, 1959, the Cuban revolution ended with Cuba becoming Communist. Fidel Castro became the president. United States citizens and government were very concerned about a potential threat so close to the American mainland.

On September 13, 1959, Russia was the first country to land a rocket on the moon. Two days later, Soviet leader Nikita Khrushchev visited Washington for talks with United States President Dwight Eisenhower. On a trip to Disneyland, the Soviet leader was refused entry, due to security reasons. But the meetings between the two leaders was seen as an effort at beginning to thaw the Cold War.

The Dutchmen opened training camp at the Elmira Arena on September 26, 1959, with thirty players. Durnan was back as coach.

Early in training camp, team manager Ernie Goman clearly articulated that the sole goal of the Dutchies would be to bring home a gold medal for Canada in the 1960 Winter Olympic Games. The organization was totally committed to that cause. His expectation was that the players would reflect that commitment.

The good news for the Olympic-bound Dutchmen was that they could bolster their team by adding really good players from other Senior A League teams, with their permission. Also, like other Senior A teams, they could draft junior level players and hopefully have them join their club.

However, as always was the case in Olympic years, professionals and reinstated professionals were prohibited from competing. Former Dutchmen Bill Graham, for example, was disqualified. He'd played in the professional Canadian Football League.

There was also the possibility that a drafted junior player could turn professional and the Dutchmen would lose him. NHL president Clarence Campbell didn't help. He said, "I wouldn't donate the best young players to that amateur outfit from Kitchener."

Unlike the situation with the 2014 Canadian Olympic Men's team, the Dutchmen would be assembled as their regular season progressed. The team with which they started the 1959-60 season would be partially remade as they made their way to the middle of February and the Olympics.

The situation presented a huge challenge for the manager, his coach and all the Dutchmen executives, but it was also a challenge for the players and their families. Some highly talented players who in a normal year would have been part of the Dutchmen team were told that they wouldn't be going to Squaw Valley.

No player was assured that he was a member of the Olympic team until mid January when the team's roster would be announced. It made for an unsettling situation with no template as to how to proceed. In 1956, the team that came to training camp had been basically the same one that eventually took to the ice in Cortina d'Ampezzo.

Butch, Laufman and Rope were back from the 1956 team, but none was guaranteed a spot. Elmira resident Bob Ertel was showing well in training camp. Daryl Sly, a highly regarded Leafs prospect, had a contract to teach fourth grade at Elmira's John Mahood School. His pay was $2900 annually. He hoped he'd stay with the Dutchmen. With a reputation for aggressive play, he was dubbed the "pugnacious pedagogue."

The OHA Senior A league in which the Dutchmen competed in the 1959-60 season had four other teams: Windsor Bulldogs, Whitby Dunlops, Chatham Maroons and Belleville McFarlands. For all of them the upcoming season presented financial challenges.

Early on the Dutchmen asked for an increased split of the gate from the Kitchener Auditorium, their home. The Maroons were in danger of folding. They had difficulty meeting their $1700 weekly payroll. The McFarlands' accounting and financial dealings during their road to the World Championship in 1959 were under scrutiny. They'd lost only one game during the competition in Prague, Czechoslovakia.

The Dunlops were the defending 1959 Allan Cup Champions, and had been the 1958 International Ice Hockey Federation (IIHF) Champions.

While all other teams played a fifty-four game schedule, Butch and the Dutchmen played forty-eight games, including some four-point games, to make for a balanced schedule. They had a really crowded calendar before leaving for the Olympics.

As their pre-season exhibition season opened, the Dutchmen carried three goalies: lanky, dark-haired Cesare Maniago; Marv Edwards; and Waterloo County resident Harold "Boat" Hurley. The results from the early games were encouraging.

The Kitchener-Waterloo Record said of Butch: "Butch Martin has been covering the ice as if he had jets attached to his blades. But this is nothing new. Butch always goes hard, even at the first of the season." The previous year Butch had his best offensive season with his team.

A young newcomer who was turning heads was nineteen year old Cliff Pennington from Winnipeg. The Dutchmen had drafted him from the Flin Flon Bombers Junior A Team. Pennington was seen as a really good NHL prospect. He, along with fifteen other junior players from across Canada were drafted by the Dutchmen with the invitation to try out for the team. Among them were Stan Mikita of the St. Catharine Teepees, and Bobby Rousseau of the Ottawa-Hull Canadiens.

The Dutchies had to pay five hundred dollars to the club from which the player was drafted if he was retained, Drafted players weren't obliged to report, but their present team couldn't hold them up if they showed up at Dutchmen camp.

In reference to newly arrived Pennington, The Kitchener-Waterloo Record reported: "The blond star from Flin Flon Bombers fitted into the K-W style like a bikini on Bridget Bardot."

In October, 1959, Durnan was announced as coach of the Dutchmen team that was going to the Winter Games.

During the early months of the season the Dutchmen were hot and cold. Durnan expressed concern about the quality of the roster, after a 7-5 loss to the Dunlops. But by November, they were on top of the league. Goalie Edwards moved on to Milwaukee of the International League. Hurley and Maniago would carry the goalie load. Sometimes Hurley's play was described as "magnificent" but Dutchmen fans were on him. His less spectacular games came at home.

Hockey players who'd been teammates were full of praise for Butch.

They described him as tough on the puck, an accurate passer, and a rugged competitor. He approached the game intelligently, had high expectations of himself, was a calming influence and was consistent in his level of play. Reports on Dutchmen's games regularly brought attention to these qualities. Butch displayed the qualities of a leader, one who led by example.

The other Dutchman mentioned regularly was Ken Laufman, often Butch's linemate. As always, he was an outstanding goal-scorer and character player. Butch and he had a great respect for each other's hockey abilities.

Butch continued to work at the family's Floradale sawmill from 7:00 a.m. to 5:00 p.m. Laufman was in the real estate business.

But going into December 1959, the Dutchmen were slumping, with the brunt of the blame heaped on Hurley. He'd allowed twenty-two goals in four games and seemed to be fighting the puck. Further, in the opinion of a team executive, some of the players were shooting harder in practice than they were in games. The Dutchmen chose a bad time to go into a slump: an Olympic fundraiser was coming.

There was another concern. The team was rotating new players into the lineup regularly to take a close look as to whether they might be able to help the club. Some felt the situation caused uncertainty. Not all players with the team were assured of being on the Olympic squad. Some observers felt that unconsciously this uncertainty showed in their performance. The lineup was seldom the same, so there was little opportunity to develop continuity or team togetherness.

Sometimes players came in groups. In one December game against Chatham, highly regarded veteran Ralph Hosking, Leaf prospect Ron Casey, and clever center Bill Wylie were skating for the Dutchmen. Even then, there were rumors that likely Hosking and Casey would be traded to the Dunlops temporarily for players who would be on the final Dutchmen Olympic team.

In December 1959, Frank Shaughessy, general manager of Canada's Olympic team, predicted four gold medals for Canadians at Squaw

Valley. He felt that Barbara Wagner and Bob Paul could win in the pairs figure skating competition. He thought the men's single skater Donald Jackson could bring home gold. Also, Canadian skier Anne Heggtveit was one of the top three skiers in the world.

Shaughessy further confidently predicted a gold for the Kitchener-Waterloo Dutchmen., but he expected a close hockey tournament, with competition from Russia, Czechoslovakia, Sweden, and the United States.

"But I have a feeling that my favorite goalie Bill Durnan will lead the Dutchmen to a gold medal this time," he said.

With the 1960 Winter Olympic Games a few months away, conversation about the Olympic movement attracted comments from many quarters.

The topic of whether the Olympics should be abolished made inroads into the press. But Jack Roxburgh, first vice-president of the Canadian Amateur Hockey Association, emphasized that participation in such tournaments helped to put Canada on the map. Canadian hockey teams had gone to Europe and helped to built up Canadian prestige. He stressed that we should be proud that hockey had become an international sport. For example, Japan's National Hockey team would be touring Canada in pre-Olympics preparation. They'd play before packed houses. The Moscow Selects would be playing the Dutchmen at the Kitchener Auditorium in January of 1960, a month before the Games.

The Dutchmen's relationship with the National Hockey League grew into one with a somewhat acrimonious flavor.

Goman expressed his anger about NHL teams signing junior players whom the Dutchmen had drafted. For example, the Chicago Black Hawks signed the richly talented Stan Mikita, the previous year's Most Valuable Player in the OHA Junior A league. Like some other Dutchmen draftees, the young star was now untouchable.

NHL president Clarence Campbell felt that Canadians shouldn't attend the Olympics at all unless they could send the best professionals instead of "phony amateurs." Unlike 2014, when NHL-connected men like Steve Yzerman and Ken Holland chose the players from only NHL teams, in 1960 the NHL was not involved at all in hockey at the international level. Campbell also felt that the CAHA hadn't put together a good management team in Kitchener that would ensure that Canada's best amateurs went to Squaw Valley.

Some CAHA executives felt that Campbell and his league were upset by not getting world-wide exposure while lower level Senior A teams like the Dutchmen did.

Back in Kitchener, in mid-December 1959, the Dutchies' slide in the league standings remained a concern for management and fans, and especially for their coach. He considered resigning but decided to continue, hoping for improved results. There were also whisperings that he might be replaced.

Dutchmen management called a team meeting to engage them in conversation about how their performance might improve. Previous to the meeting there were hints in the press about what was deemed the partying lifestyle of the youthful, charismatic Cliff Pennington. When the question of what actions might be taken for the team's improvement, Pennington suggested they meet at a King Street tavern for a few beers and talk about it.

Dick Warwick asked for a tryout with the Dutchmen, and Goman hoped to have him in his team's starting lineup at the Winter Games. Brothers Bill, Grant and Dick Warwick had become household names in Canada in 1955 as members of the Penticton Vees who won the World Hockey Championship for Canada in Germany. The Warwicks went on to play in Poland, and assisted in the development of their national hockey team. Their presence led to having more fans being turned away from arenas than there was room inside.

But in 1959 it soon became apparent that Warwick was out of shape. His significant international experience might help, but the Dutchmen needed a player who could step into the lineup and make a positive difference immediately. Warwick wasn't signed on.

The Dutchmen manager openly wondered if Warwick's arrival had more to do with him wanting to take over as coach of the Dutchmen, knowing full well he couldn't make it as a player. The manager said, "So Warwick is definitely through with this club. I wish we had never seen him in the first place."

Earlier, while he was still on good terms with the Dutchmen. Warwick had advised that the Russians remained the team to beat. Their coach Tarasov's philosophy had changed and he now believed that the individual player needed to be given the opportunity to develop in his own best light. Despite this, Warwick predicted that at the Olympics the Soviets would be playing "their old, mechanical style." Bobrov, the Russian star at the 1956 Games, had retired from the game. The Czechs had brought Bubnik out of retirement. Warwick thought he might help, but he was past his peak.

In late December the Dutchmen played the Windsor Bulldogs and lost 6-0. It was the third consecutive shutout for Bulldog goalie Don Head. The Dutchmen management took notice.

After their sixth straight loss, their tenth loss in the past thirteen games, a local sports writer felt the Dutchmen were at a crossroads. In his opinion, they lacked leadership on the ice. He called the Dutchmen "discomfited, discouraged, disparaged, and disinterested. If we can get them dedicated, everything else will disappear."

Durnan's frustration grew. Before the year 1960 arrived, he resigned from the team, following a conference with club president Oscar Wiles. The coach felt the team lacked the personnel to compete. He also pointed out the team's injuries and the need to try out extra players as agitating factors. Some members of the team's executive offered that some of the players weren't giving one hundred percent effort.

With Durnan gone, the manager needed a coach. The team approached former Leafs Joe Primeau, Ted Kennedy and Hap Day. All declined, but expressed a willingness to assist in whatever way they could.

Goman made an appointment to visit the production manager at the local Canada Skate Company in Waterloo whose name was Bobby Bauer.

"There are a great many obstacles in Bobby's way," Goman said. "I think he might take the job, though, if some of the pressure of business can be removed."

The other news was that Wren Blair, manager of the Dunlops, would be making the trip to Squaw Valley with the Dutchmen. He'd have no official position with the club, although he was called Olympic coordinator. Some grew a bit concerned in having a high-powered man, used to being in control, on board. Having Blair be available but without a defined role with the Dutchmen might be a recipe for problems down the road.

By the time the Dutchmen played the McFarlands in early January, Bobby Bauer had been introduced as the team's coach. Butch regained his scoring touch for his familiar coach, scoring two consecutive goals in the game and adding an assist. It was a good welcome back for the coach he knew so well and for whom he had great respect.

The Dutchmen won five in a row. Butch scored a goal against the Dunlops and a goal in a 3-2 win over the Bulldogs.

In early 1960, St. Michael's Junior A team had the league's third highest scorer on their roster. He was eighteen years old, and his name was David Keon. He was given a one-game tryout with the Dutchmen. Centering Laufman and Butch, he scored a goal. From all reports he was spectacular. He'd be a great lift to the Dutchmen. But the Leafs organization didn't want him to be away from his team and from his education for the length of time the Dutchmen needed him. Grasping at straws, perhaps, Goman suggested that Rope, a high school teacher, could tutor Keon during the trip. But Keon returned to his St. Michael's team.

In January 1960, the Moscow Selects arrived in Kitchener as part of their North American tour. The players were chosen from the five teams in the Moscow League. It was an all-star team, but not the team that would represent the Soviet Union at the Winter Games.

However, on the Selects roster were six players from the 1956 national team. Among them was outstanding defenseman "Soly" Sologubov. Bauer was sure Sologubov could be an all-star on any NHL team. Also on board was goalie Pushkin whose efforts in goal had a lot to do with the Dutchmen's loss to the Soviets at the 1956 Games.

The coach of the Selects was Arkady Chernyshev, the same man whose Soviet team had defeated the Dutchmen and won the gold medal in Cortina d'Ampezzo.

PeeWee said that although her husband was a calm man, she'd never seen him so keyed up for a game as he was for the Dutchmen-Selects game. He really, really wanted to win that game.

Against the Selects, the Dutchmen were wearing their official Canada sweaters: white and green with a green maple leaf on the front and CANADA on the back. The game was officiated following rules that would be in place for the Olympics: full two-minute penalties; no icing; and no body-checking in the opposition end of the ice.

Before 7000 fans, the Dutchmen won by a 7-4 score. Laufman, Rope and Butch, the only Dutchmen who'd been to Cortina, each scored a goal. The Record report said that Butch's goal was "a beauty." Vladimir Chinev played goal for the Selects. Pushkin had the day off.

The Dutchmen were happy with the win, but concerned that the Soviets had filmed the game and were taking it home to review and gain valuable information which might assist them the next month in Squaw Valley. Some naysayers suggested that the Soviets had sent a weaker team to Canada to make the Dutchmen feel over-confident.

Butch met the Selects again a few days later in Maple Leaf Gardens. The Whitby Dunlops had asked him to join them for the game. He helped them win by a 9-1 score before a sell-out crowd of over 14,000. The invitation to play was another indication of the high regard Canada's hockey community had for Butch. It would not be his last such invitation.

Goman received a check for a thousand dollars from the Montreal

Canadiens. Sam Pollock, general-manager of the Canadiens, was showing his support.

One evening a classy Canadien Junior A prospect, considered to be one of the best junior players in Canada, was leisurely leaving a theater in Brockville where he was playing for their Junior A team. A Canadiens' representative quietly pulled him aside, and told him he was going to the Olympic Games. Nineteen year old Bobby Rousseau broke into a wide smile. He'd dreamed of representing his country.

Rousseau was one of five hockey playing brothers whose home was Montreal. One hockey scout suggested that unless an avalanche at Squaw Valley took him out, Rousseau would be an NHL star. His dream was to play like the Rocket.

Now Pennington had a teammate his age on board.

But Pennington became the centre-piece of a controversy. A Toronto reporter wrote that in a conversation with the young Dutchmen, he'd said that there was dissension on the club and that the Dutchmen lacked a competent coach. However, Pennington's excellent contributions during the next few games showed no sign of displeasure. The Toronto newspaper, operating in a competitive market, was accused of questionable reporting. The Dutchmen were under great strain to finalize their roster and needed support, not unsubstantiated criticism.

As February came, the Dutchmen were finally able to get their team in place. Bobby Attersley, Fred Etcher, Harry Sinden and George Samalenko were loaned from the Dunlops to the Dutchmen for participation at Squaw Valley. At twenty-three years of age, Attersley was considered one of the best amateur centers in Canada.

The Dutchmen were required to pay the Dunlops $500 (close to $4000 in 2014) for each of the players. Butch and Samalenko had been opponents in 1956 in Paisley, Scotland when the Dutchmen played the Paisley Pirates.

As expected, the deal with the Whitby team meant giving up Hosking, their most experienced and best defenseman, for the remainder of the season. It seemed a high but necessary price to pay.

The Dutchmen were also responsible for the expenses but not the salary for Wren Blair. Bob Lebel of the CAHA offered that, although Blair's role wasn't clearly defined, he'd be an active and vociferous presence. The volatile Blair, Lebel knew, would holler and scream from the first face off, and be an inspirational leader. Lebel believed that for a team to win, they had to be fired up. Finally, in Lebel's opinion, compatibility between Bauer and Blair would be essential for the team to be successful. It might be a challenge. Bauer was a calm, rational coach.

Laufman was thinking ahead of his time. He felt it would be beneficial for hockey teams to have not only a head coach, but also assistants, handling forwards and defense respectively.

In a league game, before he joined the Dutchmen, the Dunlops' outstanding defenseman Harry Sinden received a cut on the lower part of his mouth that required over thirty stitches. It happened accidentally when Don Head of the Windsor Bulldogs, the league's best goalkeeper, caught Sinden accidentally with his stick. The Dutchmen were concerned: Sinden was sure to be the cornerstone of their defense corps.

Ironically, a relatively few days later, Head joined the Dutchmen, but was promised for only eighteen days.

But Bauer was carrying three goalies, Head, Hurley and Maniago. Head would stay. He just didn't know who his partner would be. Head and Jim Connolly, a forward with Chatham Maroons would join the remainder of the team in Squaw Valley.

The Dutchmen Booster Fan Club members were making plans for their trip to Squaw Valley. Flight plans weren't a major problem, but the closest accommodations were about an hour's drive from the Olympic Village. PeeWee and the other ardent fans were a bit disappointed. Ray Bauer, a team executive, promised he'd try his best to find something closer to the action.

At Elmira's John Mahood School, grade four teacher Daryl Sly had the first bit of news during the early morning's current events class. Finally he could tell the kids that he'd be going to the Winter Olympic Games. Mr. Davis from the Signet newspaper would be announcing it the next publication. The children thought it pretty neat that Butch Martin and Mr. Sly, both from the small community where they also lived would be playing for Canada's team. They'd keep track of how they were doing through the local Signet newspaper.

On a frosty, windblown December morning a middle-aged salesman from J. M. Schneider Foods, dapperly attired in a fashionable trench coat and wearing a fancy Biltmore hat, dropped by Cecil Capling's Garage in Floradale for a gas fill-up. He also needed instructions to the Emmanuel Bauman farm, situated in the Floradale suburbs. He said, the word "suburbs" with what Cecil later called a "big city snicker." Cecil took five dollars for the gas and stuck it into the side pocket of his oil-stained, blue coveralls, also home to his large, red handkerchief.

As the city guy was about to drive off, he rolled down the window of his white Studebaker Lark,and yelled, "Hey, isn't this the place where that Martin guy lives? I heard he's going to the Olympics."

"No, no," said Cecil, "that was four years ago. That stuff happens only once in a lifetime."

Cecil got the real story when he crossed the road to Ruggle's General Store to pick up his mail. Butch's sister Valina, with the new Eaton's catalogue tucked under her arm, paused and broke the news.

Cecil leaned on the worn wooden counter in front of an open bag of Stokes corn seed. "Holy cats!" he murmured to himself, "Butch will have another chance to send one of those Russians flying on his rear-end,"

The debate about who was amateur and who was professional had continued, especially since the Cortina Games. The CAHA in particular but also amateur hockey executives at the Senior A level were leading the charge.

In 1956, the CAHA had questioned whether Eastern Bloc Olympic participants were really amateur, as required by President Avery Brundage and his International Olympic Committee. Four years later, the concern was greater than ever and had the support of many non-Communist countries. The CAHA was strictly following the rules, insisting that all members of Canada's National Hockey Team be true amateurs, untainted by professionalism.

Sport in the Soviet Union was directed by the state, and all athletes were given financial subsidies, some more than others. It seemed clear to the Dutchmen and others that the practice broke amateur rules. The Canadians and Americans alleged that Soviets hockey players were the elite among all their players. They were given phantom jobs in the military so they could play fulltime.

In reply to the growing undercurrent of protest, the Brundage chastised the suspicious activities of sportsmen in America and other western countries. In his opinion, ninety percent if not all of the top athletes in the Games had received money at one time or another.

Rising above the debate, there remained a shared optimism in important places about the Dutchmen's chances.

Bauer said, "This time I think we'll do the job. Until this month is over, we'll let our actions speak better than our words. If we can't do it, the CAHA should send out an expedition force with bazookas in 1964."

Goman added, "We're stronger in goal, stronger on defense where half the pairings were forwards, and stronger down the middle than the team that failed in Cortina."

Butch said, "We have to be ready for the Soviets. We knew in 1956 they were a lot better than most people thought." Asked about pressure, Butch replied, "When you're playing, you don't have time to think about pressure."

Jack Roxburgh, first vice-president of the CAHA, said, "We now have one of the best, if not the best amateur teams in Canada, to represent us."

At a civic reception at Kitchener's Walper House Hotel, each of the Dutchmen received a watch, a dress shirt and a solid showing of support from Kitchener civic authorities.

Yet almost on the eve of the team's departure, a rumor came out that the Leafs were exploring the possibility of entering a Kitchener-based team into the newly formed Eastern Professional Hockey League. If plans came to fruition, the new pro team's home would be the Kitchener Auditorium, present home of the Dutchmen. The first puck would drop at the beginning of the 1960-61 season.

But Canada's team had more pressing matters to address in selecting the best team to represent millions of people who were counting on them.

The city of Kitchener was in an upheaval when a third major fire broke out in the downtown. The damage was estimated at $350,000. The loss had been $1.5 million in one of two earlier downtown blazes.

In preparation for the 1960 Winter Games, the Japanese National Hockey team, touring in Ontario, wasn't particularly competitive but Canadian fans were being introduced to customs that had never before occurred in Canadian rinks. When a Japanese player was called for a penalty, he'd bow to the "honorable referee" and skate quickly to the penalty box. Before entering, he'd bow to the "honorable time-keeper." When a stoppage of play was indicated, the Japanese player closest to the puck would pick it up and deliver it to the nearest on-ice official. The players from the land of the rising sun were making inroads into the hearts of Canadian hockey fans.

The Japanese team asked IOC officials to make sure they met the Canadians in the Olympic Tournament. The highlight of their Olympic experience, they said, would be to score a goal against the Canadians.

During the last week of January 1960, Daryl Sly introduced his grade four students at John Mahood School to their teacher for the next six weeks or so. The students promised, when Sly returned, they'd hand in their completed scrapbooks filled with pictures of the Squaw Valley Olympics. Then, with a collective wave, they said goodbye.

Sly, Butch and the others on Canada's team were about to see western Canada by train. More than two thousand hollering and hooting excited fans heated up the cold outside the Kitchener Auditorium on the last day in January of 1960. Once again, their Dutchmen would be Canada's team. They couldn't have been prouder.

Since 1928, Lishman coaches had travelled a regular route through the quiet, countryside between Elmira and Kitchener. On the cold winter morning of 1960, the drivers were headed toward the same Toronto destination as they had in 1956 with their passengers on a similar mission. Dozens of cars filled with Dutchmen fans followed.

Butch, Laufman and Rope had made a similar excursion before. Now their mission took on a greater significance. The pressure began as soon as the coaches left the Auditorium's parking lot and made their way slowly along Ottawa Street to Weber.

The uncommon motorcade's destination was downtown Toronto's Union Station. Once inside, the Waterloo County fans exploded into a never-ending rallying cheer of "Go Dutchies Go!" The snaking, pulsating parade wound its way through the increasingly congested halls, curiously observed by big city commuters with tokens and transfers squeezed in their palms, hurriedly making their way to their homes in the suburbs of Don Mills and Scarborough.

Maestro Walter Susskind was conducting the Toronto Symphony in their majestic performance of Oskar Morawetz's Symphony #2 a few blocks north in Massey Hall. But in the halls of Front Street's Union Station, Waterloo County's own "dignified" maestro led his "oom pah pah" group in musical arrangements that would never make it inside the venerable Hall. Engaging and entertaining Earl Einwechter, resplendent in his tall black hat, tails and flippers, raised his dust-mop baton and led his New Dundee's Little German Band in a spirited rendition of "Uch du Lieber Augustin."

Kitchener's Mayor Harry E. Wambold said, "We can count on this team to bring back the bacon to the city that produces the best bacon in the country!"

It was an emotional moment.

Butch boarded the train coach, dressed like his teammates in a red, yellow, green and black striped Hudson Bay jacket, grey flannels, and seal-skin hat and boots. Canada's team was on its way to an intense seven-game western Canada tour. The exhibition games would give them a comparatively brief time to gel as team and garner the confidence and support of the knowledgeable, friendly hockey fans of the Prairies.

But some changes were coming.

The Dutchmen were on a quest, one they'd begun at the Elmira Arena about five months earlier. During that time, familiar players, some with friends on the Squaw Valley-bound team were gone. New players were welcomed. But as they made their way west, there remained uncertainty about the final roster.

Goman and Bauer understood that a great goalie could make a huge difference. Goalie Pushkin of the Soviets and Ikola of the United States had proven that in Cortina. With Head's arrival in Squaw Valley, they'd have the best goalie available. But who would make the better back-up goalie?

The first stop on their western tour was in Fort William, Ontario, where the Kaministiquia River flows into Lake Superior. The Dutchmen, with Sinden on defense, Attersley up front, and other reliable newcomers, defeated the Lakehead All Stars by a 6-1 score. Rousseau got three goals, a promising sign for Bauer. Butch had an assist.

From Fort William it was a ten-hour trip west to the city of Brandon, Manitoba, located along the Assiniboine River. The temperature was minus 10 degrees Fahrenheit.

The Dutchmen played the Senior A Winnipeg Maroons in Brandon. The city was home to the much-loved Tommy Douglas before he became the seventh premier of Saskatchewan. In a viewer's poll in 2004, Douglas was named "The Greatest Canadian," venerated as the "Father of Medicare." One fan in attendance at the game said he hadn't been to a hockey since Tommy Douglas was an eight year-old in grade school.

The Dutchmen won 10-1, outshooting the Maroons 54-15. Butch had a goal and two assists. In the dressing room after the game, a Maroon player, in a witty, self deprecating remark, quipped, "We sure hemmed them in our own end, didn't we?"

At this late date, Maniago, Ted Maki and Murray Davison were disappointed with the news that they wouldn't be going to Squaw Valley.

Just off the Trans-Canada Highway, west of Regina, in minus 20 C weather, over three-hundred cheering Moose Javians met the Dutchmen at the local train station. Shortly thereafter the Moose Jaw Chamber of Commerce hosted a warm reception and a delectable luncheon.

At game time, as the Dutchmen skated out for the pre-game warmup, they were met with a rousing welcome. When they returned for the start of the game, players on the Moose Jaw Pla-Mors team, their opponents, formed an arc of honor with their hockey sticks. Pretty little Pelly Lighel presented captain Jack McKenzie with a Dutch doll, while standing tall on the red dot in the big centre circle with the "Go Dutchies Go" message painted on it.

Butch had a goal and an assist in a 9-1 Dutchmen victory.

Saskatoon was next. Saskatoon, Saskatchewan was first settled in 1893 by the Toronto Methodists, wanting to escape the liquor trade in the city. They travelled by train to Moose Jaw, then made their way north to the new settlement by horse-drawn cart. The prairies were growing rapidly. Saskatoon had a few major growth spurts, one leading into the mid 1960s. The Dutchmen arrived at a city approaching 100,000 citizens.

The Dutchmen played the Saskatoon Quakers. The 1934 Quaker team had won gold at the World Ice Hockey Championship in Milan, Italy. Bauer felt that the 1960 Quaker-Dutchmen game was a stiff test despite a 6-0 victory. Butch had two assists.

The Dutchmen were traveling via the Canadian Pacific Railway. In 1881 the construction of the cross-Canada railway had begun. Incredibly, it was completed six years ahead of schedule with the last spike driven on November 7, 1885, in Craigellachie, British Columbia. Its completion physically joined Canada from sea to sea.

Goman and Bauer hoped to build cohesiveness and camaraderie among the team members through the exhibition games. Hockey fans throughout the West were transforming the perception of the Dutchmen from a team from a city in south-western Ontario into Canada's team.

Deep in British Columbia's interior, in the Okanagan Valley, the Dutchman stopped in Vernon. The city was settled by the Okanagan people, a tribe of the Salish. Initially they named the community Nintle-Moos Chin which means "jumping over place where the little creek narrows." Vernon is known for its lakes and beaches in the summer and skiing and hockey in the winter.

In 1959 the Vernon Canadiens defeated the Dutchmen in the Allan Cup semi-finals. Leading up to the exhibition game, the Vernon coach boldly predicted that his team would win by five goals.

Butch must have heard the remarks. In an outstanding performance he scored three goals and assisted on three others in an 8-3 victory. The next day, a game report in the local newspaper, stated, "Butch Martin, the honest brakeman, who toils up front for the Dutchies, had a big night."

The Kitchener-Waterloo Record's sports page headline was, "Martin, Connolly Spark Win Over Vernon."

Newly minted as Canada's team, the Dutchmen were leaving a strong impression which was surprising to some hockey experts. Local sports reporters in the West suggested that the excellent fan support came about because they wanted to see if the Dutchmen were as awful as they were being told.

The "surprisingly talented" team travelled about seventy-five miles west to get to the city of Kamloops, at the confluence of the two branches of the Thompson River, located in the Thompson River Valley. Kamloops had a population of about 11,000 in 1960. The great Canadian poet Robert Service who wrote poems and ballads about the Klondike Gold Rush of 1897, worked in the Kamloops branch of the Canadian Bank of Commerce for four months in 1904 before being transferred to Whitehorse.

Reportedly, the Dutchmen weren't at their best against the Chiefs. But Butch, with a reputation for consistency, once again received praise from the local press: "Butch Martin was probably the most effective Dutchies' forward." People across Canada were becoming more familiar with the name "Butch Martin."

Goman received the Olympic Hockey schedule. Purposely, he was told, Canada and the Soviet Union had again been scheduled for the last game. There were high expectations that the game would be for gold and many felt certain such would be the case. Canada's almost 18,000,000 inhabitants were hoping for nothing less.

Canada's team reached the town of Trail, British Columbia. They were preparing to play their seventh game in nine days. The hotel to which they were assigned was described as "dismal" by Bauer and his manager.

In 1960, Trail was a small, smelting town, located between the Monashee and Selkirk Mountains, and divided by the Columbia River. It was named after the Dewdney Trail which passed through the area.

But Trail's reputation for winners had grown with its senior hockey teams, particularly the Trail Smoke Eaters. They'd won an Allan Cup in 1938, and a World Hockey Championship in Zurich and Basil, Switzerland the following year. In 1960 the Smoke Eaters were building towards another date with hockey glory. Their game against the Dutchmen would give them an indication of their progress.

The Trail fans were in a party mood, fueled by a seven-piece hillbilly band. But in the end the Dutchies remained perfect, with an 8-3 win.

A year later the Smoke Eaters would win the 1961 World Championship in Geneva and Lausanne, Switzerland. Sly, the Elmira grade four teacher, was with the Dutchmen in 1960 but in 1961 he helped the Smoke Eaters in their World Championship run.

The big win in Trail had a down side which turned out to be a major factor at Squaw Valley. Ken Laufman, considered by most as the Dutchmen's top star, sustained a leg injury. It was a déjà vu experience, bringing back memories of his injury sustained in the 1956 exhibition game in Czechoslavakia.

The Dutchmen were on their way to Squaw Valley. Some prominent politicians were making plans to join them, including Prime Minister John Diefenbaker, whose Tory government had passed legislation that allowed Status Indians to vote in federal elections.

Back home, excitement grew about the imminent opening of the Macdonald-Cartier Freeway between Milton and Kitchener. The Record reported that twenty-five people a year were brought to court to explain to the judge why they hadn't returned their books to the Kitchener Library. A ten year-old St. Jacobs boy was getting people's attention while playing minor hockey for Elmira. His name was Daryl Sittler. In January of 1960, Gordie Howe became the leading scorer in NHL history, passing Maurice Richard.

In 1945, the Soviet Union and the United States had been allies, jointly triumphant in their decisive victory over Adolph Hitler and his Nazi empire in Europe. But within a few years they had become mortal enemies, locked in a global struggle—military, political, economical, ideological—in what was known as the Cold War. The Olympics were seen as a non-military competition to show the superiority of the Communist way of life over that of Western culture.

American president Harry Truman had said, "The Soviets recognize the games as an opportunity to again apply its talent for twisting international gatherings into vehicles for Soviet propaganda."

But the Soviets weren't alone. Truman's successor, Dwight Eisenhower stated, "Our aim in Cold War is not to conquer a territory or subjugate by force. Our aim is more subtle, more pervasive, more complete. There are many peaceful tools that must be used in waging this fight… friendly contacts through travel, and correspondence, and sport."

Some political observers referred to the Olympic Games at the Secret Cold War. Sports competition, like the 1960 Winter Olympic Games, were indeed opportunities for political adversaries to demonstrate the success of a political system.

In his doctoral thesis in philosophy at the University of Western Ontario, Toby Charles Rider argued convincingly that the United States and the West were equally culpable with the Soviet Union and the eastern Communist bloc.

He wrote, "Modern sport has been remarkably conducive to propaganda. By its nature, sport is suited to the task. It excites nationalistic instincts, and encourages group identification. It is superficially apolitical and readily understandable. Sporting activities can take place across barriers of race, class, religion, and nationality. And through modern means of communication, sports spectacles can be transmitted throughout the world. Predicting that the Americans will use the Olympic Games for nationalistic purposes is as facile as predictions that a tornado will touch down in Oklahoma sometime in spring."

In 1955 Avery Brundage had been elected president of the International Olympic Committee at its meetings in Helsinki, Finland. He said, "In a world engaged in a titanic struggle between different political systems, it is not a simple matter to keep aloof."

In 1960, the reunification of Germany was a delicate question in international politics. The question of how to deal with the potentially explosive situation arrived in the lap of Brundage. The president and his Olympic committee ordered the East and West Germans to combine into a united Germany for the Games. Brundage also assisted in designing a unified flag that was acceptable to both sides.

Two years before the 1960 Games, the Peoples Republic of China withdrew from the Olympic movement and all International Federations.

The 1960 Winter Olympics was the first for the Union of South Africa. They sent four figure skaters. But South Africa was banned from any further Olympic competitions due to its political policy of apartheid. South Africa came back to the Winter Games in 1992.

Canada's National Hockey Team, on their way by rail to the 1960 Winter Olympic Games were aware that their matches, whether they liked it or not, would cast a much wider swath than simply winning games. Victories or losses, in some quarters would be interpreted in the context of a political ideology and a way of life.

The Cold War and the emotions it generated were pervasive forces in all cultural activities, including hockey. But hockey was Canada's sport. And Canada's team was given a second chance to have a nation restored to its proper place in international hockey hierarchy. They had had an unexpected opportunity for retribution and they were determined to succeed for themselves and for Canada.

A total of forty-four Canadian athletes were making their way to Squaw Valley. They read weather reports that carried the dismal news of warm temperatures and seemingly constant rain. Parts of Squaw Valley were flooded.

Squaw Valley, California, located in the Sierra Nevada Mountain range, remains the smallest and most improbable place in the world to ever host an Olympic Games. It was once a mining boom town. In 1960, as now, it was a ski resort, situated about fifteen miles from Lake Tahoe. In 1960 it had one chair lift, two tow ropes, and a fifty-room lodge. It had no mayor and apparently only one year-round resident—Alexander Cushing. The impressive Cushing was a Harvard alumnus and trained lawyer.

Innsbruck, Austria had built much of the infrastructure to host a Winter Olympics, and had been considered a sure thing to be the 1960 host. But in 1955, Cushing, then the president of the Squaw Valley Development Association, had travelled to Paris to show the International Olympic Committee a model of his proposed Olympic site. He explained that Squaw Valley offered a clean slate on which a world-class facility could be built, custom-designed for an Olympic

Games.

Over time, with the support of the state's governor, Goodwin Knight, and assurances of financial stability, Cushing won over the IOC members. Squaw Valley narrowly edged out the deeply disappointed Innsbruck delegation. In February of 1959, Cushing was featured on the cover of Time magazine.

However, not all Americans were enthralled. One writer said that having tiny Squaw Valley host the Olympics was like taking the Super Bowl from Cowboys Stadium in Dallas and holding it in a high school stadium in some unknown Texas hamlet.

It took five years and $20 million to build the Olympic Village. In 2014 the cost of the Sochi Olympics was about $50 billion.

Unlike Cortina, Squaw Valley, by building an Olympic Village, could accommodate 665 athletes from thirty countries. Three or four team members shared a room. Management of the teams preferred to be in separate quarters from their players. That not being the case in Squaw Valley, they had to meet in "a corner" where they discreetly conversed about matters relating to their players.

Athletes from all countries ate in the same dining area. Regularly appearing on the menu were featured dishes from participating countries.

Butch enjoyed the style of his extravert teammate Pennington. Butch said, "He was s really young guy but was kind of outgoing. He'd sit at a different table every night at dinner, and after he'd move around. He knew everybody there and he acted like he could speak every language. He couldn't but he'd kind of jabber away. He got to know everybody there."

The dining hall became a marvelous meeting place for others besides Pennington. Butch met many Canadian and international athletes over meals in the dining room. Foreign languages, customs, and politics weren't barriers to growing and sometimes long-lasting friendships.

There were many distractions. Taking in the grandeur of it all took some time. That's why the Dutchmen, like most other Canadian competitors, gave themselves time to take it all in, to feel comfortable and to catch the wonder that comes with having the spotlight of the world shine on the place where you are performing.

One event from other Winter Olympic Games was missing: Cushing and his committee had refused to build a bobsled run.

It was the first Olympics to use instant replay, to be internationally televised, and to use an ice resurfacing machine. Televising the Games provided many challenges, with its large, bulky cameras, giant studio tripods, background noises, freezing cold cameramen and technicians, and mile and miles of cable. Bonfires were lit around the cameras each night so they wouldn't freeze up.

At thirty years of age, Butch had had an eventful life already. Hockey had been an important part of it. As a young child playing on Floradale dam, he had never hoped he'd become an NHL hockey player. Neither had he had aspirations to represent Canada at a World Hockey Championship or Winter Olympic Games. Now he was at his second Games.

His record in his years with the Dutchmen was impressive. Some called him "the best Dutchman." Butch deferred to Laufman. In 2014 he said, "Kenny was so smart. He never missed. He is a guy who now would be an NHL player. But back then he was hurt by his size and the fact he wasn't really fast. Although nobody seemed to catch him when he didn't want them to. It was his hockey sense that was so strong."

But Butch himself had great physical strength and fortitude. He never seemed to tire. His accurate, playmaking and intelligent strategy brought results, but that was only a part of what he brought to a game. He impressed people with his rugged style, defensive abilities and respectful approach to the game. He was a complete player, the kind of player managers wanted to have on their teams on special trips abroad.

By the time the 1960 Winter Games began, Butch had amassed an enviable hockey record. As a captain, he'd led the Elmira Polar Kings to

OHA Intermediate B and A championships. With the Dutchmen he'd brought home an Olympic bronze medal. He was on the Dutchmen team who'd won four straight OHA Senior A championships. As a young man, with his best hockey years ahead of him, he'd turned down the opportunity to be an NHL player. He had walked away from the Dutchmen, with the decision not to play on Sundays, and had taken a year off to think things over before resuming his hockey career.

He'd also married Ethleen "PeeWee" Martin, the love of his life and most ardent supporter. She'd be leading the cheers as Butch played in the Blyth Memorial Arena in Squaw Valley.

PeeWee said, "Butch is a powerhouse on the ice. He never gets out of shape as his job is to haul and saw logs. He loves the out-of-doors and he loves rugged hockey. It always surprises people that he's such a mild-mannered, easy going person after seeing his tough body-checking."

As a Polar King, a Dutchmen and an Olympian, Butch was highly popular. His presence on the Dutchmen teams brought thousands of fans to the Kitchener Auditorium from the surrounding townships, places where people knew him by name, who'd shared a table for coffee, who'd sat beside him at church and who'd done business with S. S. Martin and Sons. He was a local boy and one of whom they were rightly proud.

Canada was cheering for the Dutchmen. But for thousands of Waterloo County residents, when Butch appeared on the ice, the spotlight was only on him. None paid closer attention than sports-loving Donnie Hoffman and James Snyder whose uncle Butch was involved in something incredibly important. How they wished they could be there!

Chat at Elmira's Etchwood Restaurant, over fries and milkshakes, after Mennonite Church Hockey League Games got folks up to speed as to how Butch, their guy, was doing in Squaw Valley.

Butch had thousands of admirers. He was a role model for thousands more.

By 1960, the year of Squaw Valley, the Mennonite view on competitive sports was in the midst of a slow but steady turn. More families had moved into urban areas where they had more time available to participate and where Mennonite children were allowed to join teams at the minor level. Some joined high school teams.

The Canadian Mennonite, the official voice of the Mennonite community, had a brief piece noting that there was a distinct possibility that Butch was the first Mennonite to represent Canada at the Winter Olympics.

The same publication article noted, "Spectator sports are big business these days. You are encouraged to participate, rather than just watch, even if you're not Rocket Richard. Compare it to doing something at church, even if you're not Billy Graham." The comments clearly signaled a cautious change in attitude among some in the Mennonite community regarding participation in athletic endeavors.

Butch's accomplishments in hockey were already far beyond what most players would attain in a career. But Squaw Valley was a gift, an unexpected second chance to perform at the highest level of amateur competition in the world. It was a long way from shinny on the Floradale dam.

Bobby Bauer reiterated his comments from 1956 concerning the pressure, "Believe me, the Stanley Cup is nothing like this! But I'm quietly confident."

Bauer's wife, Marguerite, was in agreement: "The strain is terrific."

Walt Disney, himself an international icon in the world of animation and entertainment, was hired to produce the opening ceremonies at the 1960 Winter Olympic Games. By 1960 Walt Disney Enterprises was recognized as the world's leading producer of family entertainment. He and his assistants spent the year coming up with the most elaborate and colorful panorama ever seen in the Games' history.

Disney said, "Nothing is more important than creating good will among our visitors, and we shall do everything we can to make their stay here a happy one."

The morning of Thursday, February 18, 1960, the day of the opening ceremonies, was grey and dull in Squaw Valley. There was a drizzle in the air. Walt Disney was hoping for a change in the weather.

Several hours before the ceremonies began, a blizzard hit the valley, dumping more than a foot of snow. Disney, along with all the other participants, was covered with snow. But underneath his thick, winter parka, he was smiling. Splendid sunshine followed the storm, just in time for the ceremonies. Representatives from the Soviet Union asked what chemical the Americans had used do suddenly bring on the perfect winter weather.

Including the athletes there were more than 5000 participants. The cream of the high school music world in California made up a band with 1285 members and a choir with 2650 voices. An impressive Tower of Nations and two twenty-three foot snow sculptures stood on either side of the tower. Chimes rang out as the Marine Band played "God of Our Fathers."

Actor Karl Malden, who had starred in Pollyanna that year (the first of his six Disney films,) narrated the Olympic Prayer. American speed skater Ken Henry lit the Olympic Flame. Henry had won a gold medal in five-hundred meter speed skating at the 1952 Winter Games. Carol Heiss, a twenty-year-old favorite to win figure skating gold for the United States, recited the Olympic Oath, the first women ever to do so.

United States Vice-President Richard M. Nixon barely made it on time to officially declare the games open. In November of 1960, Nixon would lose the race for the presidency to Senator John F. Kennedy by one percent of the popular vote.

20,000 balloons and more than 2000 doves of peace were released as part of the Disney extravaganza.

Canada's hockey team took in all the sights, the sounds, and the emotions of the moment. Only a few had been at such an occasion in their hockey careers. They had returned home with a bronze medal.

1960 American hockey team member Bill Cleary said, "I wouldn't trade my chance to march in the Olympic opening ceremony for one hundred Stanley Cup championships. When it was over, we all went back to our lives. That's the way we wanted it."

With the distractions in the background, the Canadians began to focus only on their task. Goman made it clear that without exception, no alcoholic beverages were to be consumed until after the competitions were completed. No one was to leave the village without permission. The curfew each day of the tournament was midnight.

Almost immediately there was controversy. The schedule for the practices for the figure skaters and the hockey teams were such that often both groups would show up at Blyth Memorial Arena at the same time. The Dutchmen often practiced on an outdoor rink. IOC president Brundage, in referring to the ice in the Arena, said, "I don't think you can expect teams who have travelled thousands of miles to play in that slush." Goman called it "barnyard." The Czech delegation thought the hockey games should be moved to Los Angeles.

Visiting newsmen complained about the one-dollar charge for parking, then having to walk half a mile to the arena.

Early on, PeeWee was staying with member of the Dutchmen management party, about forty minutes by car from Squaw Valley. Fortunately, a chalet became available in the town and she and others moved closer to the action.

Disney hired Art Linkletter to head up the task of entertaining the athletes. He was the popular host of the equally popular televisions programs "Kids Say the Darndest Things" and "People Are Funny." Nightly there were free refreshments and entertainment from stars like Danny Kaye, Roy Rogers, Bing Crosby, Debbie Reynolds, and Sammy Davis Junior. German-born actress Marlene Dietrich posed for a photo-shoot with the German hockey team.

Each night Linkletter introduced that day's medal winners and entered their names into a draw. The winner had a free call home—a really big deal in those days. One competitor was so excited about making the call that it was only when his home town operator asked for the number of the party he was calling did he remember that his family didn't have a phone.

Each evening, with the entertainment about to begin, a solitary, forty-three year old man finished eating his steak, placed his folded white napkin on his plate, and sat back in his chair. His name was Walter Cronkite. By 1962 he would begin a long career as host of the CBS Evening News. Cronkite was called "the most trusted man in news." In Squaw Valley Cronkite made history as the first television host of an Olympic Games. He narrated the Opening Ceremonies. Bob Costas, Jim McKay, Paula Zahn and others would follow in his footsteps. As CBS news anchor, Cronkite would later report on the murders of John F. Kennedy and Martin Luther King. He would end each evening news broadcast with the words, "And that's the way it is on 'February 26, 1962.'"

Butch and PeeWee enjoyed visiting the venues and watching other Canadians in the various competitions. They also loved the entertainment.

On one occasion, Butch noticed that PeeWee had drifted to the far side of the gathering in one of the public facilities. She was engaged in conversation with a handsome man who had a familiar look. PeeWee then introduced her husband to actor Tony Curtis. Curtis starred in over 100 movies, including the 1960 release of Stanley Kubrick's Spartacus.

Curtis' wife Janet Leigh came by, best known for her role of Marion Crane in Alfred Hitchcock's suspense horror movie Psycho. Butch and PeeWee had their picture taken with Curtis and Leigh, two of the biggest Hollywood stars of that era.

Blyth Arena was the scene of all of Canada's games. Fans seated on one full side were in the open, at the mercy of the outside weather conditions. The International Olympic Committee had a regulation that no official competition could be held under an enclosed roof. The

1960 Winter Games hockey competition was the first held on a man-made artificial ice surface. The roof was designed to move up and down as much as twenty-two inches, as snow and cold came, resulting in the supporting cables expanding or contracting.

The tournament arrangement was the same as that in Cortina. A round-robin series was played with the teams divided into three groups. Group A made up of Canada, Sweden, and Japan; Group B, the Soviet Union, Germany and Finland; and Group C, United States, Czechoslovakia and Australia. Hockey was gaining popularity in Australia, but they only had two rinks—one in Melbourne and one in Sydney.

The top two teams in each division entered a round-robin medal round. The remaining teams entered a consolation round.

CBS television and the hockey world focused on what they presumed and hoped the last game of the tournament would provide: an exciting, tense battle between Canada and the Soviet Union for Olympic Gold. They had not counted on the United States and "The Forgotten Miracle."

CBS had purchased the rights to broadcast the 1960 Winter Olympics for a meager $50,000. They purchased the right to the 1960 Summer Olympics for $550,000.

February 19, nine days after Bauer's team arrived in Squaw Valley, they faced off against Sweden's national team in their first game.

There was no doubt about Butch's preparedness or intensity. At 18:36 of the first period he scored Canada's first goal. As he skated back toward the centre faceoff circle with Daryl Sly at his side, Sly said, "That'll get those guys at the coffee shop in Elmira talking!"

The intensity came from both sides. Sweden star Sven "Tumba" Johansson and Sly, the pugnacious pedagogue, got five minutes each for a scrap.

Butch played his usual physical game. He lined up 6'3" Lars "Lasse" Bjorn, Sweden's star defensemen and the biggest man in Swedish hockey. The collision that ensued had some interesting repercussions.

In the Hockey News 2011-2012 Yearbook, writer Ken Campbell described the incident: "At the 1960 Winter Olympics in Squaw Valley California twenty years before his grandson Douglas Murray was born, Lasse Björn was a standout defenseman for the Swedish Olympic team. In the first game of the tournament, Floyd "Butch" Martin of Canada, via The Kitchener-Waterloo Dutchmen, knocked him clean over the board and Björn ended up with broken ribs.

"The story goes that Björn has been plotting his revenge against Martin ever since. 'I'd tell him that was a real cheap shot.' Björn said that if he ever met up with Martin today, 'I'd swallow him whole. I would have done so when it happened if I didn't lose the blade of my skate, so I was slower than usual.'"

Following the thunderous hit, Butch received a penalty and a ten-minute misconduct for arguing with the referee. Bauer was upset with the official and yelled, "How can you give him a misconduct? He doesn't even swear!"

The Canadians were victorious by a score of 5-2. Herman Karlsson, manager of the Swedish team, called the game a scandal. He said, "If they started playing hockey instead of fighting, they might find it fun." The foreign press also took issue with the Dutchmen's play, reporting initially that Björn had a broken leg. The Canadian players, and Butch in particular, were painted as goons who relied on intimidation to win games.

A small ceremony was held in the village on February 19, with representatives from Australia, Canada, Great Britain, New Zealand, and South Africa paying tribute to the birth of the new prince—Andrew Albert Christian Edward Duke of York, second son and third child of Queen Elizabeth II and Prince Philip Duke of Edinburgh.

A couple who previously lived in Floradale had moved to Squaw Valley. When they heard that a "Butch Martin" was playing for Canada, they made inquiries as to whether he was the real Butch Martin they'd known back in the village. Butch assured them he was.

Ontario Premier Leslie Frost's telegram to the team read, "Realizing that a price has to be paid for everything worthwhile in life by dedication to the task before us, by working hard toward a goal, and everyone making his proper and one hundred percent contribution...." Frost promised to wear a Dutchmen tie in the Legislature.

Canada moved on. Japan was waiting for them. Their dream was to meet Canada and that day had arrived. The Canadians scored nineteen goals. Midway through the second period, Atsui Irie of the Japanese team got free on a breakaway and scored. It was at least six feet offside but with the goal the Japanese had accomplished their mission to score one goal against Canada. The jubilant Irie received the biggest cheer of the day!

As the medal round opened, IIHF officials expressed concerns about boarding and talking back to the referees. Searching for hockey glory and the gold medal were Canada, Germany, Czechoslovakia, United States, Sweden and the Soviet Union. There were no surprise entries in the mix.

Canada dominated in a 12-0 win over the German team. Michael Hobelsberger, the German goalie made some miraculous saves in facing fifty-eight shots. Germany was outmatched, managing only eighteen shots. But Laufman's knee injury, sustained in an earlier game, was beginning to cause him more problems than he'd anticipated. Fourteen cubic centimeters of fluid were drained from his knee.

On February 24, the undefeated Canadians faced Czechoslovakia in Blyth Arena. Laufman sat out the game. His gift for scoring and his marvelous playmaking were missed. Don Head, the Canadian goalie had to be excellent as he stopped many Czech scoring chances. Many of the thirty-five shots sent his way were labelled. Pennington took the captain's place on a line with Butch and helped in Butch's two big goals in an impressive 4-0 victory. With the loss, the Czechs were out of gold medal contention. But with a vaunted lineup, they could make things uncomfortable for gold medal contenders.

The Kitchener-Waterloo Record reported on the game: "Floyd (Butch) Martin who plays like he's supped at the fountain of eternal youth, cashed two fine scoring chances as he came up with another of his consistently good games." The accolades for Butch's play continued.

The relationship between Bauer and Blair, although not rancorous, wasn't a positive one. Fortunately they got together in a rational discussion to get things cleared up. Blair felt the need to return home to help prepare the Whitby Dunlops for the playoffs. As the team's manager, he felt it was his responsibility,

On the following afternoon, the unknown and undefeated Americans faced the Canadians. The entire Canadian team was under enormous pressure but for Butch, Rope, Bauer and Laufman, the pressure was really intense. This was their time for retribution. The 1956 defeat to the Americans was something that could finally be erased with a victory here.

Canada was watching and from Newfoundland to British Columbia hockey fans were expecting their team to deliver.

Mr. Sly's class at Elmira's John Mahood School took turns in giving reports to their classmates about their teacher and how his team was doing. Excitement grew as the medal round progressed.

Laufman's leg injury was such that if this game were a league game he'd have sat out without question. But this was not a common game. He'd waited four years for this moment. With some difficulty he laced up his skates. He said, "I didn't come all this way to be a spectator." His seven-year-old son told him not to come home without the world title.

Bill Reilly, coach of the American team said, "I think we can beat Canada. We may have to be lucky but I think we can win." The American team had two sets of brothers—Bill and Roger Christian, and Bob and Bill Cleary. The Christians were widely considered the first family of hockey in the United States. John Mayasich, who had scored three goals in Cortina against the Dutchmen, was back. Most of the players on Reilly's team were from the Boston and Minnesota areas.

The 1956 American goalie Willard Ikola wasn't back. That was the good news. The bad news for Canada was that Jack McCartan was the new net-minder.

Herb Brooks, who would coach a young American team to a gold medal in the 1980 "Miracle on Ice" in Lake Placid, was the last cut as a player on the 1960 United States team that faced Canada.

Bauer said, "The tension got as high as the mountains," pointing to the High Sierras. "It makes even experienced players rubber-legged. The Stanley Cup is nothing compared to this. The heat is always on Canada. Everyone expects us to win and everyone wants to beat us."

The team that gathered in the dressing room to prepare for the Americans felt under the gun. There was silence and palpable tension in the room. Bauer's style wasn't loud. He quietly and calmly spoke to the team.

When the Dutchmen lined up for the opening face-off, 7000 boisterous pro-American fans didn't need encouragement to make noise. They made lots of noise!

Canada's first shot on McCartan beat him, but rang off the post. Canada was all over the United States. Rope remembered looking towards the Canadian zone, and barely seeing any skate marks. He thought his team was on their way to a convincing win. But the Canadians couldn't solve the American goalie who "jumped around like a bunny on a hot tin roof."

United States scored first. Then Laufman deked past McCartan, but missed the open net.

Butch remembered, "We had no luck, just no luck at all. Nothing went right." His team had twenty shots in the first period. McCartan and American-friendly goal posts were frustrating them. But as the game progressed, Don Head, in goal for the Dutchmen, came through in splendid style.

The American team was ahead 2-0 by the end of the second period. Reilly had them go into a defensive mode to effectively protect the slim lead. Mayasich, the hero in 1956, had an assist for the Americans.

With ten minutes remaining in the game, Butch set up Jimmy Connolly to put the Dutchmen within one goal. Late in the game, Bauer pulled goalie Head for an extra attacker, but to no avail. The American team and their fans were ecstatic! Mayasich said, "It was another unexpected, unbelievable experience."

Reilly said, "This was a nine out of ten performance for our team; a peak effort. Our goalie played his finest game." McCartan was sensational. Following the game, Tarasov, the Soviet team's coach rushed over to Reilly and kissed him, caught up in the euphoria that the unexpected victory had brought and the door it might open for the Soviets.

In Canada, the reaction to the loss to the Americans was generally one of confusion and dismay. This was not supposed to happen four years ago, but how could Canada's team allow it to happen a second time?

More than five decades later, a hockey game at the 2014 Winter Olympic Games in Sochi, Russia looked hauntingly familiar to Butch. In a quarter final game in 2014, the Canadians were highly favored to easily beat Latvia, who'd upset favored Switzerland a few days earlier, but It was a very frustrating day for Sidney Crosby and his teammates. Latvian goalie, twenty-one-year-old Kristers Gudlevskis stopped fifty-five of fifty-seven Canadian shots, in a remarkable display, à la Jack McCartan for the Americans in 1960. Carey Price, the Canadian goalie, like Don Head for the 1960 Canadians, made some outstanding saves although only facing sixteen Latvian shots. Only Shea Weber's third period goal gave the Canadians a 2-1 victory and saved his countrymen the feelings of utter disappointment and humiliation experienced by Butch and the Dutchmen in Squaw Valley.

Had Canada lost the Sochi game, one can imagine the Canadian reaction being similar to that after Squaw Valley.

Noted American author Margaret Mitchell famously wrote, "Life's under no obligation to give us what we expect." The Canadians' loss to the United States in 1960 showed the truth of that statement. But they had hope. They felt that the Soviets could beat the Americans in their next meeting. Then on the last day of the tournament Canada would take on the Soviets for gold. It would be theatrical drama that was about to be performed—but the Canadians could only partially write the script.

On Saturday afternoon, February 27, the Canadians attended the game between the Soviets and the United States at Blyth Arena. In retrospect, Bauer wished they hadn't. It was the featured game on CBS Television. Millions of Americans watched as their team, with another remarkable effort, marvelously defeated the Soviets 3-2. It was a magnificent sports achievement for the young Americans. Some called it a miracle.

As Butch left the arena, he clearly understood that any hope of a gold Olympic medal had once again evaporated. It was like the replay of a surreal nightmare. But he and his teammates had to recover quickly. That evening they had to be prepared for Sweden. A loss to the Swedes meant returning to Canada with no medal at all.

Mr. Sly's class needed help to sort out what was happening out in California. The folks at Bauer Felt in Waterloo had their fingers crossed for coach Bauer.

It was an unexpected struggle for Canada against the Swedes. They needed to recover from a three-goal deficit at the end of the first period. With a splendid four-goal third period, including a late-game tie-breaking goal by Connolly, they salvaged a 6-5 win.

Canada would play the Soviets the next day, February 28, to decide the silver and bronze medal winners; the same day the Americans played the Czechs where a win would assure them a gold medal.

It was to the Soviet's advantage if the Americans won over the Czechs. At the end of the second period the Czechs were leading 4-3. "Soly" Sologubov, the great Soviet defenseman was watching. Sitting in the dressing room between the second and third periods, American coach Reilly responded to a knock on the dressing room door. The man who faced him was Sologubov. He suggested that Reilly have oxygen tanks available for his team's use in the third period. Reilly was willing to give it a try. In the third period, his team scored six unanswered goals to win 9-4.

But only observers paying close attention understood that the Soviet star's gesture, although apparently beneficial to the Americans, was also self-serving. An American win over the Czechs meant that the Soviets would be declared European champions, a great honor.

Going undefeated in all seven games they played, the Americans won their first-ever Olympic Gold Medal in hockey. It was a stunning result that struck the American amateur hockey world like an unexpected and welcome thunderbolt.

Years later, after the 1980 "Miracle on Ice," their 1960 championship became appropriately known as "The Forgotten Miracle." A documentary with the same title was produced in 2010, on the fiftieth anniversary of the 1960 Winter Games.

Reports arrived that in the game between Finland and the usually polite Japanese, a free-for-all had broken out.

The last hockey game of the 1960 Winter Olympic Games was played on the last day, February 28. Canada met the Soviet Union. The schedule makers hoped it would be a gold medal game. But the gold medal had already been unexpectedly won by what some called an over-achieving American team.

The 1960 Soviet team was coached by Anatoli Tarasov, considered the father of Russian hockey. After World War II, he had put together the hockey program from scratch and was considered the genius behind its development. His "Soviet Hockey System" was largely copied from a Canadian, Lloyd Percival, a well-known and respected exercise and conditioning expert. Percival's programs had been rejected in Canada, but became the cornerstone of the Soviet system.

Previous to WW II, "bandy" was the name for Russian ice hockey. It was played with a ball, and sticks, on a rectangular sheet of ice about the size of a football field. As in football, there were eleven players to a side. Some referred to bandy as field hockey on ice, and with skates.

Tarasov's approach to ice hockey was developed from bandy, using the drop pass and constant attack, sometime retreating to develop a play. Passing, skating, conditioning and discipline were demanded.

Tarasov was asked for his prediction for the Canada-Soviet game. He said, "We are very simple people. You know I never predict the outcome of a game. We play them one at a time."

Soviet star Boblov, a member of the Soviet's 1956 team had retired. Goalie, Nikolai Pushkin, who'd stymied Butch and his teammates in 1956, was with the 1960 team.

Impressively, with an excellent start Canada took a first-period 3-0 lead and were ahead 4-3 at the end of the second. They clinched the silver medal with four goals in the third period, winning 8-5.

Canada had won a silver medal. But there was no joy in the dressing room.

Many players wiped away tears in the emotions of the moment. Some felt they'd been humiliated. Most felt they'd let their country down. There had been tremendous pressure for them to win and they felt they'd failed in that mission.

Butch, Rope and Laufman had walked this lonely, gloomy path before. The second time was no less arduous than the first.

Laufman, Canada's captain and best player sat quietly on the dressing room bench, towel around his neck and head bowed. His reverie was disturbed when Olympic organizers barged into the room all frantic and demanded that the captain remove his equipment and come out immediately to stand on the podium to receive the silver medal. They wanted to get on with the closing ceremonies. A restless crowd of thousands was waiting.

The captain wasn't in a hurry. For years he'd been the Dutchmen's scoring leader. He'd won the OHA scoring title in every league in which he'd played. He was a clutch guy, responding to playoff games with his best performances.

But at these Olympic games, severely impeded by a seriously injured leg, he was held to four assists. Butch played with him on the same line. They changed their break-out patterns so that Butch would skate back and pick up the puck in the Dutchmen zone, so Laufman didn't have to retreat farther than the blue line.

He wasn't able to be at his best in 1956 nor four years later in Squaw Valley, and was deeply disappointed.

Butch scored six goals and had six assists in the tournament.

The captain knew, as did Butch, that had he been at his best, the outcome might well have been different for Canada's team. It was a haunting reminder of 1956. Laufman's young son would have no world championship news from his dad.

In the Canadian dressing room, the captain was physically and emotionally spent. In a less-than-hurried fashion, he undressed completely, showered, dried, and then put on his clothes. Meanwhile the officials became more agitated. Thousands were impatiently waiting. The closing ceremonies were being held up by a hockey player! Finally, when he felt he was ready, Canada's captain walked to the podium and accepted the silver medal for his team and his country. It would be Canada's last Olympic hockey medal for twenty-two years.

The response in the Canadian press was anything but complimentary. A headline read "CORTINA ALL OVER AGAIN." Goman received a telegram from George Webb, a Kingston alderman: "From the birthplace of hockey, I'm calling for one day of mourning at your sorry showing. I will also ask that our flag be flown at half-mast." He received a harsh reply from Kitchener's mayor and reportedly apologized for the comments.

In an opinion that seemed years late in developing, some felt that the balance of power was shifting to other countries. Canada needed an approach, they said, that would get the best amateurs from across the country assembled months before an international competition.

Warwick, who had left the Dutchmen on less than amiable terms after a tryout, commented that in having the Dutchmen represent Canada the CAHA had sent boys to do a man's job.

The Canadians had defeated a Soviet powerhouse and had won an Olympic Silver Medal. Thinking back, Rope said that while that brought some pleasure, the team had failed in what they'd set out to accomplish at their first practice in the Elmira Arena on Snyder Avenue some five months earlier.

Gordon Juckes, president of the CAHA praised the team for keeping up their effort. They never quit. He assured Canadians that Butch's team was the best that could be gathered under the financial strain and other limitations that burdened them.

As they prepared to go home via San Francisco and Chicago, the Canadian players didn't know what to expect when they finally landed in Malton Airport. In 1960, regular folks had no computers, cell phones, or other technical devices to keep each other informed. Unfortunately, in Chicago their TCA Viscount airplane was initially refueled with the wrong fuel and the team was delayed seven hours.

Back in Kitchener, civic leaders were planning a reception for the team outside downtown Kitchener's City Hall. However, given the long delay and the relative location of Malton to their hometowns, the players did not all return to Kitchener. Some went to their homes in Toronto, while others went to the east and west in private cars.

Butch and PeeWee arrived in Kitchener at 2:00 a.m. on their own. A radio station staff member spotted them and gave them a lift to the planned reception at City Hall. A small crowd of avid supporters, including some of Butch's family, had waited for their arrival and hopefully the arrival of the entire Dutchman team. By 2:30 Butch and PeeWee were shaking hands with Kitchener's Mayor Wambold and Waterloo's Mayor Bauer.

Reporter Gerry Todd called it "The weirdest civic reception ever recorded in the Twin Cities." Butch said that after they'd shaken hands with the mayors, there didn't seem to be anything left to do, so he and PeeWee made their way to their home in Floradale.

Canada had reasons to be proud of all their athletes at Squaw Valley. Ottawa native, Anne Heggtveit won Canada's first-ever Olympic skiing gold medal in the Women's slalom. Toronto residents, Barbara Wagner and Robert Paul won Olympic gold in the pairs competition in figure skating. During the early part of their performance, the record playing their music skipped. They were allowed to restart their program and followed with a perfect performance. Donald Jackson of Oshawa took bronze in the Men's singles figure skating.

Waterloo County resident Kurt Boese represented Canada in the wrestling competition at the 1960 Summer Olympic Games in Rome. He earned five Canadian championship titles between 1958 and 1963. Come 1969, Boese began his coaching career at the University of Waterloo. He was selected as coach of Canada's Olympic team in 1972, and inducted into the Waterloo County Hall of Fame.

More than a few very impressive careers took off with the 1960 Winter Olympic Games. But the Dutchmen's 1960 appearance at the Games was also the team's farewell. Management was unable to come to a financial agreement with the Kitchener Auditorium so the newly formed minor professional Kitchener Beavers made the former Dutchmen home theirs in the newly formed Eastern Professional Hockey League.

In a twist of irony, Jack McCartan, whose heroics at Squaw Valley stymied the Canadians, was the starting goalie for the Kitchener Beavers at the Kitchener Auditorium, long time home of the Dutchmen.

Don Head followed his starring Olympic record by signing with the Western Hockey League's Portland Buckaroos. He spent most of the remainder of his career there, eventually being inducted into the Oregon Sports Hall of Fame. In 2014, on the nation-wide "Grapevine" radio show, Don Cherry told co-host Brian Williams that Don Head was the best goalie he'd ever seen in terms of handling the puck.

Bobby Rousseau, the young Montreal Canadien prospect, admitted that his nervousness negatively affected his play at the Olympic Games. He said his legs felt like rubber. But Rousseau's star was rising. In nine sparkling seasons with the Montreal Canadiens, he would win the Calder Trophy as the NHL's top rookie, be a four-time all-star, and be on four Stanley Cup winning Canadiens teams. On February 1, 1964, Rousseau scored five goals in one game.

The gregarious Cliff Pennington played over one hundred games in the NHL with the Montreal Canadiens and the Boston Bruins.

Stalwart defenseman Harry Sinden was inducted into the Hockey Hall of Fame as a builder in 1983. Sinden was the long-time manager, coach, and president of the Boston Bruins. When Bobby Orr broke into the NHL, he was the youngest player, playing for Sinden, the youngest coach. Sinden was Canada's coach in the unforgettable 1972 Soviet-Canada Summit series. In 1999 he was awarded the Lester Patrick Trophy for outstanding service to hockey in the United States.

In 1980, Bobby Attersley, as classy on the ice as off, was elected as Mayor of Whitby, in the first of four terms.

After seven years as a Dutchmen, high school teacher, Don Rope and his wife Benita founded the Cambridge Kips Gymnastic Club in Cambridge, Ontario. The club produced Olympic caliber gymnasts, including their daughter Patti, She was Canada's top gymnast at the 1976 Olympic Games in Montreal.

Cesare Maniago, who was replaced by Don Head on the Dutchmen tour to Squaw Vallley, played nine seasons for the expansion Minnesota North Stars, recording 190 victories.

Ken Laufman never made it to the NHL but he continued his scoring prowess with minor professional leagues in the United States. Butch and Ken were reunited as teammates for one year with the Johnstown Jets of the Eastern Hockey League.

Following the demise of his beloved Dutchmen, Bobby Bauer supported his brother, Father David Bauer with David's vision of a permanent national hockey team for Canada. He gathered some top amateur players to join primarily university students. Elmira's Rod Seiling was on the team before he became a New York Ranger. The team was based at the University of British Columbia, where Father David taught. The youthful group represented Canada at the 1964

Winter Olympics in Innsbruck, Austria, from January 29 to February 9.

Vsevolod Bobrov, the Soviet star who faced Butch in the 1956 Winter Games, played a prominent role in the 1972 Soviet-Canada Summit Series. He was the Soviet coach. Anatoly Tarasov, the long-time Soviet coach, took the team to the gold medal in the 1972 Winter Olympic Games in Sapporo, Hokkaido, Japan. Tarasov's star pupil, and favorite player was Anatoli Firsov. He won the IIHF scoring title four times and was selected the tournament's Most Valuable Player three times. The coach described Firsov's play: "His game is a continuous succession of brilliant thoughts." However, following the Sapporo Games, Tarasov was dismissed as the Soviet National Team coach. He lost the position because he allowed his players to be paid for two exhibition games in Japan, even though he had been instructed by his superiors not to do so.

Firsov, still one of the Soviet's dominant players, wasn't on the team that played against Paul Henderson and the rest of the Canadians in the marvelous 1972 Summit Series. To many, his absence was shocking. Some knowledgeable hockey observers felt Firsov's absence, especially in the eighth and final game, likely influenced the outcome. Laurence Martin, in his book "The Red Machine" suggested that Firsov was very unhappy that his coach, Tarasov, had been replaced, and he was not going to play for Bobrov. Martin offered that Firsov could well have made the difference in the Moscow games of the series. His replacement on the team was an untested twenty-year-old.

In a 2000 research paper entitled "Myth, Memory, and the Kitchener-Waterloo Dutchmen in Canadian International Hockey," Dan MacKinnon wrote, "Simply put, Canada's International hockey success died in 1960 with the Kitchener-Waterloo Dutchmen, not because of the Dutchmen but because Canadian hockey failings that they exposed were never properly dealt with after 1960. This is a reality under appreciated by most Canadian hockey fans. As Bruce Kidd states about the era in which the Dutchmen competed, 'The Russians, Swedes, Italians, English and Germans were building new facilities and experimenting with new techniques while Canadians indulged themselves in post-war affluence.' Complacency got the best of Canadian hockey."

The Blyth Arena collapsed from the weight of snow on its roof in the winter of 1983. It was completely demolished and replaced by a parking lot to serve the ski resort.

In the Dutchmen dressing room after a shattering loss to the Soviets, in Cortina, Butch's teammate Charlie Brooker assured him that in a couple of years that moment would hardly be remembered. Yet thirty-six years after the 1956 Winter Games, Don Rope stopped in Cortina d'Ampezzo on a biking tour of Europe. As he looked down at the Alpine Valley he was deeply moved, almost brought to tears by the memories.

The Dutchmen were the last self-contained club to represent Canada at an Olympic tournament.

A GREAT HONOR

In a tremendous honor, Sports Illustrated Magazine named Butch as a member of Canada's All-Olympic Team (Amateur Era). That takes in all Canadian amateur hockey players representing Canada at the Winter Olympic Games from 1924 on.

This is what appeared in the magazine:

THEY SET RECORDS AND BECAME LEGENDS IN THE YEARS BEFORE THE PROS SKATED INTO THE GAMES.

HARRY (MOOSE) WATSON: St.　John's,　Newfoundland　(1924) Forward—Toronto Granites

Watson was born in Eastern Canada and raised in England. In the I Olympic Games in Chamonix, France he scored thirty-seven goals in five games. Watson turned down an offer of ten thousand dollars to join Toronto St. Patricks of the NHL for the 1924-25 season.

JOE JUNEAU: Port Rouge, Quebec (1992) Forward—Team Canada

Juneau led Canada to the silver medal in the XVI Winter Games in Albertvile, France. He scored six goals and assisted on nine others. He went on to a thirteen-year NHL career. Juneau said he went to the Stanley Cup finals twice, and as much fun as that was, it wasn't like the Olympics.

WALLY HALDER: Toronto (1948) Forward—RoyalCanadian Air Force Flyers

Halder was a late addition to the team, impressing coach Frank

Boucher in a final tune-up game before the team left for Europe. He scored twenty-one goals for Canada at the V Winter Games in St. Moritz, Switzerland.

TERRY O'MALLEY: Toronto (1964, 1968, 1980) Defenseman—Team Canada

O'Malley was chosen by coach Father David Bauer, for the IX Winter Games in Innsbruck, Austria at age twenty-three. His second participation was at the X Winter Games in Grenoble, France. O'Malley became the oldest Canadian Olympian when he was on Canada's team at the XlII Winter Games in Lake Placid.

BUTCH MARTIN: Floradale,ON. (1956, 1960) Defenseman (and Forward)—Kitchener-Waterloo Dutchmen

Six years after walking away from the game for religious reasons (He was a Mennonite), Martin helped hold opponents to twelve scores in eight games en route a bronze medal in '56. In '60 he had six goals and six assists.

MURRAY DOWEY: Toronto (1948) Goaltender—RoyalCanadian Air Force Flyers

Dowey was a last-minute fill-in, after the team's original goalies failed a medical examination. At V Winter Games in St. Moritz he had a 0.62 goals against average. That, and his streak of 225 minutes twenty-five seconds without allowing a goal, remain Olympic records. Dowey wore a trapper glove, never seen before in Europe.

FRANK BOUCHER: Ottawa (1948) Coach—RoyalCanadian Air Force Flyers

Boucher's Flyers stretched the odds to coach his team on an unbeaten road to the gold medal at the V Winter Games in St. Moritz. In 2001 the Flyers were honored by the Canadian Forces as Canada's greatest military athletes of the twentieth century.

Butch had represented Canada at two consecutive Olympic Games. He'd met athletes from around the world. Thousands had watched him play the game he loved. There was no doubt about the pride his family and friends had in him. He had two Olympic medals to cherish and someday show his grandchildren.

In the spring of 1960 he returned to the sawmill for the milling season, employed again as the sawyer. It was a spring like any other spring. On Sunday mornings he and PeeWee returned to Floradale Mennonite to join in the singing of the old hymns and reconnect with friends and acquaintances. He got back into the rhythm of the community.

A few evenings a week he played softball with his buddies. Their games were played in small towns and villages in the rural areas of Waterloo County. His desire to win and his competitive spirit were as much a part of him on a ball diamond in tiny Winterbourne as they were at the Olympic Blyth Arena in Squaw Valley. A young ball player who made a good catch received as much praise from Butch as he gave a teammate when he scored in Cortina. That was Butch being Butch.

Butch was thirty-one years old. The future would bring him an Allan Cup and another try at a gold medal on the world stage. He'd move to Pennsylvania to play hockey, the place from which his forefathers came on covered wagons to clear the land and farm in Block 3-Woolwich Township. They paid three dollars an acre. He'd move to full-time coaching and return again to be a player, his first love. Amazingly he'd play his last hockey game in his seventieth year.

The decade of the 1960s brought significant social changes in Western society. Some sociologists called it the decade of irresponsible errors and flamboyance. It was the birth of reactions to social taboos like racism and sexism. John F. Kennedy narrowly defeated Richard Nixon to become the youngest president of the United States. 1961 brought the construction of the Berlin Wall. Thirty-two countries gained their independence from colonial rule. The war in Vietnam brought over 30,000 draft dodgers/resisters to Canada: some to Waterloo County. Among them were Mennonite young men. The '60s saw Nikita Kruschev expelled from office. They also brought the assassination of President Kennedy, his brother Robert, and civil rights leader Martin Luther King.

On April 14, 1960, the Montreal Canadiens defeated the Toronto Maple Leafs to take the first of five successive Stanley Cups. In October of the same year, the Canadiens retired #7, worn by Maurice Richard.

The Mennonite community continued its transition, making its way into mainstream society. Conrad Grebel College, associated with the University of Waterloo, was chartered in 1961 and taught its first classes in 1963. Mennonite author Rudy Wiebe published the novel "Peace Shall Destroy Many" in 1962. It caused controversy among some members of his faith but Wiebe's publication was a leader in the introduction of contemporary Mennonite literature into the public conversation.

With the demise of the Kitchener-Waterloo Dutchmen, Butch joined the Galt Terriers of the OHA Senior A League for the 1960-61 season.

A Lishman coach leading the parade of 125 cars to Malton Airport from the Kitchener Auditorium - 1956

KW Dutchmen - Canada's Representatives - Cortina, Italy • 1956

Bronze Medalists

Front Row (from left):   Keith Woodall, Jack McKenzie, Coach Bobby
Bauer, Ken Laufman, Denis Brodeur

Middle Row (from left): Trainer Harry Warmsley, Art Hurst, Paul Knox,
Gerry Theberge, Bob White, Beryl Klinck, Joe
Logan, Manager Ernie Goman

Back Row (from left):   George Scholes, Butch Martin, Billy Colvin,
Charlie Brooker, Charlie Brooker, Buddy
Horne, Don Rope, Howie Lee

Some of the huge crowd in front of the City Hall in Kitchener, welcoming back their Dutchmen - 1956.

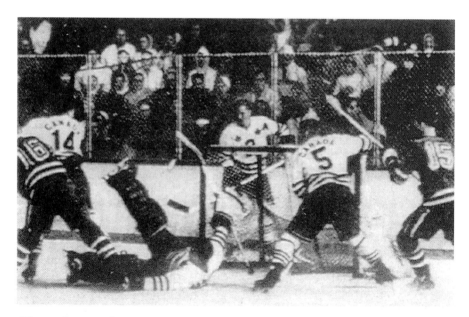

Thwarting an American scoring opportunity - 1956 Winter Olympics.

**Kitchener Waterloo Dutchmen
Canada's Olympic Representatives 1960
Squaw Valley, U.S.A.
Silver Medalists**

Front Row: Harold (Boat) Hurley, Bob Forhan, Floyd (Butch) Martin, Murray Davidson, Harry Sinden, Ceasar Maniago

Centre Row: Bobby Bauer, Doc Jim Spohn, Harry Warmsby, Darryl Sly, Gary Sharpe, Bob McKnight, Ken Laufman, Bob Attersley, Ted Maki, George Samlenco, Oscar Wiles, George Lawson, Ernie Goman, Wren Blair

Back Row: Jack Douglas, Mike Elik, Don Rope, Cliff Pennington, Chester Koneczny, Fred Etcher

Missing: Jim Connelley, Murray Bennoit

Courtesy of the Region of Waterloo Museum

Dutchmen fans preparing to go to Squaw Valley - 1960
PeeWee Martin: Front row, 5th from left.
Marguerite Bauer: (Bobby's wife): Front row, 4th from left.
Oscar Wiles: Team president, kneeling in front
Don Cameron: Play by play broadcaster - holding banner on left

Breaking through the Soviet defence - 1956 Winter Olympic Games.

Butch with a scoring chance on American goalie Jack McCartan
1956 Winter Olympic Games

Reception for Two
Butch and PeeWee greeted by Kitchener Mayor Wambold on the
right and Waterloo Mayor Bauer on their return from the 1960 Winter
Games. All other team members were travelling to their homes.

The silver and bronze Olympic medals.

PATHS OF GLORY
GALT TERRIERS AND THE ALLAN CUP

During the 1960-61 season Butch was captain of the Galt Terriers Senior A team. But in December of 1960 he was invited by the Chatham Maroons to join them on a friendly hockey tour of the Soviet Union and Sweden. He returned to the Terriers for the remainder of the season and playoffs.

One of the games in Sweden was against the great Swedish defenseman Lasse Björn's Djurgarden team. It was at the 1960 Winter Olympics where Butch's bodycheck of Björn had sent him clean over the boards. His response had been that if he ever met up with Butch he'd "swallow him whole." In Djurgarden, Butch and Björn played up the incident, including posing together on the front page of the newspapers. They had a good laugh, and Butch could report that he was not swallowed up by the big defenseman. Butch said, "Actually, he was a hell of a nice guy."

Björn played old-timers hockey. He also ran a trucking company into his seventies. He said, "My last hockey tournament was in Lake Placid in 2001. I was only seventy years old at the time, so it was really a piece of cake."

On February of 1962, a young, bright reporter with the three-year old Elmira Fair Dealer newspaper was given an assignment that made him feel like he'd won the grand prize at the local bingo night. On receiving the great news he ran across Arthur Street to tell his girlfriend,

Alice Naylor, a clerk over at Reichards Dry Goods. The Fair Dealer was trying to get a leg up on the more established Elmira Signet by doing a feature article on local hockey star Butch Martin.

The novice reporter's name was Isadore Panagapka. His father had purchased the downtown Central Hotel six years earlier. The twenty-year-old, with a maturity far beyond his age was pursuing a career in journalism. He felt very, very lucky when the Fair Dealer publisher, Henry Spletstoeser, offered him a junior position, accompanied by a modest salary.

Isadore's assignment was to get the details, and capture the excitement of the Terrier's pursuit of the Allan Cup in the 1960-61 season, but his focus was to be Butch's part in the story.

Henry's instructions to his young reporter were to drop into the Galt Arena Gardens on the night of the annual skating races. An "interesting" sports writer, John Mitchell, from The Cambridge Reporter would be in the Gardens press box gathering information for a story about the elementary schools taking part and the children who were participating.

If a child was entered into the races, he was representing his school but his name would also appear in Mitchell's write-up. The skate races were a really big deal in Galt! One year there was talk of putting a stop to the event. The citizens' response was such that the suggestion was quickly dropped.

Reporter Mitchell had a widely recognized amazing ability to remember details of games. With staggering accuracy he recalled scores, how individuals scored important goals, great plays, penalties, and spectacular saves made by goalies. He was a walking encyclopedia of facts that went back many years. He loved talking sports! And he loved smoking cigars.

Henry knew that Mitchell would be receptive to inquiries about Butch and the Terriers. Henry had contacted the big man, and was told that he didn't like making appointments. Rather he preferred people to just drop by. He'd make time for them.

Henry's information was sparse. All he knew for sure was that the Cambridge fellow would be in the press box, and he'd be wearing a Terriers' cap. Henry said that Isadore would "be knocked off his feet" by Mitchell's recall of detail. He also said he might have to keep Mitchell on topic and that he talked fast.

Here's what happened:

Isadore sits in the top row of the bleachers at the grand, old Galt Arena Gardens down on Shade Street in Galt. Beside him a grey-haired grandmother stands, wildly waving green and gold pom poms, and shouting, "Skate hard, Ricky! You can do It! Go for it, Ricky!"

Rickey's been skating perhaps a dozen times, on borrowed skates. Mrs. Langdown, his kindergarten teacher up at Dickson School always helps tie his skate laces. Dickson's got a small, outdoor rink, that's lower at one end than the other. One day of sunshine will melt it as its base is black pavement. There's not a square inch of grass on the Dickson playground. But it's the only school in Galt that has a ghost in the school's bell tower. It appears each first day of the school year and rings the bell as the children leave for the day. That's the only time the bell is heard.

The school's motto is "Where Kids Count."

Ricky's in the Galt Skating Races, held on every last Friday of February—since 1930. No exceptions! The kids, in various age groups, gather at the starting line. Then they listen for the clap of the wooden clappers, put into action by the elderly man standing behind the skaters, and out of sight. He's been the "clapper" for decades.

Clap! And they're off! Ricky skates on his ankles. And while waving at his shouting grandma, wipes out. But it doesn't matter. He was in the Skating Races! He was proud as heck wearing the green and gold of Dickson and his name would appear in next week's Reporter.

Popular Donnie Brouse, the Terrier's mascot in their Allan Cup run and frequent arena visitor shows Isadore to Mitchell's "home."

With notepad in hand, the rookie reporter climbs the ladder to the wooden press box, a relatively small space with a really good view of the entire ice surface. There's a lone individual typing in one-finger style while exhaling a cloud of smoke from a large cigar, its ashes hanging precariously, ready to land somewhere without warning. The cigar came from a box labelled White Owl that sits on a small wooden table.

The middle-aged man wears a Terriers cap, turned backwards, and tattered-looking sneakers with no socks. He also has a generous girth. Isadore would bet last week's pay that a brush cut is under the cap. Mitchell glances over the rims of his glasses at his new press box partner and nods. The eager young reporter is certain he's found his man.

The Elmira Fair Dealer young researcher gets right to it. He mentions to Mitchell that he notices the name on his cap, and asks him to tell him about the Terriers.

Mitchell doesn't miss a key punch. He continues looking straight ahead. Between puffs of his huge cigar, he tells his guest about the city's Terriers baseball team, who had an outstanding run in the Senior Inter-County League. Between 1927 and 1932 the Terriers won five Senior Inter-County baseball championships. They played in Galt's Dickson Park.

"Okay," Isadore says. "But what about the hockey team. Weren't they called the Terriers too? First, let me get you a coffee from the snack bar inside the rink."

"Don't add anything. I like it black."

The aspiring reporter makes the purchase and delivery in record time, barely spilling a drop.

Mitchell takes a generous sip, and says, "Yes, there were the Terriers of hockey—going all the way back to 1924. Do you know that in 1926 the NHL was rumored to be considering doing away with goalies? They suggested a net's width be adjusted to eighteen inches—without a goalie. They wanted more goals to be scored. Imagine hockey without a Johnny Bower or a Jacques Plante."

"That's an interesting bit of trivia," says Isadore. "But how about the Terriers hockey team?"

"Oh yeah, It's a bit confusing. There were the Terriers of the Canadian Professional Hockey League, the Ontario Professional Hockey League, the Ontario Hockey Association Senior A League, the Ontario Hockey Association Senior B League, and the Intermediate A League."

"Sounds like you know a lot about Galt hockey teams," says The Fair Dealer rookie.

"Well, yes. I don't want to brag, but when it comes to hockey, I've got an encyclopedic mind. Give me a hockey season, a team, or a player who played for a Galt team and I'll give you the details. Want to know the name of the Terrier short-stop in 1930?"

"Let's stick to hockey," says the Elmira resident. "How about Butch Martin? Ever hear of him?"

The cigar ash drops suddenly, landing on the protrusion of Mitchell's midriff, rapidly brushed aside, as he bolts out of his chair, and utters a four-letter word, spoken loudly enough to cause Ricky's grandma to break out in laughter.

"Are you kidding me? Captain of the Terriers Senior A team in 1960-61, the first year of Senior A operation here. Came over from the Dutch......Hey, I bet you're the kid from Elmira. Henry said you'd be dropping by. Butch came over from the Dutchmen with five other guys. Len Gaudette, our arena manger, invited them. Len was the team's manager too. I heard that Butch turned down an offer to go to Johnstown, Pennsylvania that year, so he could be with us. His buddy, Kenny Laufman went to Johnstown, you know, for the 1960-61 season. Probably won the scoring title, as usual. Butch could have used him on his forward line with the Terriers. But little Billy Wylie, a Galt born guy worked with Butch like a charm. Bet Wylie wasn't more than one-hundred-and-fifty pounds. They scored some beautiful goals on fantastic passing plays. One of The Cambridge Reporter's sportswriters called some of the creative moves breathtaking. Sometimes the fans gave them a prolonged ovation."

"You said Butch was the captain," says Mitchell's guest. "How did that work out? I'm from Elmira. When Butch was a captain of our hockey team, the Polar Kings, they were the OHA Intermediate B champions. He was the heart and soul of the team."

"Great NHL captains like George Armstrong and Jean Beliveau say you lead by example. You always work hard. That was Butch. He led by example. Don't know how many comments I saw in the local Cambridge Reporter newspaper, praising Butch about being an 'honest brakeman' or being the team's most consistent player. Things like that. I'll tell you what Butch the captain did for those '60-'61 Terriers. By the time Christmas rolled around they were sitting fifth out of six teams. Butch wasn't with them for all the games. He was on a European tour with the Chatham Maroons. Only Woodstock was behind the Terriers. Butch's Elmira buddy, Byrle Klinck, played for Woodstock. He was great goal scorer for a defenseman. The league leaders were the Windsor Bulldogs. Now listen to this. After Butch got back, from January 1, 1961 to the end of the season the Terriers won thirty-two out of thirty-eight games. They ended up one point behind that Windsor bunch who had Joe Klukay. Played about twelve years with the Leafs in the NHL before he arrived in Windsor. A lot of the Terriers' turn-around had to do with Butch."

He finishes the coffee in chug-a-lug style, and wipes his mouth with the loosely fitting sleeve of his crumpled, green sweater.

"What magical thing did Butch do to make that happen?" asks Isadore. "I know it was tough to get the puck off him. He could throw a body check and he could work. He knew all about work; worked at the family sawmill for years. Don't know where he got the energy, even at thirty, to work in the bush all day, drive from Floradale, and then play a tough hockey game. There were some pretty long distance road games to places like Chatham, Windsor and Strathroy."

"Butch scored: seventeen goals in eleven games. He picked up the rest of the team. That's another sign of a great captain. For a while there he had a seven-game scoring streak going. Butch's twentieth goal was a beauty, a game winner against Chatham Maroons. Wylie, and Bob McKnight, the third guy on that line, really helped with Butch's goals. Some nights they were awesome! Lloyd Roubell was the coach, a bit of a joker too. He knew he was fortunate to have a man of Butch's character as captain. The coach played a lot of years in the American Hockey League. Came from North Bay originally. They teased him a bit about his full name: Lloyd George Harold Christopher Roubell.

"By the way, there were a few Terriers with brush cuts like mine. There was Butch, Joe Hogan and Bobby Mader, the gentleman, and cattle buyer from Breslau. Mader, an assistant captain, started scoring goals, just like Butch. They had about fifty points each by the end of the year."

He opens the box and reaches for another White Owl. After a few futile attempts, he gets it lit and exhales a puff of smoke that floats over the cheering crowd.

"I don't want to appear to be rude," says the always polite newsman. "But I'm going to offer an observation. I want to put it as politely as I can and I know it's going to sound awkward anyway it comes out. But here we go. When you speak, and you blurt out all this super, detailed information, it just blows me away. I'm glad I know short-hand. How do you do this?"

"The short answer is I don't know. No one really knows. I just think differently from most people. Some of my friends think I'm a savant, one of those people who have the astonishing ability of reciting entire books or telling you what day of the week your birthday falls on, regardless of the year. I'm not like that. But I have an exceptional memory. The experts call it Hyperthymesia, although mine is not a true case. People like me have an amazing capacity to recall specific personal events or trivial details, including a date, the weather, and in this case the detailed events of a hockey season. One lady with true Hyperthymesia says her memory is like a movie that never stops."

Isadore ponders the words, but continues. "Like the good leader he was, Butch made Ab Martin, Frank Carroll, Fred Plestch, Harry Neale and the rest of the team improve their play too. I bet you didn't have many complaints about that bunch."

"I only had one complaint. They had trouble getting the record with 'The Queen' playing properly down at the old barn. We'd be standing there, all quiet and straight, and it would start a few lines into the song and after some scratchy efforts finally get it going. Got so bad I wrote a letter to my boss, the editor of the Reporter. I told 'em they should dust off the old organ. Take a look through the window and to the right. It just sat there. Things got better. And guess what, they got some heaters into the old barn finally, so you didn't half freeze."

"I'm sorry," Mitchell says. "Did you say Ab Martin? Wasn't he from Elmira too? Used to skate around like a buzz-saw some nights. Some games he was the best player on the ice. One night he and Butch each had two goals and an assist against Woodstock. Ab had a bit of tough luck late in that '60-'61 season. Broke a bone in his arm. Kept him out for a while. But he was married to a nurse, so he got looked after pretty well I should think. Wouldn't play on Sundays, you know."

Henry was right, muses his young employee. This is as amazing man. And as his boss also said correctly, he occasionally wanders off topic. Isadore continues. "Butch seemed like a sort of calm player. He appeared to have things under control. That's the sign of a good captain too, don't you think? He just seemed to go about his business out there."

"I think when Butch got upset the next body check he gave was a doozy. Guy he hit probably had to gather himself off the ice. Saw him pretty upset one night. It was a game in Woodstock. I went to some away games if they weren't far and if my son would drive. Well, anyway, towards the end of the game, some Woodstock fans started yelling at our excellent goalie, Boat Hurley. It got so bad that they started throwing empty cans and stuff at him. Butch skated towards them and had his stick in the air. That's all he did, other than maybe yell a few words he learned up there on the streets of Floradale. Ha! That was the end of it. Never seemed to get really upset with his teammates. But the trainer told me that Butch would say things like, 'Come on, you can do better out there.' The thing about Butch was that he demanded so much of himself that it bothered him when others weren't doing the same."

"There was something sort of interesting about that Terriers team," says Isadore. "Elmira, where I live, was well-represented. Butch lived close by in Floradale. Ab Martin was a banker in town. Frankie Carroll worked for Ontario Hydro. And both lived in Elmira. Darryl Sly was a teacher at John Mahood School in Elmira. To top it off, Fred Pletsch married an Elmira woman who lived a few blocks from Ab's home where he grew up. Butch knew them all well and all of them had great respect for him."

"Yes, I remember them all. Frankie was a big, strong defensemen who'd block shots like no one else. In a game against the Strathroy Rockets, I counted twelve shots he blocked. Hurley must have loved him! We lost Sly for a while. He went with the Trail Smoke Eaters to the 1961 World Championship in Switzerland. Came back in time for the playoffs, with a gold medal around his neck. The Terriers borrowed Pletsch from the Chatham Maroons, with two other players for their Allan Cup run in that 1961 season."

"When Butch played for the Polar Kings he'd sometimes be on the ice for most of the game," says Isadore. "Did that ever happen with the Terriers?"

"Some nights the Terriers had as few as ten or eleven players. Wylie coached a minor team so that kept him away. There were injuries. There was illness, and sometimes players had work responsibilities. Rubell used Butch a lot on those nights. One night against Woodstock, Butch played pretty well every minute of the first two periods. Never seemed to get tired. He must have been in great shape!"

A washroom break would be welcome. But the rookie stays focused. "With a contact sport like hockey, injuries are bound to happen. How did Butch make out with that on the road to the Allan Cup?"

"I only remember one time when an injury kept him out of some games. The Terriers were playing Rouyn-Noranda Alouettes in the

Allan Cup quarter-finals. The great Dave Keon came from that area. They were the Northern Ontario Hockey Association winners and were allowed to pick up six players from other teams in their league. Anyway, in the second game, Butch somehow got a cut on his foot that needed stitches. A bit of cloth got in there too to irritate the wound. And they also discovered a broken bone in his foot. He spent some time in the hospital. The Terriers were doing well so they kept Butch out for the rest of that series and all of the games in the next series against the Ramblers of Amherst, Nova Scotia. The Terriers could have used Butch. The Ramblers were a rough and tumble bunch. Butch would have gotten their attention! Must have been tough for him to sit out. He was such a competitor!"

"Okay," says the Fair Dealer's rising star. "Help me out here. How did the Terriers get from playing in their Senior A league to playing against a team from Quebec and a team from Nova Scotia?"

"The answer to your question is a long story. I'll try keep it brief. In the championship series in their league, the Terriers beat their season nemesis, the Windsor Bulldogs, in four straight games. Mader got three goals in the first game. Butch's forward line scored eleven points in the third game. Being they were now the league champs, they entered the Allan Cup playoffs. They took out Rouyn-Noranda in three straight games in the Allan Cup quarter finals. And that took them into the Amherst series undefeated. That was now the Allen Cup semi-final. I should add that the Ramblers had lost only nine times in their sixty-game league schedule. The Terrier-Rambler games were all played in the old barn in Galt. Our guys took them out in four straight games.

The Terriers didn't lose in eleven straight playoff games. Mader got eleven goals in those games. His remarkable effort was welcome with his captain having to sit out. One of the games got really heated. It got so bad that some really angry, somewhat inebriated fans entered the ice ready to do battle. In the final game a fan threw a live rooster on to the ice. Ha! Maybe it was one of those farmers from up Woolwich way who brought it along! By beating Amherst, the Terriers were the eastern Canadian Senior A champions or Allan Cup semi-final winners. Getting tired of me yet? Want to hear about Friendy Graham, Terriers baseball legend of the 1920s?"

Isadore chuckles. "Sure, if you're finished with the hockey Terriers. But I'm betting there's more. Are you sure you're not making this up?"

Mitchell takes off his Terrier cap, runs a hand through his brush cut, then places the partially finished cigar into the empty paper coffee cup, and smiles. "I understand why I come across that way and you're not the first to ask that question, even in a humorous manner. But this is me. Anyway, with the wonderful career and experiences that Butch has had, there's no need for fantasy.

Okay. Remember the Terriers were aiming to be the best amateur team in Canada in 1960-61? On their way they beat Windsor, Rouyn-Noranda and Amherst without losing a game. Next series was the final one against the Winnipeg Maroons, winners of the Senior A Western Canada championship. The winning team would be Allan Cup winners and crowned as the best amateur team in Canada. All the games were home games for the Terriers."

"I've heard a few stories about Bill Juzda, a defenseman for Winnipeg. Apparently he was a tough guy, not dirty, Just tough." It was getting more difficult to take notes with Mitchell's detailed responses.

"I want to tell you two main things about that Winnipeg series. First, there's the Juzda story. Bill played in the NHL with the New York Rangers and the Leafs. He was an All Star and won the Stanley Cup with the Leafs in 1950. He had excellent defensive skills. But what he did best was lay out players with clean, bruising body checks. He and Rocket Richard had an ongoing battle. He was called Rocket Richard's 'Anglo Nemesis.' After his NHL career he returned home to Winnipeg and joined the Maroons. By the time they arrived in Galt, he'd been with the Maroons seven years. He earned his living as an engineer with the Canadian Pacific Railway."

Isadore asks, "How'd Juzda do against the Terriers? Seems like he'd be quite intimidating, the kind of player the Terriers forwards weren't use to meeting. Did he get in some good body checks?"

"During the first few periods of the first game he was having fun, and got in some really good body checks, crashing into players and sending them flying. But in the third period Butch got to work and that seemed to take the steam out of him. Mind you, Bill was forty years old. As the series went on he just wore down."

"You mentioned two things. What was the other one?" The aspiring journalist fleetingly has thoughts that this could be a first page article in the Fair Dealer, with his name in the byline.

"The other one is all about Butch. Keep in mind he wasn't at his best in the final series, still bothered by his injury. But he played in every game. The Terriers won game one 3-1. In the very important second game, Butch got the Terriers first goal. It was a great game with outstanding goaltending. The game was still tied after the first overtime period. Then about five minutes into the second overtime, Butch got the puck on his backhand, spun around and in the same motion his shot beat the goalie for the winner. Best and most important goal I've ever seen him score. Could have been the turning point in the series."

"There he was being a great captain again, doing what great players seem to do: score important goals. That's the type of thing Armstrong would do for the Leafs. How'd the rest of the Allan Cup series go?" asks the reporter as he shakes his hand to ease the stiffness.

"The first two games were in Galt Arena Gardens. But they took the third game to the Auditorium in Kitchener. Over 7000 fans were in the stands. But the Terriers lost 2-1, the only loss in the series. Galt won the third game 4-2 at home. And Hurley shut out the Maroons in the final game 3-0. Butch scored in that game too. There was a long lineup for tickets for that final game. About 3600 fans got in."

"Must have been a great celebration!" adds Isadore.

"Yeah, downtown bars were hopping. The most prized picture in my Terriers' scrapbook is the one with Butch being presented with the Allan Cup. My gosh, he looked happy! There's a visual of mine that will never go away. I'm just sorry that I didn't get his autograph."

"Mr. Mitchell," says Isadore as he stands up to leave. "I've got to be on my way. I'm a rookie in this business and I am very grateful for your time and information about Butch. It's highly unlikely that I'll ever again meet as remarkable an individual as you. You're amazing! Just one more question. How do you feel the Terriers, Canada's team, will do at next month's World Championship?"

"My money is on Canada. But I've been around long enough to know that in international competition, anything can happen. Butch could tell you about that."

He lights another White Owl and balances it between his lips, unlit. It wobbles up and down as he talks.

"I wish you all the best, you and the other folks at the Fair Dealer. I've never met Henry. But give him my regards. This business can wear you down. But the people you meet, like Butch, make it all worthwhile."

The veteran and the rookie shake hands. Isadore has the feeling he's just been welcomed into a club. But he'll never smoke cigars.

In 1997, the 1961 Allan Cup-winning Galt Terriers would be inducted into the Cambridge Sports Hall of Fame.

LONG DAY'S JOURNEY INTO COLORADO SPRINGS

1962 IIHF CHAMPIONSHIP

At the beginning of the 1961-62 season, Butch was in Johnstown Pennsylvania, playing for the Jets of the old Eastern Hockey League. His Galt Terriers, as winners of the Allan Cup the previous season, had the honor of representing Canada at the 1962 IIHF World Championships in Colorado Springs and Denver, Colorado. In preparation they went on a cross-Canada tour. Butch joined the Terriers in Trail, British Columbia and stayed with them until the end of the tournament, after which he returned to Johnstown.

Elam Foell from the village of Glenn Allan, a fifteen-minute drive from Floradale, accompanied the Terriers across Canada and at the tournament. He was a forty-two-year-old bachelor, and owner of Foell's Farm Fresh Foods in the village. Elam was well-read and had been an outstanding student at Elmira and District High School where he'd graduated from grade thirteen with honors. He loved literature and writing. Evelyn Davidson, his English teacher, saw a lot of potential in her student. She encouraged him to seek out a vocation as a journalist. But Elam was a home town guy, content with his situation in life.

The Glenn Allan-born man was also an ardent hockey fan; he followed the Dutchmen and Terriers closely and travelled to many of their games. Given his predilection for research and writing, he relished getting behind-the-scenes information. He shared these stories with guys who'd come over from Dorking, Macton and as far away as Hawkesville every Saturday night to talk hockey. All were big fans of Butch and had followed his hockey career for years.

With reliable help to manage his store, Elam felt he could take an extended vacation. And the Terriers had room to accommodate him. It would be a once-in-a-lifetime experience! He'd never been on a train. Heck, he'd only travelled on a Lishman bus between Elmira and Kitchener a dozen times.

Jack Rowland, manager at the Royal Bank in Elmira was a hockey fan. He was also impressed by the way Elam ran the business, especially the financial end of things. He helped Elam work out a plan to obtain a loan and pay it back in reasonable installments. That meant he could travel with the Terriers without financial concerns. An unnamed benefactor paid for all his expenses during his stay in Colorado Springs.

Elam was a very close friend of the Ruggle family in Floradale, owners of Ruggle's General Store. They'd been in Floradale since the late nineteenth century. Butch lived next door to the store and would frequently share his hockey stories.

Elam had a brilliant thought! Why not get a note to the Ruggle family from time to time? They could post it on their small bulletin board and the community would be right on top of the progress of Canada's team and Butch.

No wonder he'd been an honors student!

To :   The Proprietor
       Ruggle's General Store
       Floradale, Ontario

Sent from: Moncton, New Brunswick
February 2, 1962

Dear Ruggle Family,

I've been enjoying ham and scrambled eggs with my coffee in a small, friendly café not far from Main Street in this beautiful place. As I was draining my third cup, it dawned on me that before I left home I made a promise to get my first note to you within a few days of our travels. Sorry, I'm a little late. The Terriers have already played two hockey games on their eastern Canada tour. They plan to play about sixteen games across Canada before the World Championship Tournament in Colorado during the first part of March. We're traveling east in the first part and then making our way west to the site of the tournament.

I remember last spring how enthused Butch's family and friends were when the Terriers won the Allan Cup. There were three carloads of us Butch fans from the Floradale and Glenn Allen area that stood for a good hour to get those precious tickets. That was a good time wasn't it? I'll never forget it. I still have the picture of Butch receiving the Allan Cup. What a scene!

This hockey season is the first one when Butch won't be playing In Elmira or Kitchener, and be home each night. PeeWee and the Martin family will really miss him. You'll miss him too, dropping in there for a Pepsi and telling you how his team is doing. Elmer and the other guys at the sawmill need to hear how many goals and assists their sawyer has made!

As you know, Butch is in Johnstown Pennsylvania with the Jets. The general manager John Mitchell had a long-standing offer for Butch join his team. He sealed the deal after he saw Butch play in the Allan Cup finals last spring.

Johnstown is about three hours west of Lancaster where the Martin family has its roots. In the early 1800s their ancestors made the long trek to block Three, now Woolwich, by Conestoga wagons pulled by oxen. They purchased land for three dollars an acre.

I'm glad to hear that PeeWee can make it down to Johnstown each weekend.

I'll get a brief note to you regularly to post on that bulletin board beside your cash register. When people pay for things like seed or binder twine, you could draw their attention to the notes. Some of the Old Order Mennonite fellows who attended S. S. #5 with Butch have followed his career in hockey. They played shinny with him on the dam! "Big" Anson Bearinger, who has a Holstein herd just west of Wallenstein, often inquires about his former Floradale school chum.

The Johnstown team agreed to allow Butch to play in the World Tournament. He'll join the Terriers in Trail, British Columbia.

I hope I'm back in time for the maple syrup season! I'll want a gallon of amber—the same as the last twenty years!

Sincerely,
Elam Foell

Sent from: Amherst, Nova Scotia
February 3, 1962

Hello Floradale friends.

Amherst is a pretty town of about ten thousand people, situated right by Cumberland Basin. Imagine many, many Floradale dams all in one and you'll have an idea of the size of the Basin. Amherst is only a few miles from the New Brunswick border and forty miles from Moncton. There are many impressive historic buildings here including the First Baptist Church, an outstanding stone structure on the main street.

I've been browsing through some local history and was surprised that the Russian revolutionary Leon Trotsky was in prison here in 1917. Amherst was also the home of Charles Tupper, Canada's sixth prime minister. He held that office for sixty-nine days in 1896.

I've been to Toronto with Butch and Elmer to an NHL game. But that's the extent of my travels. So this chance to travel extensively is precious. I can hardly believe that this is happening! I hear similar comments from the hockey players. These "Bluenosers" and "Bogtrotters" are living up to their fun and friendly reputation.

Amherst people say there are no hard feelings about the ruckus at the playoff game last spring. Things got a little out of hand at the Galt

Arena Gardens. They clearly want to put that behind them.

Two nights ago, about fifteen hundred fans saw the Terriers easily beat the Halifax Wolverines 8-1. Before the game we saw the Citadel and the Town Clock, and fog rising from the harbor.

The next night we were in Moncton and we worked hard to beat their Beavers 7-6. They're in the Nova Scotia Senior League. Moncton is located in the Petitcodiac River Valley and has about forty-five thousand residents. A lot of people are employed at the Canadian National Railways engine repair shop, the largest in the Maritimes.

Tonight the local Ramblers lost 7-0 to the Terriers. Their team may have been shut out, but their fans love them. The Ramblers are still a scrappy bunch. They have an arena only three years old. Manager Len Gaudette surprised us with the news that he once played hockey for an Amherst team.

We've been treated to hodge podge, Nova Scotia's hearty traditional stew, and Alexander Keith's India Pale Ale. What a great combination!

So the first three games haven't been too tough, although Moncton made it interesting.

Some of your customers have met Bob Mader at the cattle auction at Kitchener Stockyards. Bob is with the Terriers again. He's got a lot of family help to look after the farm in Breslau. Bob's scored a lot of goals in his Senior A career and he's a man of great character. Butch and Bob led our team to the Allan Cup! But this past summer they were on opposite teams in the North Waterloo Rural Softball League whenever Elmira played Bob's Breslau team: the winners of ten consecutive league championships.

Maple Leaf fans will know forward Tod Sloan. He's joined the Terriers for the World Tournament competition. Word has it that he turned down an offer of three hundred and fifty dollars a week to coach in San Francisco. He could be a key addition!

I spoke with my sister Vi who said that Frank Malinsky, pastor at the Lutheran church in Floradale will be retiring. The congregation will miss him. I hope his health is well. With his stature, and powerful voice, he kept the parishioners awake!

Warm Regards,
Elam

Sent from: Toronto
FEBRUARY 13, 1962

A lot has happened since my last note. We returned to Ontario on February 6 to play at Varsity Arena, down on bustling Bloor Street in Toronto. The more experienced Terriers beat the young Varsity Blues, the University of Toronto's varsity team, 10-2. It was a close battle until the third period when our guys exploded for seven goals.

In the game's program it stated that the University's 1928 varsity team, coached by Conn Smythe, won Olympic gold in St. Moritz, Switzerland.

After the Varsity game and a good night's sleep, we travelled to Wallaceburg. The scenic Sydenham River runs through the town of about eight thousand. Butch played against the Hornets, their Senior B team when he was with the Polar Kings. This time the opposition was the Chatham Maroons. Butch toured with them in Russia and Sweden last year. The Terriers lost to the Maroons 8-4 and were a little disappointed with their performance.

News came to the Terriers team manager Gaudette that the European hockey teams going to the IIHF Tournament wanted ex-professional players to be banned from participation unless they've been reinstated amateurs for three years. He told them bluntly that if that was the case, the Terriers would immediately withdraw. But the tournament needs Canada. So the rule was quickly changed. The revised rule states that pros had to be reinstated by December 31, 1961. Politics is always involved, it seems. I hope this is the end of it!

Today, the Terriers gathered at busy Union Station in Toronto, located on the South side of Front Street between Yonge and Bay. This is the busiest transportation centre in Canada. Not all the players who'll be playing at the World Championship are with us. A few will be joining us later when we get further west.

You know how well Boat Hurley plays goal. He's having some difficulties getting away from his job as an accountant at Bauer Felt in Waterloo. He was last year's most valuable player with the Terriers. We'd really, really miss him. Hopefully he'll join the team with the other late arrivals.

What a lively going-away celebration! About twenty car-loads of loyal and enthusiastic fans cheered loudly, and carried colorful "Go Terriers Go!" signs. I think the door man over at the stately Royal York Hotel might have heard them! Galt mayor, Mel Griffith wished the Terriers luck, and a pipe band marched them, in their bright red jackets, to the train. There were lots of hugs, shaking hands and pats of the back: even a few tears.

Our tough guy defenseman, Butch Keeling, said that like me, this would be his first train ride. The Terrier's equipment man put twenty-two dozen hockey sticks on board. The players want a lie four—in their minds it's the perfect weight for a stick. None of the players wear anything but CCM Tackaberry skates.

Bob Mader's wife, Ina is expecting their fourth child. And Sue, Harry Neale's wife, is expecting their first child. Her due date is today! Harry was also with the Terriers last season. Bob and Harry for sure will be hanging around hotel lobbies and front desks nervously waiting for the good news!

I borrowed a book about Pennsylvania from the Elmira Library. Alice Morden, the always-friendly librarian kindly let me keep it for the entire trip. There will be no overdue fines! It has a good section about Johnstown, and Cambria, the county in which the city is located.

Manager Gaudette and coach Rubell keep in touch with what's happening with all the players who'll be joining the team along the way, including Butch. They don't mind my inquiries.

I've heard a bit about Butch already. The league he's playing in is the Eastern Hockey League. He doesn't think it's quite the caliber of the Senior A League back home.

My reference book says that Johnstown is known as the city of floods. Also, thousands of their citizens are employed in the Bethlehem Steel Mills, by far the main employer in the city.

Gaudette says they like their hockey rough in Johnstown, as does the rest of the league. The danger is that apparently some of the tough guys get carried away and use their sticks as weapons in fights. Makes you concerned about injuries. But as we all know, Butch can look after himself. And he's got far too much "Floradale common sense" to get involved with crazy stuff like that. We also need him healthy for the World Championships!

Our trainer has visited Johnstown while on vacation and eaten at the famous Coney Island Restaurant. Their specialty is super hot dogs with chili sauce. This may surprise you. Johnstown claims to be where whoopee pies originated. I thought those delicious treats were only made in Woolwich Township! People in Pennsylvania called them gob cakes when they first came on the market.

Valentine's Day is coming up! I'll miss receiving those beautiful hand-made cards the Old Order Mennonite children bring into my store. Over the years I've gathered a large collection.

Thinking about all of you,
Elam

Sent from: Moose Jaw, Saskatchewan
February 18, 1962

Greetings.

I celebrated my birthday yesterday in Saskatchewan, the province in which my four older brothers were born. I enjoyed a slice of neapolitan ice cream, always our childhood birthday dessert.

Saskatchewan, where the view goes on forever, receives more sunshine than any province in Canada. It's also the only province that stays on the same time the entire year. I'd really like to be here in late summer, when the thousands of acres of golden wheat are ready for harvesting. What a beautiful sight that must be! David Rosenberger, from up Lanigan way told us he farms 4500 acres of land!

Moose Jaw's the wonderful city where Butch and the Dutchmen were treated so well back in 1960. It's situated on the Moose Jaw River, shaped like a moose's jaw! The city has lots of small villages and large farms around it and is the railway junction of agriculture in the area.

The Terriers are playing the Moose Jaw team tonight.

But I've lagged behind a bit. I'll get you caught up.

On Valentine's Day the Terriers were shut out 3-0 by the Port Arthur Bearcats in front of about twenty-five hundred fans. Our team just couldn't get anything going. The big news up there was the possible amalgamation of Port Arthur with Fort William. Most people seem to be in favor. But it could be ten years away. The guys as S. S. Martin's may know that this area has many sawmills associated with the expansive pulp and paper industry.

We spent eleven hours on the bus going from Port Arthur to Fort Frances. Things were getting a bit testy. To top it off the local newspaper sports writer reported that after seeing the Terriers game in Port Arthur, he felt they were the worst team to represent Canada in five years.

Our hockey team showed 'em! The Fort Frances Lakers got the brunt of it. The Terriers beat them convincingly 8-2-with an exclamation mark!

Fort Frances, in the Rainey River District, is close to the U. S. border. Butch's brothers Dick and Elmer would love this place as it's renowned for fishing and hunting. The town of Fort Frances is connected to International Falls Minnesota by the Fort-Frances-International Falls International Bridge.

Fort Francis civic officials hosted a delectable dinner. Manager

Gaudette introduced coach Roubell. He told the amused crowd that the coach would likely tell them that Fort Frances was his hometown. Before every game, regardless of where it is played, the coach reportedly starts his pre-game speech in the dressing room with, "Fellows this is my hometown. My entire family is here today and I know you don't want to disappoint me in front of them so..........." He enjoys bringing a little levity to the proceedings.

We travelled by bus across the Bridge into Minnesota. The fun kept up. Coach Roubell used the bathroom and the players somehow locked him inside. The immigration officer asked if anyone was in the washroom and the episode ended. Mr. Roubell likes to have fun but he is highly respected having played over a decade in the American Hockey League.

We arrived at Warroad, Minnesota, situated about 140 miles south of Winnipeg. Its population is 1300. That is less than half the size of Elmira! Boat Hurley arrived. Great news! Now we need to find a back-up for him.

About half the town of Warroad came to the game between their Lakers and the Terriers. The arena has natural ice, so it was really cold-the coldest building I've ever been in! The wooden stands were makeshift with sand underneath them. What an unusual place! I sat shivering in the crowd, clutching a hot coffee, and heard many complaints about the three-dollar admission fee; apparently jacked up for this special event. The Terriers won 7-4 in a pretty competitive game. But it didn't raise the temperature!

Too bad Butch wasn't with us. Gordon Christian and his brother, Roger play for the Lakers. The Christians will meet Butch in Colorado Springs as they're both on the American National team. Gordon played against Butch at the 1956 Winter Games and Roger played against him at the 1960 Games. Both remembered Butch. The brothers started the Christian Brothers Hockey Manufacturing company in an old building just off the highway that goes through Warroad.

In a good-hearted manner they asked if we remembered who won those two United States-Canada games. We reluctantly admitted that we did. This place is called "Hockey Town U.S.A" because of all the good hockey players they produce.

Next note I'll tell you about the Terriers game in Winnipeg against the Maroons and tonight's game with the Moose Jaw Play-Mors. The Terriers have a lot of games packed into a short time. The coach joked that he'd either get the team in shape or he'd "kill 'em."

Judging from the weather reports, you have it cold enough for skating on the dam. Remember when Henry Metzger from the fourth line of Peel brought his eight children to the dam for skating one Sunday afternoon, all crowded onto his buggy? They brought along a huge plastic bag filled with popcorn.

I'll be in touch again soon. Give my regards to Cecil Capling, over at the garage.

Your friend,
Elam

Sent from: Saskatoon, Saskatchewan
February 19, 1962

Hi friends in Floradale,

It's winter, so rural Saskatchewan looks like a never-ending sun-drenched, glistening, blanket of snow. It's really quite beautiful! This area is known for its potash, oil and gas, diamonds, and uranium. Saskatoon has a population of about one hundred thousand. Tiny Guernsey, where my parents had a farm in the tough 1930s, is about ninety-minutes east of Saskatoon. Their farm is now a potash mine.

The atmosphere in Winnipeg for the game against the Maroons was electric! Over twelve-thousand cheering fans attended, hoping for some measure of revenge for the Allan Cup loss to the Terriers.

Thirty minutes before game time, Harry Neale proudly announced that his wife, Sue had delivered a baby boy. That caused some back slapping in the dressing room!

Big defenseman Bill Juzda, the rugged body-checker, and former NHL player of the Maroons is in his last year of hockey. He's slowed down somewhat, so wasn't handing out as many body checks. But he's still strong defensively and is really good in his own end of the rink. His Maroons won 7-4, urged on by the crowd's encouragement. We definitely could have used Butch's rugged style out there.

But we had a reason to celebrate! Harry Neale handed out cigars after the game! He said he played the first period in a daze.

Through the bright lights of the city of Winnipeg I saw the glow of the Golden Boy statue on the dome of the Manitoba Legislative Building.

This is Blue Bomber football country! How can we ever forget last year's Grey Cup game at the CNE stadium in Toronto! The Tiger Cats and Bombers were tied 14-14 at the end of regulation time. In overtime Kenny Ploen, the Blue Bombers outstanding quarterback, ran in for the winning touchdown. It was awesome!

We arrived in Moose Jaw where they opened a beautiful new arena in September of 1959. The great jazz trumpeter and singer Louis Armstrong and his All Stars entertained at the opening. How great is that! They've nicknamed the arena "the can" because of the shape of its roof. Too bad I can't send you pictures!

The Moose Jaw community was as hospitable this time as they'd been four years earlier with Butch and the Dutchmen. But their PlayMors beat the Terriers 4-3. After the game our team was down a bit. It was their fourth loss. The media will likely pick up their usual chant about Canada not selecting their best team to represent them internationally. Be ready.

The Terriers were guests of these wonderful westerners at a scrumptious roast beef dinner. They also assured us that the community of Moose Jaw would be rooting for us all the way. It was a great and glorious send-off.

In 1908, Moose Jaw had a series of underground tunnels built. Their original purpose was to hide thousands of Chinese who were railway workers and escaping persecution during what was called the Yellow Peril. In the 1920s the tunnels were used for rum running during the era of Prohibition in the United States, also for gambling and other illegal activities. In the late 1920s notorious gangster Al Capone had boot-legging operations here.

The Terriers are really looking forward to their game in Trail, British Columbia against the Smoke Eaters. They won the World Hockey Tournament in Switzerland last year. Their coach Bobby Kromm doesn't think our team will be much opposition. It will be a good test to see where we're at. That's when Butch will be with us, as well as Ted Maki. Butch would like to leave Johnstown earlier. But we won't see him until the game in Trail.

The Terriers are also eagerly anticipating two exhibition games at Squaw Valley, where the Dutchmen competed in the 1960 Winter Olympics. It will be very special for Don Rope, Boat Hurley and Butch. The games will be against West Germany, the only ones against a European opponent before the World Championships. Our team plans to stay in Squaw Valley for five days.

Here's your Johnstown update. The worst flood was in 1889 as result of a dam on the Little Conemaugh River giving way. It's known as the Great Flood. The devastation seems simply unimaginable. Over two-thousand people died, including ninety-nine entire families. About sixteen hundred homes were destroyed and four square miles of downtown buildings collapsed into the water. They have experienced other floods. But fortunately none was nearly as damaging.

Johnstown today is a bit of a drab city, as a result of all the impurities escaping through the smoke stacks at the steel mills. But the mills are the heart and soul of the city. They employ about twelve thousand. Johnstown's also been called America's most affordable city. There's a quite prosperous farming community around Johnstown. Their potato crop is the second largest in the United States.

During World War II, German prisoners of war located in Johnstown, were used as labor in making bomb shells. The casings for the atomic bombs dropped in the war were also made there.

We'll soon hear from Butch himself about how the hockey's going.

Manager Gaudette got news that the Soviets may not be attending this year's World Hockey Tournament. The Terrier management stated clearly that their team is going to the World Tournament in Colorado regardless of what the rest of the world decides. I like that.

We're playing the Saskatoon Quakers tonight.

Mr. Ruggle, I hear you've got a new neighbor across Floradale Road, what with Ward Schwindt buying the feed mill from Ishmael Bowman. He'll do well. Ward's had a lot of good experience in the feed business at Eli Martin's Mill in Elmira.

I bet your store is abuzz today with the news of American John Glenn's three orbits around the earth: the first American to travel in space. For me, that's very, very, difficult to comprehend. Makes you wonder what's going to happen ten years from now! Maybe they'll land on the moon someday!

Missing you all,
Elam

Sent from: Edmonton, Alberta
February 21, 1962

Hi folks.

Thanks for posting these notes, Mr. Ruggle.

Things seem to be going well at my store in Glenn Allen. Young John Debold from just west of Dorking is looking after the management responsibilities. Katey Starr from a farm on the Sixth Line of Peel is helping with the banking and accounting. I have no worries about Foell's Farm Fresh Foods!

Saskatoon, where the Terriers played last night, is a real hockey town! Right now their Gump Worsley is playing goal for the New York Rangers. Tough guy Lou Fontinato is from here and is also a Ranger. He played in Guelph as a junior the year after Butch left. Also, Orland Kurtenbach from Saskatoon is playing with the Boston Bruins.

Yesterday afternoon, Bob Mader announced the birth of a new son, Calvin Robert! His wife Iva and their other three children are doing well. Bob is such a great family man. I'm sure at this moment he'd like to be snuggling Calvin.

The Saskatoon team is called Quakers because of the Quaker Oats company, the largest employer in the city. The game lacked excitement and the Terriers looked sloppy, playing what the coach described as their worst game of the tour. The score was 3-3. But the Terriers at their best would have dominated.

The coach had the team out on the ice at ten o'clock this morning for a stiff workout. But he cut off things early. He said the guys looked so strong that he didn't want them to leave their best game on the practice rink.

Yesterday we travelled from Saskatoon to Calgary. The Terriers played against the Calgary Addison Builders, Alberta's only Senior A team. They play in an intermediate league and weren't strong opposition in their 10-5 loss. Manager Gaudette admitted that even with the win his team was playing poorly; but feels they've got the "horses" to do well at the World Championship Tournament.

Aarron Bean, a beef farmer and hockey fan from Tofield, Alberta, told us about the Alberta Hutterite colonies consisting of up to about one hundred and fifty people each. They have grown to sixty-five colonies. The Hutterites live communally, operate farms of thousands of acres, and run very successful businesses with products like eggs and turkeys. They are under the Anabaptist umbrella like the Mennonite groups in Woolwich Township. Under their leader Jakob Hutter, they broke away from the main Anabaptist group in 1527 in Tyrol, Austria.

Aaron said that people in Alberta are a little concerned about the growing number of Hutterite neighbors, especially as they seem to remain aloof from the surrounding communities. They also have concerns about the quality of education provided for the children. And they're buying up a lot of the best land. I would love to visit a colony.

We've heard that Butch is doing very well in Johnstown, scoring more goals than usual!

Right now the steel industry is in somewhat unstable condition across America, with ongoing strikes. That's hitting Johnstown and Bethlehem Steel as well. The average rate of unemployment in the city in 1961 was over eighteen percent.

The population of Johnstown is about 55,000. Our coach said that the Jets average about three thousand fans a game in their Cambria County War Memorial Arena.

There are some Mennonite churches in the area of Cambria County where Johnstown is located but not nearly as many as in Lancaster and Franconia Counties of Pennsylvania. However, there's a Mennonite High School in Johnstown.

We're staying at the beautiful Macdonald House Hotel in downtown Edmonton. It was built in 1915 in the style of Canada's large railway hotels. We're in good company! Prime Minister Diefenbaker is at the hotel for a week-end conference. The hotel was named after Sir John A. Macdonald, Canada's first prime minister.

Edmontonians are crazy about their Eskimos Football team and their star quarterback, Jackie Parker. He refused a very rich contract with the National Football League's New York Giants, to stay in Edmonton, because his wife loves living here. The Eskimos last Grey Cup win was in 1956, their third in a row.

We all know how much Butch loves football!

My regards to Pastor Rufus Jutzi at Floradale Mennonite church, and the rest of the congregation. I'm sure PeeWee is keeping him up to date.

Wishing all you folks were here,
Elam

Hi.

After a few days down time the Terriers played the University of Alberta's hockey team, the Golden Bears. Pre-game comments by an Edmonton journalist about the Terriers were a little cruel, and duplicitous. He felt they showed very little talent in playing against what he called far inferior competition throughout the West. However, it's incomprehensible why a Canadian journalist would make the following comments: "The Terriers would have trouble beating the Hong Kong All-Stars on a bad day." That comment brought more laughter than anger.

The attendance at the game understandably was poor, likely because of this man's comments. But they appeared to motivate the Terriers. The guys didn't hold back, winning 14-0. Don Rope and Bob Brown each scored hat tricks.

We've had some stunning and disappointing news! Reports from the International Ice Hockey Federation say that it appears certain that Russia, and possibly Czechoslovakia, will be boycotting the World Hockey Tournament. They are two strong hockey powers! The Czechs came second to Canada in last year's tournament. Russia placed third. Our guys were so much looking forward to playing against both countries. It also would have been a reunion for Butch with players he'd met in the 1960 Olympic Games.

There's also some scuttlebutt that, because of that situation, Sweden is considering withdrawing, with the Netherlands not far behind. All the uncertainty is taking its toll on our players. But they're determined to keep going and to make their families, Waterloo County and Canada proud of them.

We know America represents western democracy, and the Soviet Union represents the communist bloc, in the Cold War. And, not surprisingly, sports on the world stage have been a part of the political maneuvering involved with that. International sports competitions, like hockey, have been used to supposedly show the superiority of one political system over the other.

But the situation this time, as we understand it, is the North Atlantic Treaty Organization's reaction to the building of the Berlin Wall last year, dividing the city into two diametrically opposite political German populations: the communistic east and the democratic west.

East Germany and West Germany each want to have teams at the tournament.

But the United States was unable to grant visas to the East Germans until the NATO travel office in West Germany allowed them to travel in NATO countries. It appears that the permission isn't forthcoming.

By withdrawing from the tournament, the Soviets and Czechs are showing their support to the East German people.

In the 1961 championship, the West Germans were forbidden by their hockey authorities to take the ice for a game against East Germany. They wanted to avoid the possibility of honoring the new East German flag should that team win.

The Soviets would come, they said, if a different venue was found.

Canada's response was that Edmonton, Calgary and Toronto have offered to host the tournament in place of Colorado Springs and Denver. I didn't know until today that Kitchener-Waterloo made a serious bid to host the tournament before it was awarded to Colorado. They'd planned to use Maple Leaf Gardens and arenas in Waterloo, Elmira and New Hamburg. Wouldn't that have been something!

The Terriers added frustration here in Edmonton is with the Canadian Amateur Hockey Association. The CAHA has arranged for the team to travel by train from Edmonton to Trail, British Columbia. That's a sixteen-hour trip! The players would much rather travel by airplane.

John Sofrack of Saskatoon has come on as the back-up goalie to Boat Hurley. Elmira's Frankie Carroll, and also Lloyd Mercer aren't with the Terriers now. But they were important parts in last year's Allan Cup run. In what to me is a classy gesture, the Terriers are paying all their expenses to attend the World Tournament as supporters.

Time to get packed for the trip through the Rockies via "flight" Canadian Pacific Railway.

This note was more politics than hockey but I hope it gives you a bit of an insider's view, rather than depending entirely on the news media.

I'm loving every minute of this adventure!

Elam

From: Trail, British Columbia

February 27, 1962

Hi everyone,

We made it to Trail! We were on the train about sixteen hours, as predicted, and another three hours on the bus and ferry. It was tiring for everyone. Bill Wylie said, "You've heard of friendship seven? This was friendship ceases!"

But what a wonderful experience to see the majestic Rocky Mountains; lakes sparkling with ice waterfalls, caribou, elk and snowy owls, sunny, blue sky and huge parcels of land covered with glistening snow. Cole Bowman, the artist, would love it.

Trail is a small city, in a beautiful valley, split into two parts by the Columbia River. It's in the Kootenays Region. We're only six miles north of the American border. We can see the Monashee Mountains in the West and the Selkirk Mountains to the East. The city is on the slopes, but the main street is flat.

There's a lot of excitement for the big game tonight, with a playoff type buzz In the town. The game's about two hours away, and I see Butch has just arrived from Johnstown. Good to see him! He's looking great!

The Trail Smoke Eaters have played thirty-eight league games this season without a loss. Some feel they could be 1962 Allan Cup winners. Also, they were the 1961 IIHF world champions in the tournament in Switzerland. Their outstanding goalkeeper, Seth Martin, was selected at the top goalie. A few locals at the Mountain View Coffee shop said that the Terriers will have to keep "Pinoke" McIntyre, and Adolph Tambellini in check. They are hometown fellows and good goal scorers. The folks here sure love their Smoke Eaters!

For the first time on the tour the Terriers have all players on board. There are no serious injuries, although Bob Mader's still recovering from a separated shoulder. Boat Hurley's returning to top form in goal.

Darryl Sly played for the Trail team last year. Remember him? He was a teacher at John Mahood School, and was a teammate of Butch's at the 1960 Winter Olympics with the Dutchmen. Darryl is with the Rochester Americans in the American Hockey League.

The Terriers off-ice outfit is a red coat, white fedora, and black overshoes. One observer said, "They look a forest fire out of control." That was good for a laugh! Coincidentally the Trail team has identical red coats to ours.

I'm looking forward to seeing the line of Wylie, McKnight and Butch reunited.

Due to the confusion and political maneuvering around what teams will be going to the tournament, our much anticipated visit for five days to Squaw Valley has been cancelled. The CAHA is hustling to arrange a few exhibition games to keep the team sharp. It's unfortunate, isn't it, that political decisions encroach on games and affect player's lives in this way? The animosity grows among the politicians but I think the players just want to play hockey.

To the Terrier's great credit, although greatly disappointed, they remain totally focused on their commitment to win. I hope all Canada gets behind them! They deserve support from Newfoundland to British Columbia.

I'll get another note out tomorrow after we've heard from Butch.

Hoping that all of you are well.

Elam

Hello everyone,

Suddenly it feels like spring. This afternoon the temperature reached fifty degrees!

Last evening's game was by far the best of the tour. It was exciting and well-played! The Terriers broke the undefeated streak of the Smoke Eaters with an exciting 3-1 victory. Boat Hurley was simply sensational in the first period. The Terriers scored two goals and then Butch scored the third on one of those picture passing plays with McKnight and Wylie. It looked like old times at the Galt Arena Gardens!

Manager Gaudette had high praise for Butch, noting, "He was his usual bull-dozing self and dogged worker whose aggressive play sets up goals." He was really pumped! He was convinced that the Terriers would bring the championship home without losing a game. What a great way to end the cross-Canada tour! Everyone was full of enthusiasm and positive vibes.

The Trail civic leaders hosted a lavish dinner. Just as we'd stuffed ourselves with spaghetti and meat balls, they rolled out the southern fried chicken. Smoke Eaters coach Kromm was gracious in defeat and wished the Terriers good-luck.

Butch looks well and says he's enjoying his first year in Johnstown, with the obvious exceptions. He really misses PeeWee, but is glad she can make it down on the weekends. He also misses the guys at the sawmill, and his sister Valina's brown-sugar-sprinkled coffee cakes. This is the first hockey season where hockey is his only job: also quite a difference.

Pretty well all the teams in the Eastern Hockey League have playing coaches. Steve Brklacich is that guy for the Jets. There's some rumors that he might retire from playing and get into full-time coaching somewhere.

The fabulous Ken Laufman and Butch are teammates again. It looks like Ken's on his way to another scoring championship. Butch likes the Jets goaltending duo. Marv Edwards plays most of the games. And young Gilles Villeneuve presently is his backup. Butch has no doubt they'll be NHL players. The Jets are having a good season, and in a position to do well in the playoffs.

We inquired about the rough stuff. He said any rumor we've heard is probably true! It's not that there's a lot more fighting. It's just that many of the fights are vicious. Each team has at least one, big tough guy. Some owners refer to them as "animals." A fellow named John Brophy is the most notorious. The Jets have John Lumley who plays the same role. These guys rack up well over three-hundred penalty minutes a season.

You won't believe this! Remember Wally Kullman, that tough guy on the Bridgeport Vets team when they played against the Elmira Polar Kings? He's the playing coach of the New Haven Blades in the same league as Johnstown.

A big change for Butch is the long road trips. There's lots of bus traveling time, sometimes starting off in the early morning. When Jets guys complain Butch tells them this is nothing! For years he showed up at the sawmill at seven in the morning, worked until five, and then played a hockey game at night. That seems to put an end to the complaining.

The Jets are in the southern division with Greensboro Generals, Philadelphia Ramblers, and Charlotte Checkers. There's also a four-team northern division.

John Mitchell, the general manager of the Jets, is also general manager of the American team Canada will meet at the tournament. Also, Butch's Jets teammates, Dick Roberge and Don Hall are on the American team. Roberge and Ken Laufman were tied for EHL scoring championship last season, each with 116 points.

I don't know what team we're playing next, but for sure they're going to squeeze in two more games before the tournament starts.

Hoping you're not snowed in!
Elam

Hi everyone,

We've arrived! The Terriers are now Canada's team. The spotlight of our great country will be on them. I think I'm more excited than the players!

This is quite a place! It's going to be our team's home. The stylish Broadmoor Hotel is part of a very large, rather lavish resort. Think of the land of a one hundred-acre farm, times thirty. That is about the size of this entire complex. The hotel is on a square acre of land.

American business tycoons, high profile politicians and other people in the upper American social stratosphere visit this impressive place.

There are twenty-eight new cars available for the use of the teams. That's first class service!

This is a new and very exciting experience for me. I'll be mingling with over three-hundred people from thirteen countries. Their view of the world, language and heritage will be substantially different from mine. I'm really eager to broaden my knowledge.

Most tournament games will be played in the beautiful Broadmoor World Arena, part of this awe-inspiring "playground."

We see people lining up putts on golf courses, swimming lengths in a pool, dining on steak and red wine in restaurants, purchasing tickets to see Jimmy Stewart in the movie To Kill a Mockingbird or going for leisurely strolls.

We're in the East central part of Colorado, in El Paso County. To the West are mountains; there are flat plains to the East, and desert to the South. We're about 6500 feet above sea level and right at the base of Pike's Peak. It rises to over 14,000 feet.

Our hockey players went through some dire times to get to this wonderful moment. At the start of this season, things weren't going well in Galt. The future looked bleak. By the end of October, a total of only forty-five season's tickets had been sold. Often fewer than four hundred fans showed up for a home game. There were fewer than that the November night I was there when the Terriers beat the Stratford Indians 15-1. The Terriers had the smallest average attendance in the league. Galt's image in the sporting community was deteriorating. The concern was so pronounced that management was considering moving the club to another southern Ontario City.

The Terriers have never received a salary. In late November they were given their portion of cash from the share-the-wealth arrangement. Each received a total of twenty-five dollars. The winners of the 1961 Allan Cup, preparing to be Canada's team, appeared to lack any substantial financial base to move forward with confidence. Things were gloomy.

But through lots of effort and remarkable ingenuity the community got behind the club. Eventually they raised $19,000. That's amazing!

Canada's team also played exhibition games back home for which they were paid very well. These funds went towards their travel expenses. One game was against the RCAF Flyers in Trenton.

So here we are!

The Canadian government and Prime Minister Diefenbaker announced that five million dollars was designated towards the promotion of physical fitness and amateur sport across the nation. Our team asked for twelve hundred dollars. They received nothing.

Enough of this rant! Arrangements were made for Canada to play in Omaha, Nebraska against the Knights of the International League. The five-hour flight was an escapade, featuring two hours of severe turbulence. Once we hit an air pocket and suddenly dropped over one hundred feet! In the end, a lot of the guys, including me couldn't handle eating anything for quite some time. The long train and bus ride to Trail didn't seem so bad after all!

The Knights and Canada played a spirited game in the Ak-Sar-Ben arena. (Try saying that backwards.) Our guys won 5-1. Most of the

Knights are from western Canada.

Here is bit of trivia. Omaha is the birth-place of raisin bran, scrumptious butter brickle ice-cream, and the Reuben sandwich. Actor Henry Fonda grew up there.

Our final hurriedly planned exhibition game was at the Broadmoor World Arena against the Colorado College Tigers. This is their original home. Canada easily handed the Tigers their thirty-fourth straight loss. It ended up 11-1. Management would have preferred stiffer competition in the last test before the meaningful games begin.

NHL star Bill Hay is a former Tiger. In 1960 he was the NHL's Calder Trophy winner as the league's top rookie and was an NHL all-star. He plays with the Chicago Black Hawks as a line-mate of the great Bobby Hull and clever playmaker Stan Mikita.

I think the guys will be happy to take it easy for a few days. They'll have a few practices. They've played eight games in eleven days, and have done a lot of traveling in a short time.

We'll be touring the headquarters for NORAD-the North American Radar and Defense Warning System on a base not far from Colorado Springs.

Butch is rooming with our team manager. Fortunately, at this point the team seems healthy and ready to go, with only a few players recovering from minor ailments. Dr. Berkeley, the team's physician and president, is with us. Bob Spooner, the hard-working Booster Club president, arrived yesterday.

Last evening we heard an enthusiastic and enlightening address by Mr. W. Thayer Tutt. He's an avid sportsman, very wealthy, and has longstanding connections to the Broadmoor and the state of Nebraska. His ancestors made millions from gold mining in the Pike's Peak area in the late nineteenth century. Mr. Tutt is hosting and generously financing this World Hockey Tournament. His budget is five hundred thousand dollars. He promised one-hundred-and-fifty dollars per player or three-thousand dollars per team to assist with expenses, regardless of from where they travelled.

Coach Roubell told the team to enjoy themselves because when the tournament starts there will be a midnight curfew and no swimming! There will be a fifty-dollar fine for any player who doesn't adhere to the rules. Concerning his team's strategy, the coach said, "We'll play it rugged and let them know we're from Canada."

Denver is about sixty-five miles from here. Our team will have to travel there for some of their practices and their first game. That will mean getting out of bed at about six o'clock in the morning!

Thanks for continuing to post these notes. It gives some of the Floradale and area people a bit of a picture of the experiences Butch is having. It's amazing how many places that hockey has taken him since his days as a mascot for the Floradale Indians.

I hope everyone is over the flu and the sniffles; those nasty, unwelcome ailments that linger much longer than we like.

Elam

Sent from: Broadmoor Hotel
Colorado Springs
March 6, 1962

Hi folks,

The official story here is that the Soviets and Czechoslovakians aren't participating in this World Championship Tournament. Eastern bloc countries like Romania, Italy, and Poland are giving their support by joining in the boycott. But the organizers haven't closed the door, should they change their minds at the last minute. They have a variety of schedules ready that could include any number of the teams.

Any idea of changing the venue has been scuttled. Vasily Napanikov, a representative from Russia, tabled a motion with the IIHF to have the tournament deprived of official recognition. But the motion was received too late to conduct a vote. The absence of the Soviets and Czechs could mean a loss of about one-hundred thousand dollars for Mr. Tutt.

We've been here only a few days, but honestly, I don't think these hockey players are interested in the political stuff. They just want to get on with the competition and represent their countries to the best of their ability.

Canada will be in the "A" division with Finland, Norway, United States, Great Britain, Sweden, West Germany and Switzerland. They'll play each other once and the medal winners will be determined by total points at the end. There's no overtime, so some games might end with a tied score. Goal differential can enter the picture. That's how Trail won the 1961 championship.

Coach Roubell says his major concern is the Swedish team. In the history of the Winter Olympic Games and IIHF Tournaments, Sweden has never beaten Canada. He'd rather this not be the first time! He also has concern about the effect of the high altitude on the players' breathing. He's considering making oxygen available.

There's a second or "B" division with Japan, Austria, France, the Netherlands, Australia, and Denmark. The medals will be determined in the same manner. The Japanese are already picking coach Rubell's brain about game strategy.

Each player from Australia had to pay five hundred dollars of his own money to get here. One man quit his job to come. Hockey's a fairly new sport in Australia and they lack facilities. They're on the ice for about one hour a week. IIHF president J. F. "Bunny" Ahearne paid ten thousand dollars out of his own pocket to ensure the Australians got here.

The Aussies brought with them boomerang and koala bear souvenirs. I've got a koala bear packed in my luggage and will "allow" it to leave when I reach Floradale.

The guys from down under sure have fun! One player said their motto was, "We're not here for a long time, but for a good time." They've challenged other teams to swimming races. But their special rule is that at the end of each lap you must kick back and enjoy a beer!

Addison Robinson, a bright young fellow from the Queensland area of Australia, told us that his country really does well in tennis and swimming. Their Margaret Court is expected to be one of the best female tennis players in the world. In the 1956 Summer Olympics in Melbourne, Australian swimmers took home eight of thirteen available gold medals.

Australia has sheep and cattle farming but farms need lots of irrigation. Addison says the biggest pests for farmers are rabbits; that's after he'd said a spirited "G'day" and a few "Good onyas."

The team from the Netherlands could use Zenas Buehler in goal! You'll remember that Zenas spent a year playing hockey there.

The Dutch coach said they had to literally drag forty-year-old Joost Van Os out of his easy chair to play goal for them. A few former Waterloo Siskins, Pat Adair and goalie Gary Millman, who play hockey in Holland could really help them. But they're still Canadians!

All in all, it looks like it's going to be a tournament of keen competition and good will. The hockey will be very important, of course. But the growing, informal relationships among the players off the ice, in the long run, might have equal significance. You know, as well as I do that when Butch talks about the tournaments he's been to, his stories are about the people he met along the way, much more than the games.

Maybe Bob Mader will do something special for his new son, although Bob's been bothered by a nagging injury and is recovering from the flu and bronchitis. Knowing Bob, he'll show up for that first game, ready and eager to play.

That gives you an idea of how things are organized here. And don't bother yourself about some newspaper sports writers who are bemoaning that the Terriers aren't good enough to represent Canada, or similar stuff. We've heard that before, haven't we? Canada is represented by a first rate team. They'll make us proud!

But think of how you might feel if Butch walked into your store carrying a gold medal! I bet there would be Pepsis for everyone: courtesy of Ruggle's General Store, of course!

Canada, our guys, open against Finland on the eighth of this month and West Germany on the tenth. There's excitement and anticipation in the air as our team prepares for the first drop of the puck! This competition is much different from the Olympics. Here, hockey is "the only game in town." Also, with only Canadians and Americans in the NHL, winning this tournament carries a great honor. On the world stage it carries much greater significance than the Stanley Cup. National pride is on the line.

I'm really, really looking forward to the first game. Although I'll have to rise early because the game's in Denver. I want to hear "Our Land" (Maamme) the national anthem of Finland played.

If you're in Elmira in the next while would you drop by Brubacher's grocery store and tell Noah and Clarence that things are going well. Clarence was the ticket-taker at the Polar King games. Both were Polar King fans and very fond of Butch.

Eagerly anticipating the first game! Go Canada! Go Butch!

Elam

From: Boadmoor Hotel

March 11, 1962

Greetings again from Colorado,

Canada met Finland in their first tournament game. After all the traveling and all the exhibition games the guys were ready for a meaningful game. I was so excited, that I got up at about 5:00 a.m. so I'd be in time to catch a ride to Denver.

The teams lined up at the blue lines for the opening ceremonies. The intention was to play the national anthem of both countries. But things didn't go well, so they played "God Save the Queen" four times. It was a bit of an awkward moment for those in charge, and a moment of humor for the players.

Bob Mader scored a beauty first goal three minutes into the game: a great way to celebrate the birth of a son back in Breslau! Butch's line was clicking pretty good. He had a goal and an assist. Automatically, it seemed, I rose from my seat to cheer when Butch scored. I was the only one among the spectators to react in that way. I'm sure I'll do it again. Ex-Leaf Tod Sloan scored twice and assisted on two more goals. The first two goals of the game were scored in less than two minutes. In the second period we scored two goals within seventeen-seconds! Our guys won handily by an 8-1 score in a pretty tame game. Kaltalo, the young Finnish goalie, said, "Some of the Canadian shots were like bullets!" Lasse Oksanen was the best of the Finns.

Coach Roubell felt his team looked tired and also had breathing difficulties. It got him thinking more seriously about using oxygen. Joe Wirkunnen, the Finnish coach felt the effort was good from his team. The players had some complaints about what they called rough and chippy ice. But it was a really good start.

I met Finnish supporter Jussi Laine from the town of Uusikaarlepyy, Finland. Given the language problems we could only manage the exchange of our names and the identities of our hometowns.

Last night our second game of the tournament was at the entirely enclosed World Arena against the West Germans. The World Arena is only a year old. It's sparkling clean and beautiful, with red carpets in the aisles, striking paintings of wild life on the walls, and wooden seats. The original arena opened in 1938. Formerly it had been an open air riding academy.

There are plans in place of gave a memorial erected on the grounds of the arena. Just one year ago the entire United States Figure Skating Team was killed in a plane crash while on their way to the 1961 World Championships in Brussels, Belgium: a huge tragedy. Some of its members trained at the Broadmoor. The arena is on its way to becoming a major player in world class figure skating training and competitions.

I hesitate to bring politics into the story of this tournament. However, in the case of West Germany, that would be to disregard the significance of what's happened in the last six months in their country. This team and their country have gone through some exceedingly traumatic times.

During the night of August 12, and early morning of August 13 of last year, soldiers and construction workers strung barbed wire all across the border of East Berlin and West Berlin. Berliners were shocked. This barrier stopped all East Berliners from crossing into West Berlin for any reason, including entertainment, sports games and other activities. About sixty thousand East Berliners could no longer go into West Berlin to continue employment. Families, friends, and loved ones were separated by the barrier.

Around August 15 a more permanent structure made from concrete blocks and topped with barbed wire was erected. The wall, about ninety-six miles long, is a symbol of the Cold War, between communism, like in East Berlin, and democracy, like that lived out in West Berlin. The wall also symbolizes what Winston Churchill calls the Iron Curtain.

That situation is hard for us to comprehend, isn't it? Some of the West German (Federal Republic of Germany) players have been effected on a personal level by this action.

It's a reminder that while we may have issues with "Dief" and our government, we're also free to come and go as we please.

The West Germans speak highly of their long serving chancellor, Konrad Adenauer. His admiration was most pronounced when he brought home the last of the prisoners of war from the USSR— known as "The Return of the 10,000."

Some of the German players and fans speak English quite well. That's good, because my command of our "Woolwich German dialect" doesn't take me far into a conversation. We sat with a German middle-aged couple, Dieter and Elisabeth Freitag from near the Ehrenbreitstein Castle, close to the Rhine River. They had a lot of fun with my rather futile attempts at German. You'd be acquainted with some of the German hockey players names; like Muller, Schultz, and Reimer. Friz

Muller from Floradale might be a relative!

Joe Hogan didn't play in this game because of flu, and Sloan sat out, resting after suffering a thirteen-stitch cut in the game against Finland.

Canada had another pretty easy time of it, winning 8-0. Butch and Bob Mader had a goal each. The Canadians had over fifty shots on the West German goalie. Unfortunately their top goalie, Wilhelm Edelmann sustained a broken jaw during a practice. They were not allowed to bring in a replacement. Young Werner Basson filled in and under the circumstances played admirably.

Butch was one of the players who used oxygen. After, he said, "Maybe it's in the mind, but I felt better."

So we're off to a good start. But Sweden is also undefeated. They won a close game last night against the Americans. The score was 2-1. Tonight we play Switzerland. They were originally slated for the "B" division, But with the boycott by some teams, the Swiss were elevated to the "A" division. You'd think that it shouldn't be too tough a game. Yet the pressure is on us to keep winning.

Many of you folks and I can trace our ancestry back to the Cantons of Bern and Zurich in Switzerland, as can Butch. That's where the Anabaptist (later Mennonite) movement, the radical wing of the Protestant Reformation, began in 1525.

The Canadian Mennonite magazine announced that the Mennonite World Conference is having an international assembly in Waterloo County from August 1-7 this year. The meeting place for the over 8000 expected visitors will be the Kitchener Auditorium, former home of Butch's Dutchmen Senior A hockey team. Given his journey with hockey, and the Mennonite's historical stance on competition in sports, Butch should find the choice of the site of the assembly rather interesting.

There will be more countries represented at assembly than at this World Hockey Tournament. At the first such assembly there were five.

I'll have more about Switzerland, and its hockey team in the next note.

I know Easter Sunday isn't until April 22, but I'm glad I'll be back in time to be with my family on that special day.

Elam

Sent from: Broadmoor Hotel
March 12, 1962

Hi everyone,

I was in touch with my cousin Curtis. He was in your store to buy some seed, and caught up with news about Butch. Thanks for your diligence in posting my notes.

Last night we played the Swiss team at the strikingly impressive World Arena.

I haltingly tried out my Pennsylvania Deutsch with Emma Zellweger, one of the friendly Swiss fans. Fortunately she's from the German-speaking area. Thanks to her patience and good sense of humor, we understood each other fairly well. Emma refers to her language as Schweizerdeutsch. About seventy per cent of the Swiss population speaks German. The second most spoken language is French, and then Italian. Less than one per cent speak Romanish which is a descendant of the Latin language spoken by the Roman Empire.

Emma and her family live in Wengen, in the mountains close to Zurich, where the Anabaptist (Mennonite) story began. She finds it fascinating that Butch, a Canadian, has roots in her home country. Emma is a friend of Rene Kleiner, the Swiss goalie.

Before there were any artificial ice-making plants in Switzerland, the teams from the mountainous communities, like Wengen, were superior. That's because the natural ice lasted longer in the colder, higher elevations which extended their hockey season.

Emma gave me a bar of that wonderful Frey's Swiss dark chocolate. Guess who has already devoured it!

Not much was expected here from the Swiss team. They'd lost to Sweden by a score of 17-2. But they surprised our boys and caught them a bit off guard. They checked tenaciously. But similar to the other games thus far, there was little rough stuff. Finally our guys broke through on Kleiner and won 7-2. He stopped about fifty shots.

Butch looked impressive in collecting two more goals but in the end was disappointed in how the team performed overall. He said, "Boy, I'm sure glad we didn't play Sweden tonight."

You can be assured that Butch is having a very good tournament and is obviously highly regarded on the international hockey scene. He really wants to be part of something that was just out of his reach twice before.

Everyone is looking at Canada's game with Sweden tomorrow night as the key game. We're considered the two strongest teams and each has gone undefeated. The winner of the game is heavily favored to take the gold medal.

Butch was asked how he thought the game would go. He replied, "How will we do against the Swedes? It will be a terrific game!" I can't wait for the puck to drop!

Coach Roubell is confidently predicting a Canadian victory by two goals. Arne Strömberg, coach of the Swedes, fears his team will make too many defensive errors. He figures that if his team is going to win, they'll need some lucky goals.

Einhard Almquist, a young, congenial, English speaking Swedish sportswriter from the town of Sandviken, told us that back home the Canada-Sweden game has generated an immense amount of interest. It's going to be shown on television at 4:30 a.m. their time. Half of the population—more than three and a half million, will be watching.

Swedes call their national team "Tre Kronor" (Three Crowns). The three crowns are on their team jerseys. The Tre Kronor emblem is also on the Coat of Arms of Sweden.

Sven (Tumba) Johansson, over the years, has been Sweden's best offensive player. He's over six feet tall and about two-hundred-and-ten pounds. The only criticism about him is that he tends not to pass as often as he should. Butch played against the Sweden star in Cortina and Squaw Valley. He'll line up against him again tomorrow.

During the 1961 IIHF championship, Trail Smoke Eaters beat the Swedish team 6-1. Trail went on to win the gold medal. Sweden ended up fourth. The Swedish contingent was unhappy with what they described as unsportsmanlike behavior of the Smoke Eaters. Roubell's optimism comes partially from knowing that his team beat basically the same team of Smoke Eaters just a few weeks ago in Trail.

Sweden's one goal victory over the United States was the result of a very intense game. Eiinhard said that the result was relished but made more so since the arena was packed with cheering Americans.

After tomorrow's game, Canada and Sweden both have three games remaining. But our team is looking no further than tomorrow, Without the Soviets and Czechoslovakia here, it opens the door for countries who weren't considered in the elite group, to do better than expected. But I really think our boys will come through.

If a Woolwich farmer bought land around Colorado Springs, he'd experience a shorter growing season and a shortage of precipitation. So there's a fair bit of irrigation. Corn, alfalfa, and small grains do quite well. There is also a large amount of rangeland where wildlife like the black bear, big horn sheep and yellow-bellied marmot (largest of the ground squirrel family) roam. That is why we see the paintings of wildlife on the walls of the Arena.

I'll be in touch soon to bring you news of a victory. (I hope!)
Elam

Here we go.

I wish I could give the Martin family and the rest of you better news. But our team was defeated by Sweden by two goals. It was a very, very tough loss. Knowledgeable hockey fans observed that Canada was by far the better team. But that doesn't bring any points.

There remains some hope. We must win each of our three remaining games and hope that Sweden loses at least one game if we have any hope of coming home as champions. We can only control the games in which we play.

Before the game began, the teams exchanged pins, as is the custom in international hockey.

When the Swedish star player Ulf Sterner jumped in the air after scoring the first goal of the game, it seemed to be an omen of what was to come. We couldn't believe what was happening. By the end of the first period, our guys were behind by a stunning 4-0 score. Canada had scoring opportunities, but Swedish goalie Lennart Haggroth made some saves that were simply sensational.

Our fellows surprisingly played a different style of game from what we'd seen them play in earlier games. They were very, very aggressive and played a physical style that resulted in them being short-handed more than usual. They received eleven out of the fifteen penalties. The usual skating and passing game couldn't be maintained what with all the time spent in the penalty box. Yet there was no doubt that they were giving their best.

Butch gave us hope by getting our first goal, making it 4-1. That caused a stir on the bench and among the Canadian spectators. With a tremendous effort our guys remarkably drew within one goal. It was a really impressive try at a comeback. We Canadian fans were on our feet cheering! I'm usually a reserved fellow, but I was up hollering like the rest. Winning no longer seemed impossible. But we needed the second-hand on the game clock to slow down!

Late in the game, coach Roubell frantically motioned to goalie Hurley to come to the bench. An extra forward hopped over the boards. We put on a lot of pressure. But we needed a break, like a deflected shot, or the puck going off a skate and into the net. Anything! We came so very close to scoring.

Then Nils Nilsson got the puck on his stick, just outside Sweden's blue line. Immediately he took a shot towards our empty net. As the puck slid along the ice, our defenseman made a tremendous effort to extend his stick and send the puck into the corner of the rink. But it swiftly swished along the ice, on its way to bringing unbridled joy to one players' bench and a figurative stab in the heart of those wearing the maple leaf on their chests.

We Canadian fans just stood in silence, not wanting to believe what the score board told us. I can't imagine what emotions our team was experiencing.

Einhard Almquist, told us that Sweden's legendary play-by-play announcer Lennart Hyland became very emotional as he described the long shot into the empty net to the millions of the now wide-awake county folks back home. Hyland shouted into the microphone-"Den glider i m -a- a -a -a -a -a- a -a l!" (It slides into the n- e -e- e -e- e -e -e- e-t!) The final score was 5-3 for Sweden.

The winners deserve the praise. Tumba Johansson, Sweden's leader and a hero at home, played very well and the skillful Ulf Sterner and Nils Nilsson each scored twice.

Youthful goalie Haggroth stopped four Canadian breakaways and had at least three shots go off his arm that he didn't see coming. But, as we all know, when a goalie is playing well, luck seems to be with him. Yet Canada missed a wide open net at least three times. Tumba called his goalie the hero of the game. Haggroth had replaced regular goalie Kjell Svensson.

Einhard counted sixty Canadian shots on the Swedish goal. Haggroth is just twenty-two years old, and an engineering student. It was "his best game ever" at the best possible time.

The jubilant Swedish players proudly lifted smiling and arm-waving coach, Stromberg onto their shoulders and jubilantly paraded around the arena. Einhard said you had to be a Swede to really understand how wonderful that moment was! Back home in Hudiksvall the folks would be raising lots of pints of Carnegie Porter in celebration.

I spoke to a Canadian team member later in the evening. He said that the dressing room was entirely silent after the game. Players just sat and looked at the floor. He felt that the team, in playing it rough, resulted in needless penalties, himself included. He went on: "We could have won, I'm sure if we'd have played our normal, fast paced and passing game."

There were some of our players suffering with various injuries. But he didn't feel that took away from scoring chances missed. "We just couldn't put the puck into the net. Their goalie was really their whole team."

It was indeed a very big win in Sweden! A Swedish newspaper called it the biggest win in the history of Swedish international hockey competition. Johansson called it the happiest moment of his life.

Coach Roubell said that clearly the better team didn't win. IIHF president, and Canadian citizen Robert Lebel said, "Even if I am Canadian, I am proud of you. You deserved victory. You were the better team."

In the last seconds of the game, with the outcome certain, Orlander, a Swedish forward, skated beside Butch and taunted him by leaning in close and laughing derisively. In an instinctive reaction, Butch jabbed the blade of his stick into Orlander's mid-section. Orlander staggered to the bench after a few minutes of contortions on the ice. Less than a minute later he was back on the ice joining in the victory dance. Butch received a five-minute major penalty. He apologized for the action following the game. Today, he, coach Roubell and manager Gaudette appeared before an IIHF committee and Butch was reprimanded for his action. But there is no suspension.

The Canadian players, dejectedly, but hopefully, say all they can do is make certain they win their three remaining games.

I expect that the Toronto Sports writers at The Globe and Mail, and Star, are at their IBM Selectric typewriters, composing vitriolic diatribes about Canada's team; and about the CAHA for sending what they will describe as an inferior team, to this IIHF tournament. Be prepared.

But, friends in Floradale, we're not done yet! As we all know, strange things can happen in one game. Which makes any confident prediction as to how this tournament will end a shaky premise.

Canada plays Norway, Great Britain and the United States. We absolutely have to win each game!

I've driven around the countryside and have found villages as small as Floradale. A few of them are Green Valley Falls and Calhan. Outside the small village of Palmer Lake, on Sundance Mountain, is a large, man-made star, 500 feet across. The thousands of bulbs that light the outline are lit for the entire month of December and other special national occasions. I'd like to be here during Christmas to see that!

How are your plans for those plate glass windows and new front for the store coming along?

I hope everyone is well back home. We're still enjoying ourselves— and have our fingers crossed. Quite a drama will unfold here during the next few days!

Elam

Sent from: Broadmoor Hotel
March, 1962

Hi friends,

Canada is internationally loved!

In fact we're running out of Canadian souvenir pins. They seem to be among the most prized possessions. We're also giving away miniature hockey sticks, note cards and team pictures. That gives you an idea of Canada's stature in the international hockey world. But the good folks in charge of the glitzy souvenir program here have said our team is from "Gault." (Canada is also forgiving.)

Dr. Berkely, our team's very capable physician, has come down with pneumonia. He's receiving attention at a medical clinic in Palm Springs. We anticipate he'll be back with us soon, hopefully feeling much better.

One local reporter described our game, against Norway, as a massacre. Butch scored three times (I rose from my seat three times to cheer!) and assisted on two others in a 14-1 victory. We played the puck and skated. There was no need to add a physical dimension. Our back-up goalie John Sofrak, was given a chance to play. But he wasn't tested severely. The Norwegian team came in tenth at the 1961 IIHF tournament. But even with the loss, their record here seems to point to a loftier finish.

Oddvar, an uncle of the Norwegian coach and sometime hockey player from Vestfold County, told us, through an English-speaking friend, that the team has poor training facilities and lacks artificial ice operations. He'd like to see Canada play Norway in European football. (Oddvar has a good sense of humor!) I told him I didn't think that would happen soon!

He and I exchanged a Norwegian krone for a Canadian dollar. What do you think a krone will buy me at Ruggle's?

The next game, our second to last, was against Great Britain, or Team GB as they're known by their fans. Sweden had beaten them 14-0. GB's only win here was against Finland. All the "lads" play on club teams back home. Altrincham Aces and Brighton Tigers have the most representatives on the team.

Newlyweds, James and Ruth Philips, from Sale, Cheshire in the English midlands took in the game. They have a friend on Team GB so included a stop-over. They're on the way to their honeymoon destination in San Diego, California. Today the temperature there is seventy degrees. The newlyweds love ice hockey but are "really, really in love" with the Manchester City Football Club.

Our team coasted through the game. Coach Roubell said they were saving themselves for the big game against the United States. Butch scored another goal in a 12-2 win.

Some bits of information: With his impressive play here, Lennart Haggroth, the Swedish goalie has been put on Boston Bruins negotiation list.

Sweden, Switzerland, Austria and Germany are looking for Canadians to take over their national development programs and handle their national teams.

We've noticed at the games at the World Arena that many of the women parade in late, adorned in mink: sort of an impressive "fashion show" for us hockey fans.

All youngsters playing hockey in Europe must wear some type of helmet. How do you think that would go over with the Elmira minor hockey teams?

The Golden Bee is an English-style pub located in the basement of the International Centre on the Broadmoor Hotel grounds. Authentic English ale sells for ninety-five cents a pint. I've enjoyed some rich Samuel Smith's Nut Brown Ale, brewed in Tadcaster, England, a market town in North Yorkshire.

Coach Roubell spent an hour with the Japanese team, an interpreter, and a blackboard. He explained about playing the slot, body checking, penalty killing, and other tips. The Japanese team is preparing for the "B" championship game against Holland.

After beating Australia by a lopsided score, France bluntly told them they shouldn't return to international competition unless they can bring a competitive team.

We have one game left. It's against the Americans. It's going to be televised on CBS and CBC. Broadmoor World Arena is going to be rocking with American supporters! By the time Butch hits the ice for that game, he'll know if it's for gold or silver, as Sweden's final game will be played before the Canada-United States match. There's a lot at stake, especially for Butch. He doesn't want a repeat of Cortina and Squaw Valley games.

I am very nervous about this game! I have a sister who is married to an American from Pennsylvania, who just happens to be a hockey fan. She'll be cheering for her home country. You can guess for which team her husband will be rooting.

I'm not sure why, but for me, it's just tough to lose to the Americans in our sport.

The next note will be my last. In a way, I've been living in a surreal world here. But getting back to friends and family in Glenn Allan and Floradale will be great!

Your friend,
Elam

Sent from: Broadmoor Hotel
March, 1962

Get ready to proudly welcome Butch home with another silver medal!

Incredible, isn't it, that your tiny village of Floradale has one of you who has now earned two Olympic medals and one World Championship medal? I'll bet that fifty years from now this will still be a story that Butch will be asked to tell to school children in Waterloo County, as he shows them his medals.

When Butch lined up for the faceoff against the Americans, he already knew that Sweden had won the championship. But knowing that didn't take away from the importance of the game he was facing. On many levels, it was very important to beat the Americans and restore Canada as being superior in the "only sport that counts" in our great country.

There were 3495 loud and boisterous fans at the Broadmoor World Arena for the game. A great roar went up as the Americans skated onto the ice. They looked like determined bunch.

Our small group of Canadian supporters was huddled together, hollering as loudly as we could manage, and waving our arms madly when Boat Hurley confidently skated towards his goal crease, hitting his pads with his stick and carrying his face mask. He was the only goalie here who wore a mask.

The American team had a roster that listed five players who were born in Canada. All of them play for teams in the Eastern Hockey League, where Butch plays. Two of them are his Jets teammates.

There was great anticipation as the referee deftly dropped the puck and skated backwards, leaving the center-ice face-off circle. We had no idea what the next sixty minutes of hockey would bring. Our team was favored to win but so were the Dutchmen at Cortina and Squaw Valley when they'd played the Americans. One ring of the puck hitting a goal-post......one deflected shot............another hot goal keeper...............a questionable penalty......could turn expected victory into unexpected, bitter disappointment. Butch had been down that road before.

But as the game unfolded, our fears disappeared. Canada, for the most part, returned to the style of play they seemed to find most effective: fast skating, accurate passing, stellar goal-keeping, and avoiding penalties that resulted from overly aggressive play.

The final result was a convincing 6-1 win. Canada looked like the best team in the tournament—which was what most knowledgeable observers thought. I heard no concerns expressed about rough play, like when we played against the European teams.

That doesn't mean they're complainers. It's just that they play a different style and aren't used to the more rugged North American approach to the game. When some European players had their forward movement thwarted by a defender, they'd often whack their sticks against the boards to get the referee's attention.

But we also know that coming in second place isn't good enough for some Canadians. It is tantamount to losing.

There remains an "If only we'd beaten Sweden" thought that will likely haunt our players and Canadian fans for a long time. So we may hear it again from the sports writers and commentators. Frankly, the players don't know what to expect when they return to Malton Airport. I hope there will be a good sized crowd to welcome them.

As for Butch, there's nothing to say that isn't praiseworthy. He has always said that he plays hockey because he enjoys the game. He's certainly shown that again in Colorado. He gave it his best in every game—just like he always did at the Elmira Arena, Kitchener Auditorium or Galt Arena Gardens. I am very proud of him, as I'm sure his family and the rest of you are. When people ask if he comes from Galt, I quickly and enthusiastically reply, that no, no, no, he's from Floradale! But we need a magnifying glass to find it on the map!

My hope is that should Butch and PeeWee have a family and possibly grandchildren that they will get to read articles and see pictures that will help them appreciate what their father and grandfather accomplished in international hockey—the wonderful people he's met, the sights he's seen, the unusual experiences, the euphoric feeling of winning and the silent loneliness of losing, and becoming a better person for having been a part of it all.

We also want to congratulate the team from Sweden. Their welcome home will be amazing! Manager Gaudette was hoping to arrange an exhibition game with the Swedish team before they left North America. But they had to stay on schedule, so the game won't happen. Stafford Smythe of the Leafs is talking about a possible Canada-Sweden game at Maple Leaf Gardens. That would be great! It's probably a dream, but maybe someday a Swedish player will even play for the Leafs!

We've traveled thousands of miles, slept in a lot of hotels, eaten in many restaurants, met many wonderful people, and played a seemingly endless number of hockey games since that first game in Halifax. We've travelled by almost every imaginable manner. And we've felt the brunt of the continuing Cold War and its effect on international sporting events.

It has been a wonderful and unbelievable experience. I'm glad I made the decision to see Butch more than hold his own among highly acclaimed international players. Watching from outside of the dressing room, I've seen that the glory of winning a medal comes with a lot of hard slugging, extraordinary effort, many personal sacrifices, and a roller coaster of emotions on and off the ice. Some players have struggled with injuries and illnesses, but have motored on. There may be a few players walking with limps as they exit the plane at Malton. From where I sat, every member of Canada's team handled all of the adversity exceptionally well.

It has been a life-changing experience.

Makes me proud to be a Canadian! And yeah, Floradale!

See you soon.
Elam

(The Japanese beat Holland 20-2 in their "B" championship game. About half of their goals came from placing a man in the slot about twenty feet in front of the net—just like coach Roubell drew it on the blackboard! They gave him one of their winner's medals in appreciation.)

AFTERWORD

On June 17, 2014, Robert Ruggle died suddenly, at age eighty-seven. He was the fourth generation owner of Ruggle's General Store in Floradale. He'd sold the store in 2008 to Bonnie Lou Martin.

The United Stated finished in third place in the 1962 IIHF tournament. But it was the beginning of a decline in United States hockey. Its prominence was stunningly regained by the 1980 "Miracle on Ice," a completely unexpected gold medal at the Winter Olympic Games in Lake Placid, New York.

In October of 1964, fifty-seven East German citizens, including three children, escaped to West Berlin through an underground tunnel that started from a home in East Berlin.

In 2014, twenty-three years after the collapse of the Soviet Union and the end of the Cold War, Prime Minister Stephen Harper said, "As unfortunate as it sounds, it's increasingly apparent to me that the Cold War has never left Vladimir Putin's mind: I think he still thinks in those terms."

The governments in Moscow and Prague were in agreement about the boycott of the 1962 tournament, but their relationship would not always be marked with such amity.

Twenty car loads of fans greeted the Terriers on their return to Malton Airport. Manager Gaudette said it felt like the team had won the championship. The reception was totally unexpected and was described as simply wonderful. Galt mayor, E. M. Griffith said, "The citizens of Galt are proud of the honor the team has brought to the city."

A sportswriter from Colorado Springs wrote, "So to hoarse-voiced Roubell and to Butch Martin, who was perhaps the best of the Canucks, and all the rest of them, we say, 'Good try.'"

Len Taylor of The Kitchener-Waterloo Record wrote, "I wonder if Butch's hockey career will last long enough to get a fourth chance to win for Canada. He was Canada's best forward, in our books. If he wants to return home, I hope there is a team in the Twin Cities who can use him."

A Galt reporter wrote, "Butch, who was magnificent and tireless in every game, was the Terriers best two-way forward. He was probably a five-minute major away from being voted the tournament's top forward."

Terrier forwards Bob Mader and Don Rope announced their retirements at the conclusion of the 1961-62 season, capping off outstanding careers in the OHA Senior A league.

Butch's Terrier teammate Harry Neale went on to coach the Buckeyes Hockey Team at Ohio State University. Later, he was coach of the NHL's Vancouver Canucks for six years. Previous to the NHL job, Neale coached in the World Hockey Association for seven seasons. In 1986 he began a career in broadcasting as color man with Bob Cole for NHL games. They broadcast twenty Stanley Cup finals. On June 11, 2013, Neale was presented as winner of the Foster Hewitt Memorial Award by the Hockey Hall of Fame. Known for his witty comments, in the 1981-82 season with the Canucks, he said, "Last season we couldn't win at home. This season we can't win on the road. My failure as a coach is I can't think of any place else to play."

Thayer Tutt died on June 2, 1988, in Colorado Springs. A new World Arena was built in 1998.

THE GOOD THE BAD AND THE UGLY
JOHNSTOWN

At the conclusion of the 1962 IIHF tournament, Butch returned to the Eastern Hockey League Johnstown Jets and their home, the four-thousand-seat Cambria War Memorial Arena. Under playing coach Steve Brklacich, the Jets won the Eastern League championship and the Atlantic City Boardwalk Trophy. They defeated the Greensboro Generals 4-1 in the final series. It was the Jets' third straight championship.

The Jets were managed by the spirited, gregarious, enthusiastic and vociferous John Mitchell. He'd been the Detroit Red Wings chief scout for many years before joining Johnstown, a Red Wings farm team.

In the 1961-62 season, the Jets Ken Laufman totaled 128 scoring points. Butch had thirty-seven goals and forty-one assists. Both were league all stars. It was the last season that the two ex-Dutchmen teammates played on the same team. Laufman moved to the Portland Buckaroos of the Western Hockey League, where his scoring prowess continued.

The Johnstown Tribune-Democrat newspaper referred to Butch: "Martin was rated among Canada's top amateurs. His speed, agility, and durability are that of a much younger player."

The Johnstown Jets played in the old Eastern Hockey League. Contained in the league's intriguing history is a deluge of stories that were generated by occurrences among its players and its fans, culminated in the release of the 1977 movie Slap Shot.

The Cambridge War Memorial Arena, where Butch played with the Jets was the site of all the hockey action in the movie. Sports Illustrated rated Slap Shot as one of the top ten sports movies. Former long time Detroit Red Wing player and Galt native Kirk Maltby said of Slap Shot, "In junior, I think it was probably on the television every bus trip we ever took."

Slap Shot was chosen to close the Cannes film festival on May 27, 1977. At the conclusion of the screening, there was a brief pause, followed by polite applause. Famed actor Paul Newman starred as coach Reggie Dunlop of the Charlestown Chiefs hockey team whose home rink was the Cambridge War Memorial Arena.

Asked whether Slap Shot presented an accurate picture of the EHL, Butch replied, "It was a little exaggerated. But it was pretty close." Regis Philbin, popular American morning show host, said of Slap Shot, "If that was what hockey had come to, Idi Amin should be its commissioner and Adolph Hitler and Joseph Stalin should be resurrected to settle WWIII on the ice."

The Eastern Amateur Hockey League had begun in 1933 because of the initiatives of Thomas Lockhart, a Madison Square Garden promoter who had a keen feel for publicity. He promised the league that he'd have three teams calling the Gardens home on Sunday afternoons. A problem arose when the three teams needed forty-eight Sunday afternoon home dates, but there were only sixteen available. So Lockhart made up phony games and published the game reports in the newspaper. He'd put down somebody's name for scoring a goal and add an assist or two. In the 1933 program he printed the following—

"Extra Games Will Be Played At The Assigned Practice Hours At The Gardens And Will Not Be Open To The Public." The league completed its schedule and the playoffs.

The EAHL was exceedingly popular. Fans could purchase a ticket to a game at Madison Square Gardens for twenty-five cents.

Lockhart excelled at publicity stunts. In the 1930s he hired Olympic

Figure Skating champion Sonja Henie to perform between hockey periods. He also booked an ice-skating grizzly bear as entertainment. The bear was used to roller skates so Garden staff had to locate ice skates to fit his huge paws. The bear's owner guided him on a leash. Suddenly the bear took off and dragged his owner from around the ice. The fans were enthralled!

By 1953 the EHL appeared to be gasping for air. Teams in New York, Boston, Atlantic City, and Washington were in dire financial straits. There was also a new team in Johnstown, Pennsylvania—the Jets. The team had been started by former NHL player Wally Kilrea and made up of free agents and cast-offs from former EAHL teams. By the 1954-55 season the league had three full-time and two part-time teams. The EAHL was reborn as the Eastern Hockey League.

It was in the "old" EHL where Butch played for the Johnstown Jets, one year as a player and two as a player-coach. A sportswriter for the Johnstown Tribune-Democrat warned him that the EHL was full of outstanding players trailing off drastically when elevated to the coaching rank.

Especially in his final year, Butch cut back on his playing time, giving a large crop of younger players more opportunity for to gain experience and develop. Butch said, "The young guys had the desire and the ability to win."

Butch was an all-star each of his three years with the Jets.

Much has been written about happenings in the league, most of it dwelling on its most colorful characters: the goons. Team owners said every team needed at least one "animal." There were fights on the ice, fights in the stands and occasionally fights among players and fans. But there were also many skilled players who stuck to hockey. We would do a discredit to the league and those players if they were left out of the conversation. Ken Laufman is likely the prime example of such a player. However, there were also very good young players who picked up and returned home, in some cases opting to go to school full time, rather than risking intimidation and injury.

The old EHL mainly gained its notoriety from the sometimes vicious, sometimes bizarre actions of the guys who came to fight.

Chuck Miller, highly respected author and photographer from Albany, New York published a two-part article on the EHL, entitled "From Atlantic City to Toronto." The sub-title of part two is: "The Jets, the Comets, Southern Expansion and Well-Worn Knuckles." Miller spoke to EHL players who played in the 1960s in researching his articles. That was the era in which Butch was a Johnstown Jet.

Miller's articles provide the context and the experiences, many of which Butch encountered in various degrees.

"Travel in the Eastern League was an arduous endeavor in the 1960s with the league expanding ever southward to include the Nashville Dixie Flyers, Knoxville Knights, Greensboro Generals, Jacksonville Rockets, and St. Petersburg Suns. So buses were used. Teams travelled all day and night, ripping out seats in the back of the bus so players could sleep on mattresses. They might drive for a day and a half nonstop. Two drivers would take turns at the wheel. Sometimes a coach or manager drove to help out.

"A player would ride all night and still put his all into a game, trying to score goals around a league of enforcers, policemen—in other words goons. The goons usually fought each other. But often they were vicious fights. Players played every game, never sitting out with a separated shoulder or a bum knee. The only time you missed a game in the old Eastern League was if they had to cut your leg off and it took them one day to get you a new one. So you missed the game that night. The Eastern League was the enforcer's breeding ground and players moved from it to the NHL with bruised knuckles and black eyes. Imagine yourself as an Eastern League centre on a road trip. Your first stop is New Haven, and Blake Ball is on defense for the Blades. Ball spent six years as a defensive end in the Canadian Football League before taking up hockey professionally and accumulating twelve-hundred penalty minutes in four seasons. Now you are at the Long Island Arena where John Brophy holds court. Brophy led the EHL in penalty minute four times between 1960 and 1965—each time with a different team. Once he was suspended for half a season for knocking down a referee. Now for a southern swing to Knoxville and player-coach Don Labelle. He was so tough, they once said that during a playoff game it took three Nashville skaters to take him out of the game—and that was when Labelle was in street clothes and behind the bench. Back through Clinton—and there's Indian Joe Nolan, a full-blood Ojibway from Sault Ste. Marie who never met a forward he didn't like—to break in half. Later Nolan became a respected linesman.

The Commack Arena on Long Island was a tough one to play in. The worst part was that you used to come down one end of the building, and the dressing room was all the way down at the other end. So you had to walk between the stands. Many nights the players walked back to back so the fans wouldn't take punches at them. One night in New Haven, something happened, and all of a sudden chairs come flying out on the ice with fourteen visiting team players trying to dodge them. Some nights at the Clinton Arena players would pick up chairs and throw them back into the crowd."

A Johnstown sports writer said that the New Haven arena "was one of the darkest, dingiest, most ominous hockey palaces the sport has ever known." In a comment that would leave him seeking a new job in 2014, he said, "The Blades' wives looked tougher than our team."

On Friday, November 22, 1963, all EHL teams and their fans observed a moment of silence in honor of United States President John F. Kennedy who had been assassinated in Dallas, Texas earlier that day.

The Commack Arena was so cold one night, that the fans lit a bonfire to keep warm. On one occasion the Long Island Ducks got to New Haven just before game time. The equipment guy didn't have a chance to wash their uniforms. So they started the game with a big brawl.

Butch survived. He said, "There were a lot of crazy guys."

The Tribune Democrat referred to it as "a battle unmatched in Johnstown's fourteen-year history." It took place on February 15, 1964. Only a second remained in a game between Butch's Jets and John Brophy's Philadelphia Ramblers team, coached by future NHL coach and manager, John Muckler. The teams lined up for a face-off, considered in most games a brief formality. The Jets were leading 5-0.

The newspaper report said that instead of going for the puck, Brophy deliberately injured Jets defenseman and former Waterloo Siskin, Larry Johnston, by spearing him in the right eye. The two swung their sticks at each other. A general melee followed with a Long Island player coming from the penalty box and striking a Jets player over the head with his stick. There were no helmets in those days. What followed was chaotic, with multiple fights and stick-swinging. Johnston had returned to the Jets bench but jumped onto the ice again to "successfully" get at Brophy, resulting in facial cuts that left him looking like "a bloody mess." The chaos lasted about twenty minutes.

Ron Howell who Butch knew well played for the Philadelphia team. As the stick-swinging continued, he skated to center ice and waved to have Butch join him. Howell said, "Come out to the centre circle, Butch. These guys are crazy. Don't go over to the bench; you'll get hit by a stick." So the friends talked things over calmly as the melee continued.

The Jets were assessed twenty-five minutes in penalties; the Ducks eighty.

Following the game, the referee filed a charge against Long Island coach Muckler for encouraging his players to continue fighting, and for verbal abuse of the referee. Brophy received a suspension.

Butch said that the next Jets home game against the Ramblers team was sold out days before it took place. The fans were anticipating a rematch of the earlier battle. But as is often the case in such instances, it was one of the tamest games of the season.

During his time with the Jets, Butch suffered a broken nose as the result of a high stick from Brophy.

Once, on his way to the ice for a pre-game warm-up, Brophy leaned into the opposition team's dressing room and said, "Don't consider this a threat, boys, but I'm coming after each one of you."

Brophy, the intense competitor, eventually coached the Toronto Maple Leafs for two seasons during the era of Harold Ballard. He is second to the great Scotty Bowman in total games coached in professional hockey. Muckler was involved with professional hockey for over fifty years, including thirteen years as a player in the old Eastern Hockey League. He was a part of five Stanley Cup championship teams, in various roles.

Brophy's comments about Slap Shot were, "They got it down to a tee. That's the way minor league hockey was played in those days. From the bus trips to the brawls, there were some pretty wild times,"

In November 1963, Butch scored four goals in a league game against the Ramblers. Pat Quinn, who would become a player, coach and executive in the NHL, played for the Knoxville Knights in the EHL. Former Leaf goalie Turk Broda coached the Charlotte Checkers.

In 1963, EHL president Lockhart invited the Soviet Union to send their Olympic hockey team to come to the United States for five games against EHL teams. One of the games was against the Johnstown Jets, in Butch's first year as player-coach.

Butch was finishing some business at the Jets home arena when he heard his name called from down the hallway that he'd entered. The voice sounded familiar, as did its accompanying accent. As he approached the man who had called his name, Butch was somewhat taken aback; he was a short distance from the iconic Soviet hockey coach Anatoli Tarasov. He'd met Tarasov on numerous previous occasions at international tournaments and games. The coach was in Johnstown with his Soviet national team to play against Butch and his Jets. He inquired if Butch might consider accompanying his team on a tour of the city, something he gladly took on.

Butch had played well over a dozen times against Soviet teams. But having Tarasov as his rival coach, in a game in which Butch would also play, was very special. Johnstown thought it was special too.

On the night of December 21, 1963 a full house, filled with anticipation, but unsure of what to expect from their Jets, weren't greatly concerned when the Soviets scored the first goal. But by the time the first intermission arrived, some had left the building, frightened to guess what the end result might be.

Also, Jets fans, who liked their hockey rough and tumble, had to be content with international rules that didn't allow body checking in the offensive zone. It appeared that the Jets took some time to get used to that change as well.

The Soviets, always on the attack, relentless in skating, precision-like in passing, scored eight unanswered goals in the first twenty minutes. Discouraged, but not deflated, Butch led the charge with two goals as his team played much stronger second and third periods. The final score was 9-6 for Tarasov's team, a respectable result given the Jets' precarious start to the game.

The Soviet team went on to take Olympic gold at the 1964 Winter Games in Innsbruck, Austria, winning all seven games. Tarosov developed and coached remarkably skilled players. Among them were Boris Mikhailov, Valeri Kharlamov, and Alexander Maltsev. He was the biggest factor in the development of Vladislav Tretiak, considered the best Soviet goalie of all time. In 1974 Anatoli Tarasov was inducted into the Hockey Hall of Fame as a builder. He was the first Soviet so honored.

Tarasov, as coach of the Soviet National team, believed strongly that egotism on the ice was the gravest of all sins. Martin, player-coach of the Johnstown Jets, fully supported and lived that statement throughout his career.

On New Year's Eve of 1963, coach Eddie Jeremiah and the United States National Hockey Team visited Cambria County War Memorial Arena to meet the Jets. The Americans were considered a dark horse at the Winter Games of 1964 that would begin twenty-nine days later.

The Johnstown Tribune-Democrat's report on the game noted, "The usually quiet Butch Martin was doing an unusually loud amount of coaching from the coach's box. The coach also gave a two-hander across the back of an American player after he'd been high-sticked in front of the U.S.A net." The Jets led the EHL by eleven points. Their good play continued in beating the Americans 4-2.

In the 1962-63 season, the Jets lost in the first round of the playoffs. Butch's season statistics were a very impressive forty-four goals and sixty-five assists. Although cutting down his playing time considerably in the following season, his totals were thirty goals and sixty-five assists. The Jets lost to Greensboro Generals in the second round of the playoffs.

Butch played five games with the Pittsburgh Hornets of the American Hockey League. The Hornets and the Jets were both part of the Detroit Red Wings farm system. Butch had a two-week stay at a Red Wings training camp getting acquainted with the people with whom he'd interact as a coach of a Red Wing development team.

Elmira resident Don Duke, and St. Jacobs native Dave Garner played games with the Jets under Butch's coaching. Bob Ertel, also of Elmira, played with the EHL's New Haven Blades for three full seasons and part of a fourth, all during Butch's time with the Jets. NHL goalies Ed Johnston, Marv Edwards and Joe Daley all had stints with Johnstown.

In the 1963-64 season, Butch's last in Johnstown, the Jets' Larry Johnston set a team penalty record of 405 minutes. The ex-Waterloo Siskin, to the surprise of many, spent almost five full seasons with the Detroit Red Wings, Kansas City Scouts, and Colorado Rockies of the National Hockey League.

But bigger than any goal he'd scored or medal he'd received was the news Butch got on Tuesday, November 12, 1963, when he returned to his upstairs Johnstown apartment after a Jets game. Slipped under his door was a note telling him that his wife PeeWee had given birth to a beautiful daughter.

The following Saturday his Jets played in New York and Butch came home to be with his wife, and for the first time hold his precious infant daughter, Kelly.

When Butch returned to Johnstown, seven-year-old Kevin, the team manager's son, presented him with a sawed-off hockey stick that he'd worked on for a week. It was a gift for Kelly, the new and warmly welcomed addition to the Martin family.

At the end of the 1963-64 season, Butch returned to Ontario, with an additional important reason to be home.

Kelly says, Before I was born, my parents were living in Floradale with Pop and the family, near the sawmill. Dad had gotten a contract with the Johnstown Jets, which meant he moved to the United States to play. Mom was working at Uniroyal in Elmira, so she stayed behind. But every Friday night she would drive by herself to the Buffalo airport to catch plane to Johnstown. In those days women didn't really venture out on their own. But PeeWee was dad's biggest fan, so never missed a game. Each Sunday she would be back on the plane to Canada, drive back to Floradale, and be at work on Monday to again become the "voice of Uniroyal." Their dedication to each other, to their work and their families was instilled in me from an early age.I remember talking to my mom in later years, when I was expecting twins, and asked if dad had been there when I was born. She said, "No Kelly, he was playing in Johnstown and couldn't come home." Then she smiled and said, "You really should have dual citizenship you know, because you were American-made but Canadian-born."

My dad didn't get to see me until I was ten days old. It was the day of my dedication at First Mennonite Church in Kitchener. Apparently Dad had never held something so small in those big paws of his. Mom and Dad stood before Reverend Johnston for my dedication, with Dad holding me tight. Apparently I had grabbed hold of his tie and pulled. This action tightened the tie around his neck. He never said a word. According to my aunts, "Floyd was so proud that day, his face was flush with excitement." Whether it was excitement or the choking effect, Butch had bonded with his little girl.

BLADES TO GLORY
THE KITCHENER RANGERS

In 1963, the New York Rangers were concerned about the financial situation with its Junior A operation in Guelph, the Guelph Royals (formerly the Biltmores). Application for a Junior A team in Kitchener was made by a committee headed up by Clarence D. (Buller) Pequegnat. Former Dutchmen coach Bobby Bauer and manager Ernie Goman were also members. The Royal's team was relocated to Kitchener and shortly thereafter became the Kitchener Rangers Hockey Club.

Kitchener had had Junior A hockey teams previously. The Kitchener Greenshirts played from 1922-38, and from 1951-54. The Boston Bruins Hall of Fame Kraut Line of Bobby Bauer, Woody Dumart, and Milt Schmidt played with the Greenshirts during the 1922-38 era. The Junior A Kitchener Canucks of which Elmira's Ab Martin was a member, had the Kitchener Auditorium as their home from 1954-56.

In their initial season of 1963-64 the Rangers were coached by Steve Brklacich, the player-coach of the Johnstown Jets during Butch's first year with the team. The Rangers ended the season with nine wins, forty-one losses and six ties. It placed them last in a league of eight teams.

Brklacich was let go and the Rangers coaching job was offered to Butch by Rangers General-Manager Brent Madill. Butch signed a two-year contract and was back in the Auditorium, the site of his glory days with the Dutchmen.

Butch said, "It is good to be home and close to my wife, and my baby daughter, Kelly. And then there are the bus trips. It's got to be better up here. The longest ride is Montreal. Down in Johnstown the only trip shorter than the one from Kitchener to Montreal was to Philadelphia. I'm going to miss playing, but so far I've enjoyed standing at center ice blowing the whistle."

The Kitchener-Waterloo Record staff wrote, "If Martin can get the Rangers to play the style of hockey he displayed while a member of the Dutchmen, then his team will be destined for great things. Martin was one of the best two-way performers in these parts in the last decade."

When Butch stood behind the Rangers bench at the Kitchener Auditorium, he was taking on a role that was a first for him. In Johnstown he'd played as well as coached. Here, coaching was his sole responsibility, his full-time job.

He'd sat on the bench in front of him, next to the ice at the Auditorium for dozens of games. Frequently he was tapped on the shoulder to go out on a power play or kill a penalty by Dutchmen coaches Bill Durnan or Bobby Bauer. But now he was doing the tapping. This was his opportunity to explore coaching as his next step in his hockey career. It also put him back into the New York Rangers organization, where he'd been as a Guelph Biltmore.

Butch coached the Rangers in their second year, when the club was struggling, coming off a tough season. He was helping put the building blocks in place for a franchise that grew into one of the most successful in the OHA Junior A League. The Rangers would win their first Memorial Cup eighteen years later.

The young men before him were all hoping to find their way to the NHL with only positions on six teams available. Butch did his best to have them land a spot in the lineup of the New York Rangers, the team with whom he could have played had circumstances been different in his life. Emil "The Cat" Francis was the newly appointed manager of the NHL Rangers. Red Sullivan was their coach.

Elmira's Rod Seiling played his first of ten years with the NHL Rangers in 1964-65. Rod's grandfather Ab was on the executive of the Elmira Polar Kings when, with Butch as captain, when they won the OHA Intermediate B championship. Rod's impressive NHL career as a defenseman spanned sixteen years.

Butch experienced some major losses before the Junior A season began. On June 5, his father Seranus died at the age of seventy-six. Pop Martin had lived a good life as a loving father and successful businessman. With his quiet, reassuring and calm demeanor he garnered great respect from his family, church and business communities in Waterloo County.

On September 16, Bobby Bauer, the man whom Butch greatly admired and who had had a major influence in his life from his days with the Guelph Biltmores and the glory years of the Dutchmen, died suddenly of a massive heart-attack. He was forty-nine years old. The Kitchener-Waterloo Record printed pages filled with tributes to the former great hockey player, great coach and great man. One came from NHL President, Clarence Campbell, another from Woody Dumart, Bobby's linemate on the famed Boston Bruin Kraut Line.

Sports reporter, Len Taylor said of Bauer, "He gave us a belief in the rational man and the proof of the effect of a sane argument. He felt the results of 'Lady Luck' but wasn't disposed to alibi. He was simply an outstanding human being."

Both his father Seranus and coach Bauer made important impacts on Butch, as a man, and as a man who played hockey.

As the Rangers season began in October 1964, the small community of Listowel, thirty minutes west of the Kitchener Auditorium, opened the doors to its new arena. Five years earlier, the previous arena's roof collapsed from a buildup of snow. Seven hockey players, aged ten, eleven, and twelve, and the town's recreation director were killed. Almost an entire team of equally young players were in an adjoining dressing room, and blessedly were unscathed by the tragedy.

The pursuit of the league championship or Memorial Cup wasn't a realistic goal for the Rangers of 1964-65. But the team was competitive and boasted some individuals who were top performers. A regular league game attracted around three thousand fans. Fifty years later, the Rangers of 2014 always played at home in front of more than seven thousand fans. But they too were in a rebuilding phase.

The play-by-play radio voice of the Rangers in 1964 was Don Cameron, on Kitchener station CKCR. Cameron arrived in Kitchener in 1958. One of his most cherished times was broadcasting reports back to Kitchener from the 1960 Winter Olympics at Squaw Valley. In 2014 the seemingly ever-youthful, ever-enthusiastic Cameron still broadcast Rangers games over 570 News radio. In fifty years of broadcasting, his excellence in his craft remained strong.

Hamilton's CHCH television station broadcast all the Red Wings home games, which meant it was a time for young men to get new skate laces and have well-groomed hair.

Butch's Rangers captain was Alex "Sandy" Fitzpatrick, born in Paisley, Scotland, where Butch and the Dutchmen had played their first exhibition game on their way to Cortina. On this developing Ranger team, Fitzpatrick scored a remarkable fifty-one goals. He eventually played twenty-two games in the NHL.

The most popular player on Butch's Rangers was Gary Sabourin, who later spent eight years with the St. Louis Blues and Toronto Maple Leafs. Butch also helped in the development of sixteen-year old defenseman, Mike Robitaille. He stayed three full seasons with the Rangers before moving on to the NHL where he played 382 games for four different teams.

But the brightest light in the Ranger's organization was a "scrawny kid" who, at sixteen, with determination and hockey smarts, was making a surprising impression with Kitchener's Junior B Greenshirts. Butch was able to call him up to the Rangers for seven games.

The kid's name was Walt Tkaczuk. He would become the first German-born player in the NHL. In the 1967-68 season, Tkaczuk was awarded the Red Tilson Trophy as the Junior A League's Most Valuable Player. He spent fourteen years with the New York Rangers and two years as that team's assistant coach. His minor hockey team coaches would never have predicted success of that proportion.

Butch's 1964-65 Rangers were in a league with the Niagara Falls Flyers, Toronto Marlboros, Peterborough Petes, Oshawa Generals, Montreal Junior Canadiens, St. Catharines Black Hawks and Hamilton Red Wings. The league, with an abundance of talented players, was literally a dress rehearsal for the NHL. The Canadiens coach was William "Scotty" Bowman, who went on to coach in the NHL from 1967-2002, winning eight Stanley Cups.

Bobby Orr totaled ninety-three scoring points for the Oshawa Generals in the 1964-65 season. In his book "ORR" he clearly explains a young hockey player's introduction to high level competition like the OHA Junior A League. He writes, "One of the hardest parts of becoming a hockey player is leaving home. Think of yourself as a fifteen- or sixteen-year-old packing a suitcase and heading off to a strange city. You end up billeted in the home of a complete stranger, attending a school you've never heard of. The group of friends, the pack of wolves you've grown up with suddenly vanishes. The safety net of friends you've come to depend on is replaced by strange faces in the hallways of your new high school. You're playing for a new hockey team in a huge, unfamiliar rink, being cheered or booed by people you don't know. You're traveling from town to town. You've got bigger, older guys needling you every night, trying to get you to drop your gloves, trying to see what you're made of."

Orr was fourteen when playing as a rookie for the Oshawa Generals. Without the junior draft there was great advantage to getting to really good young players early. But it was only through the persistence and salesmanship of Wren Blair that Orr signed with the Generals and became part of the Bruins organization. Blair's frequent stops at the Orr home in Parry Sound aided his cause. Butch and the Rangers met Orr when he was sixteen.

Junior A players, in the 1964-65 season received a stipend of forty dollars a week.

Butch signed an A form with the New York Rangers in his final year as a junior in Guelph. Orr signed a C form, which completely assigned his rights to the Bruins.

In Butch's one season of coaching the Rangers, the Toronto Marlboros' young defensemen Jim McKenny was considered the second best defense prospect after Orr. Some expected him to be as big a star. McKenny played for the Leafs for almost eight years. Peter Mahovlich, a Hamilton Red Wing, went on to a sixteen-year NHL career. Jacques Lemaire of the Junior Canadiens went on to a Hall of Fame twelve-year career with the parent Montreal Canadiens. Lemaire's Junior Canadiens teammate Serge Savard spent seventeen years with the Canadiens, also on his way to the Hall of Fame.

But the Junior A season of 1964-65 belonged to the Niagara Falls Flyers, coached by the iconic Leighton "Happy" Emms. The Emms family moved their Barrie Junior A Flyers to Niagara Falls in 1960 and retained ownership.

Emms played as a professional hockey player for more than fifteen years. He spent eight years as coach of the Barrie team and in 1964-65 was in his fifth season as coach and owner of the Niagara Falls Flyers. He was General Manager of the Boston Bruins from 1965-67. Before the start of the 1966-67 season he promoted Butch's teammate on the 1960 Dutchmen Olympic team, Harry Sinden, to be coach of the Bruins.

All but three members of the 1964-5 Flyers team impressively graduated to the NHL. One of those three played in the World Hockey Association. The Rangers faced a Flyers roster with future NHL stars such as Jean Pronovost, Bernie Parent, Rick Ley, Bill Goldsworthy, Don Marcotte, and Derek Sanderson. Predictably, Emms' team won the league championship although the Marlies were a formidable opponent. The Flyers went on to win the 1964-65 Memorial Cup, defeating the Edmonton Oil Kings in the championship series. It was the Kings' sixth straight appearance in the finals. The 2014 Oil Kings defeated the Guelph Storm to win the Memorial Cup.

The Rangers got their first win of the season against stars Danny Grant and Mickey Redmond and their team, the Peterborough Petes.

By November of 1964, the Rangers followed up a three-game winning streak with a close 4-2 loss to the powerful Marlies. Future Leaf Brit Selby was the Marlies; top goal scorer, and Brian Glennie, also destined for the Leafs, helped McKenny anchor the defense.

On Friday, October 16, 1964, the Ranger Blue Line Club hosted a Butch Martin Night at a reception after his team played the St. Catharines' Black Hawks. Butch was honored and thanked for his accomplishments in hockey both locally and internationally.

By February 1965, the Rangers were battling the Black Hawks for the sixth and final playoff spot. On February 6 a season-high crowd of 4200 watched the Rangers as they hosted the Marlies. The Blue Line Club had a special recognition of former Dutchmen players and officials including Butch.

In the closely contested game, a shot by the Rangers' Ken Gratton was indicated as a goal by the goal judge but was ruled no goal by referee Hugh McLean. The technology for replays hadn't yet arrived. McLean's unpopular ruling was met with a chorus of boos and with debris thrown onto the ice by the angered fans. McLean was hit on the head by a bag of peanuts. In a fit of anger, the goal-judge stormed off from his post behind the goal and was replaced by a substitute. No one had previously seen such a pronounced reaction from a game official.

On February 9, the Rangers hosted the powerful Happ Emms-coached Niagara Falls Flyers who were in a battle for first place with the Marlies. in what was considered an upset, Butch's team was victorious by a 7-5 final score. The Flyers coach wasn't happy as his team really needed the two points that a victory would bring.

Emms made an official protest to the OHA on the grounds that H. M. Bob Crosby used language that had a detrimental effect on his Flyers players. Crosby had no connection to the Rangers other than in his role as manager of the Auditorium. He'd gone to the penalty box area and reportedly used obscene language directed at the penalized Flyers players, although he denied the accusation. It was considered one of the most unusual protests in the history of the league, and no disciplinary action was taken.

Between the first and second periods of a Ranger game on February 22, 1965, Kitchener resident John Sehaure accomplished a feat of some historical significance. For the first time since the beginning of the season, the puck he shot from center ice entered the small opening in a board covering the front of the net. His reward was a jackpot of $110. Fifty years later the size of the hole appeared to have remained unchanged but participants could shoot from the blue line, thus closer to the net,

On March 5, the Rangers were officially eliminated from playoff contention in a 5-3 loss to the St. Catharines Black Hawks. They finished with nineteen wins, thirty-two losses and five ties. That was a ten-win improvement over the previous season, but not good enough to retain Butch as coach.

BIRTH OF A SALESMAN

A week later, Orr Automobile, with locations on King Street in Waterloo and Weber Street in Kitchener, introduced Butch as the newest member of their sales staff. Under his picture in The Record were these words, "Butch is looking forward to seeing all his friends and to be of service to you in choosing a new or used car or truck. Come in and see him soon." James Orr was the owner if the dealership, which was eventually taken over by his son, James. Vince Scherer was the vice president at Orr—and was also ticket chairman for the Rangers hockey team.

Ironically, four years earlier, Scherer had arranged to have a group picture taken in front of an Orr business building. The group of thirteen, all members of the Dutchmen Blue Line Club supporters, were preparing to travel together to Squaw Valley. Standing beside Scherer's wife Anne in the photo was PeeWee Martin. Neither she nor any other supporter could have predicted that in four years Scherer would offer her husband a job at his company. Nor could she foresee that Butch would become one of the automobile company's top salesmen.

The Martins and the Scherers became lifelong friends.

On April 10, 1965, the first Elmira Maple Syrup Festival was held. Organizers were expecting two thousand visitors. Over ten thousand showed up. By the year 2000 the Festival was in the Guinness Book of World Records as the World's Largest Single Day Maple Syrup Festival, with an attendance approaching seventy thousand.

By 1965, eighty thousand people in the area of Kitchener-Waterloo could, for the first time, dial long distance directly to anywhere in North America. Trump cigars sold for five for twenty-five cents at the Walper Tobacco Shop on King Street in downtown Kitchener.

In 1965 Orr sold and serviced Chevrolet, Oldsmobile and Cadillac cars. Butch's hiring was a very astute move for the company. It was also a tremendous opportunity for him. When his picture appeared in The Record announcing his hiring, he was immediately recognized by thousands of people who'd seen him play hockey or heard about his experiences in international tournaments and games. They'd never read a write-up or commentary that had anything but praise for him for what he'd done on the ice. His coaches trusted him. He could be relied on to give a consistent effort regardless of the circumstances. He performed for the success of the team, not in a pretentious style. And, regardless of his sports successes, he'd remained grounded as a regular hometown guy.

That was the Butch Martin that people who dropped by Orr knew they'd see and who they could trust in negotiating the purchase of a vehicle. His excellent reputation preceded him to the showroom. Orr was a success story in the world of automobile sales in Waterloo County. With Butch on board, their reputation and sales potential were instantly enhanced.

In 1965 Canada and the United States signed the Automotive Products Trade Agreement. The agreement removed tariffs on automobiles and parts. Companies like General Motors increased their production capacity dramatically. Thousands of jobs were created. In Canada, the automotive industry replaced pulp and paper as the backbone of the economy.

In 1965, a Waterloo County couple could proudly drive off Orr's lot in an Oldsmobile Cutlass purchased from Butch for around $3500 plus five percent sales tax. Their appearance that evening at Preston's Leisure Lodge for a one-time Tommy Dorsey Big Band concert no doubt turned heads.

Advertisers of the Cadillac of the 1960s used phrases like: "Cadillac elegance," "Precision engineering," "Most distinguished car in the world," and "Stylish, luxury finish," One commercial for the car said it "will call up in us a rare and pleasant emotion." Elvis Presley drove his famous pink Cadillac and gave Cadillacs away to his family and friends. By 1965 the car's famously long rear fins had pretty much disappeared. Butch sold such a car for around five thousand dollars.

In 1965 only fifteen percent of women purchased cars. Toyota introduced two models to North America in the same year and sold only 755 of them.

A popular television commercial for General Motors line of Chevrolet cars in 1965 featured Lorne Green, Dan Blocker, Michael Landon and the remainder of the cast of the wildly popular television series Bonanza. The show told the story of Ben Cartwright and his sons as they defended their ranch and helped the surrounding community.

In 1965 Butch was a rookie car salesman with no experience or training in sales. His career lasted forty-five years at the same dealership.

Waterloo resident Tom Schnurr worked in the same car showroom as Butch for all but three of those years. Tom had changed careers as well, moving to Orr from a Dutch Boy Food Store in the Twin Cities.

In 1990, Orr Automobile was sold to the Stedelbauer family and the company took on the new ownership's name. Their permanent home was 20 Ottawa Street North in Kitchener. Company president William Stedelbauer remained in the General Motors family and continued sales of Chevrolet, Oldsmobile and Cadillac.

Butch and Tom were members of a staff of ten salesmen, under the supervision of Wayne Martin, who was vice-president and general manager of the dealership.

Butch had earned his reputation from playing hockey. His colleague and friend Tom wasn't a hockey guy but the two became close friends in business and in life. They were the top salesmen at Stedelbauer for many years. Their customers tended to stay with one dealership, and Butch and Tom had many repeat purchasers. They regularly coached buyers in moving up in car models.

Schnurr experienced Butch as a fairly quiet and reserved man. Interestingly, their many conversations seldom included hockey. But he suggested to Butch that he should bring his Olympic medals in to work. Butch's reply was that he wasn't even sure where he'd put them. Eventually he stored them in a glass jar. A close friend of Butch built a plaque on which he could display his medals and awards.

It was Kelly who felt the need to preserve Butch's photos, medals and news stories.

Tom and Butch were "old school" in their vocation. The usual shift for sales staff was from 9:00 a.m. to around 2:30 p.m. but Butch and Tom knew they couldn't make a fulltime wage from what they considered to be a part-time job. Regularly they put in sixty hours a week, often working three evenings a week. "Getting to the top of the sales board didn't just happen," says Schnurr.

Butch didn't leave his competitive spirit on the ice—it came into the vehicle showroom. He did what he had to do in order to get the last few car sales that would make him the #1 salesman or bring him an award from General Motors or the dealership. Schnurr felt the heat of the competition but it never negatively affected their relationship.

In forty-two years, Butch never broached the topic of his missed opportunity to play in the NHL. But there were hints, however small, says Schnurr, that it might have been a decision about which he had a measure of regret.

Neither was Butch's Mennonite upbringing and its effect on his life and career brought up as something detrimental. "There was no woe is me," said Schnurr.

Butch was happy in his new job and ecstatic about his young daughter. He famously said, "We're not going to spoil Kelly. We're just going to give her anything she wants."

Kelly picks up the story: My mother was the youngest child of Vietta and Elmer Gerber. She had a brother, Stewart, and was also blessed to have a sister, Doreen. With the family moving often, the fellowship of the church was a constant connection for the children. The girls began singing in the choir, and soon found a regular spot in the Sunday services, with Doreen singing soprano and PeeWee singing alto.I remember many Sunday mornings when i was a young girl. We would make our way to First Mennonite Church and walk to a pew on the left at the front. There I would stand for every hymn, in between the hockey player and the woman with the beautiful voice. Before the second song ended, Mom gave Dad "the eyes" and he would stop singing. She loved music and she sang beautifully. One winter afternoon a monster snowstorm hit the Region of Waterloo. Stedelbauer closed at noon. Schnurr invited the sales staff to his home. The guys relaxed, swapped stories and had a few beers. By midnight everyone was on their way to their homes.

By the next morning the severity of the snowstorm had diminished considerably and the sales staff at 20 Ottawa Street all reported to work. Butch pulled his buddy aside and told him that on the way home the previous night his car wheel had caught a rut well off the pavement. In the ensuing moments, he had ended up being trapped in his vehicle. Fortunately, a concerned and kindly woman had stopped to assist, and had driven him home.

By the time he reported to work the next morning, Butch remained shaken by the incident. He said, "I could have killed someone and that someone could have been me." He continued. "You know, Tom, I never had a drop of booze for the first twenty-five years of my life. If I didn't drink then, I probably can make it through the next twenty-five without taking a drink." Schnurr has no doubt that Butch kept his promise.

Kelly says, As the daughter of a Grand Sales master, our family reaped the benefits of many contests my father would win. There were new gadgets like color television sets, tickets to Rangers games, and trips. Houghton Rust Control did a lot of business with Orr Automobiles in the mid-seventies. Russ and Jean Houghton had a contest with the grand prize being a trip to Montreal to see the Leafs play the Habs. All an Orr salesman had to do was sell the most undercoating on new cars.

I didn't know about the contest at the time, until Butch was proclaimed the winner. The trip included a train ride to Montreal, tickets to the game, and staying at a hotel across from the famous Bon-Adventure Underground Shopping Mall. I thought my parents had won the lottery!

I was sitting in school on the day my parents planned to leave. I was called to the office and I wondered why. I was a good girl and feared the office, as most kids did. My dad greeted me, "Your mother can't go today. What do you say, want to come along?"

"But I have school," was my reply. "Not if you say yes," was his.

In two short hours I was packed and sitting at a window seat, embarking not only on my first train ride, but my first weekend alone with my dad. Butch had been a great dad, attending all my plays and concerts, coming home from work early to teach me how to throw a baseball—but this was different. For the first time my mother wasn't along. She was the one who soothed me when I was ill, helped me when we went to Pennsylvania to see my Uncle Dick and Aunt Melba and rescued me when I fell into the pond at church. Dad took a backseat during those crises but always gave me an encouraging pat on the back with his words of wisdom, "It's okay honey; happens to the best of us." You see, Dad was a man of few words, but you always knew he loved you,

So off we went. Dad treated me like a princess that weekend, held doors open for me, ordered for me at dinner and endured countless hours of shopping underground. I had my babysitting money and bought my very own makeup. As I got ready for the hockey game that night, i liberally applied my newfound treasures. Butch never said anything bad to anyone and that night was no different. He said, "My little girl is all grown up."

I don't remember who won the hockey game. I didn't really care. I was the winner that weekend. I had graduated to a new stage of life with my dad. And like my previous stages, he would always be there for me.

When we finally got our luggage off the train Dad said, "Well that was a great weekend. We'll have to do something nice for the Houghtons."

I always kept what my dad said in the back of my mind. It took about thirty-five years. But I finally accomplished that task: I said, "Yes" when their son Tom asked me to marry him.

Butch got back to combining work with hockey. He returned to Guelph Arena Gardens where he'd played Junior A for the Biltmores. This time he was playing coach of the Guelph Regals in the OHA Senior A league. Butch's friends and fellow Woolwich Township residents Don Duke, Frank Carroll and Dave Garner were with the Regals. It was also somewhat of a reunion for Butch with former Senior A teammates "Boat" Hurley, Butch Keeling, Lloyd Mercer and Ron Howell who were on the Regals roster.

In an early season column, Hugh Bowman, Sports Editor of the Guelph Mercury newspaper wrote, "The last time Guelph Regals played before a hometown audience, there was close to 3,500 customers in the pews; most of them pleasantly surprised at the caliber of hockey and most of them realizing for the first time, what they had been missing all season. Unlike the early part of last season, no one this year is talking Allan Cup. Under the direction of the hard-driving (Butch) Martin, however, this could be the year when the talk is replaced by action."

Opposing teams had members with whom Butch had previously played. This included former Dutchmen and Galt Terrier teammate Bill "Wiggie" Wylie who was coaching the Galt Hornets. Joe Hogan, Butch's Galt Terrier teammate, was also with the Hornets.

In his final year, Butch's Regals finished fifth in a league of ten teams. They were eliminated in the league quarter-final series by the Collingwood Kings. The Kings were led by Claire Alexander, who went on to play parts of three seasons with the Toronto Maple Leafs. The Orillia native was known as the "Milkman" because he gave up his job as a milkman in the town to sign a professional contract with the Leafs.

In the 1968-69 season Butch coached the Guelph Junior B team.

Kelly says: My earliest memories of watching my dad play hockey came when I was about seven. Sundays during hockey season would involve a trip to Guelph. Dad was player/coach of the Guelph Regals. Mom and I put on our best outfits and made the drive to Guelph with Dad. It was a quiet ride, with much concentration and focus. We'd be dropped off at Auntie Mary's home while Dad continued on to the arena. After a couple hours playing with her kids, we'd all load into the cars, because it was nearly game time. On our arrival at the arena, we'd bypass the line of people, be greeted by the staff, and make our way to our assigned seats with other players' families. Those were the days when players didn't wear helmets, so I could always spot my dad the minute he stepped onto the ice for the pre-game skate. Dad would immediately find a puck and fire a blistering shot at the glass I was standing behind to startle me. Then the biggest smile would come over his face. He'd nod at me to assure me he was aware of me being in the crowd. Then his game face would take over and it was all business on the ice.

Mom always made sure we were in our seats before the game started. According to her, Dad was very superstitious. After warm-up, he'd take his place, second from the boards for the national anthem. If any teammate tried to take that spot along the blue line, he'd muscle him out of the way. One night Mom and I weren't in our seats by the time the national anthem began, and the team lost. It was a very quiet ride home from Guelph. From then on, for any game, whether it was my son's, my dad's, or the Leafs, I'm always in "my spot" before the puck drops.

But win or lose, my favorite time came after the final whistle. I ran down to the bench and an usher lifted me onto the boards in front of the team bench. My dad skated over, took off his gloves and put me on his shoulders. He'd be dripping with sweat and smelling like a locker room but he'd skate me around the arena like I was his prize trophy, until the Zamboni driver chased us off the ice. I truly believe that's why arena smells never bothered me, even as an adult, because they brought back childhood memories of some of the greatest times of my life.

Throughout my life, I've learned by example. Compassion is one of my most valued traits. And I believe it's because of Butch's example. The first time I remember witnessing an act like this was in Guelph when I was about seven. I'd hang around the skate/stick room after the games, waiting for Dad. Connie, a sweet, kind, older man tinkered about the room. Some people called Connie "slow" But he loved hockey. When the boys left the dressing room, Connie would always say, "Good game" or "Get 'em next time." Most of them would walk past. When Dad came out he'd always make time for a little chat. Connie admired Dad for what he did on the ice. I admired him for what he did to always take the time for a special man.

ALL THE KING'S MEN
DONALD JOSEPH "SKY" KING

When Don King, the new barber in Elmira, met Butch for the first time in 1963, they soon found a common interest in sports. Don loved baseball. His brother, Mike, owned the Brantford Red Sox of the Inter County Baseball League. Ray, another brother, had become a Catholic priest.

When asked if an appointment was needed for a haircut at his shop, Don replied, "Your appointment is when you walk through the damn door!"

Don also enjoyed hockey, and was a good judge of young talent. Ten years after opening his barbering business, he worked with highly regarded hockey coach Gerald Forler in the successful launch of the Elmira Junior B Sugar Kings hockey club. Forler's brother Claude was also an important partner. In their first year, they won the league championship.

Don went to Butch for the purchase of any automobile he drove. He'd also regularly drop by at the car dealership to chat with Butch.

While Don was respected for his sports smarts, his fame came from the many humorous, often intense conversations at his barber shop, under his capable and animated direction. The shop had a vintage decor, a manly smell of shaving cream and the ambience of a sports bar.

Butch dropped by regularly. The folks down at the town hall might spend months trying to find a solution to a local matter but the fellows gathered at Don's shop on a Saturday afternoon would have the answer within a few hours. They had the solution to the problems of the Toronto Maple Leafs, political decisions at all levels, and which sulky driver was the best up at the race track at the Elmira Fair Grounds. Don enjoyed horse-racing, and regularly showed up at the track on Friday evenings, after he'd locked the shop door.

What made the congenial conversations and occasionally heated debates enjoyable were Don's witty remarks, one-liners, laughter and colorful opinions. He was the acknowledged master of ceremonies in the regular Saturday afternoon King's Court at his shop at 8 Arthur Street.

So if you, unwittingly perhaps, dropped by the shop for a Saturday afternoon haircut, you'd likely spend considerably longer in the chair than you'd anticipated. Making pointed motions with his scissors to emphasize his words, Don occasionally needed to take a moment to turn around to offer his opinion, give some sage advice, or take a drag on his cigarette that had been balancing precariously on the edge of the counter. Legend has it that Don would occasionally get so wrapped up in the debate of the day that he'd forget about the man sitting in the barber's chair.

Butch, Don, and Tom Schnurr went to Blue Jays games together. Often Butch would drive, and he and Tom would pick up Don outside the barbershop to go to the evening Jays game. One evening a local man entered the shop just as Butch was parking out front. Butch was surprised when Don appeared at the car door in only a few minutes. Don jumped in and said he had given the guy a quick, "light dusting." The remark set the tone for an evening of good times and cordial relationships. That's what Don did well and was one of his personality traits to which Butch was attracted. At the Jays games, Butch and Tom would frequently lose Don for a few innings. He'd be off "holding court" somewhere in the stands.

Don was known as "Sky" to Butch and others who knew him well. He was first given the nickname by the son of the Baptist pastor in Elmira.

"Sky King" was the name of an American television adventure series at the time.

With Don, I was a member of Elmira's first slo-pitch team. Unanimously, we chose "Sky Kings" as our team's name. Sky loved being on the ball diamond, blocking grounders big-league style at first base, making his way unsteadily under an infield fly, or dragging his bat with him to first base after he'd hit the ball.

While playing in the infield, Don would ask how many were out, or what inning it was pretty much after each batter. His inquiry may have been intended for his teammate Lorne, but Don would yell out "Bush, Ab, Del, Earl" and sometimes successfully end up with "Lorne" or even "Harry"— although Harry wasn't even on the team.

Don's brother Mike named one of his race horses "Don King."

Don was a friend of the local member of the Ontario Legislature, and had close ties to the Elmira Seiling family who sent two sons to the National Hockey League. Butch's Polar King teammate Cole Bowman was a friend. Ken Seiling, in 2014 Waterloo Region's long time Chair, played the church organ at the wedding of two of Don's children. When the local newspaper publisher first moved to Elmira, he used Don's office to store his files.

As the decades passed, Butch called Don every morning from his sales office on Ottawa Street in Kitchener. Their close friendship never wavered.

Don worked at his barber shop until the day of his death. Downtown Elmira was never the same after they closed the doors to his shop for the last time. Featured articles in local newspapers appropriately honored Don and spoke highly of his contributions for forty years to a community that he loved and who embraced him and his family.

His funeral was at Elmira's St. Theresa of Avila Church, where he'd never missed a Sunday mass. Butch was honored to be a pallbearer. Coach Forler gave a moving eulogy.

CITIZEN MOE
MURRAY IRWIN "MOE" NORMAN

In 1955 and 1956 Moe Norman won back-to-back Canadian Amateur Golf championships. He also won ten provincial championships in five Canadian provinces. After 1979, Moe won seven straight Canadian PGA senior championships. By the end of his magnificent golf career, he'd won fifty-five tournaments, held thirty-three course records and scored seventeen holes-in-one.

In 1956 Moe was invited to the Masters Tournament in Augusta, Georgia where he withdrew after scoring a seventy-five and a seventy-eight in the first two rounds. He returned to Augusta in 1957 but missed the cut by one shot. During those heady years, professional golfer George Knudson, said, "Moe Norman is the best golfer in the world—period." In 1995 Moe was inducted into the Canadian Golf Hall of Fame.

Tiger Woods said, "Only two golfers have ever owned their swings: Moe Norman and Ben Hogan." Moe was widely recognized as the one of the greatest ball strikers in the history of golf.

Professional golf legend Lee Trevino said, "When you're talking about Moe Norman, you're talking about a legend—a living legend. The public doesn't know Moe Norman. But you ask any professional whether you're in Australia, the United States, or Great Britain and they know him. He's a legend with professionals. I think he could have won all tournaments around the world. I think he's that good. I think the guy's a genius when it comes to playing the game of golf."

For years Moe went from tournament to tournament across Canada driving a Cadillac. Frequently Moe's car was also his sleeping quarters. His first cars were sold to him by Vince Scherer. When Vince retired, Butch took over Moe's file and sold him a new Cadillac about every second year. They established a close friendship that only ended at the time of Moe's death in 2004.

Moe had many quirks. Unfortunately, some would suggest, people commented more about his quirks than his golfing ability. At the 1957 Masters, golf great Sam Snead gave Moe a forty-minute lesson at the practice range. Moe immediately put his lesson to work and proceeded to hit about eight hundred golf balls. His right thumb swelled so severely that he was in excruciating pain and only played one round and missed the cut. He said it was the last lesson he took.

Moe was awesome at tapping the ball on the face of his driver. Once an onlooker told Moe he'd give him a dollar for every bounce over one hundred. Moe stopped at 192. He didn't have the heart to take more of the man's money.

Moe said he played on 434 golf courses, and his record for most golf balls hit in one day was 2207. He never got married, never owned a telephone and never saw a doctor until he was sixty-eight years old. One day while chatting to Butch and Tom Schnurr in the Stedelbauer showroom, Moe was called to the phone. It was an awkward moment as handling a phone was a rare occurrence for him.

Lorne Rubenstein, a Canadian golf journalist, authored a book entitled "Moe and Me" in 2012. Rubenstein got to know Moe very well and described him as the Glenn Gould of golf: "As a child the pianist already knew that his art could transform him to a rarified and exclusive world—and he experienced an 'inner rapture' while playing."

Moe put it this way, "Hope and fear, hope and fear, that's how people play golf. Not me. No, not me. I see happiness. I see happiness."

Moe was self-taught and never read a golf book. He played golf the way he dressed: unconventionally. Once in a tournament, Moe's caddy told him he could reach the green with a driver off the tee and then a nine-iron. Moe hit his ball off the tee with a nine-iron and hit the green with his driver. Another time, rather than playing a lay-up shot in front of a creek, he bounced his drive across the bridge that crossed the creek. Moe played golf in a hurry. When he approached the ball he hit it immediately, with no warm up swings. Butch commented, "Moe was rushing to nowhere."

Moe loved winning golf tournaments but his shyness and social awkwardness were detrimental to his acceptance into the golfing fraternity. He also shied away from the formal parts of the game, like giving a brief statement when receiving his trophy and his earnings from a win. Rubenstein wrote, "The game hurt him. Its conventions drained him."

Butch and PeeWee asked Moe to give Kelly some tips to help her improve her golf game. Any stories about Moe hadn't reached her. As he worked with her at the practice tee, she found the experience "magical." Moe was the first eccentric person she'd ever met. She'd bump into Moe over the years at Butch's work. While Moe was clearly uncomfortable in some adult company, he loved to interact with children. He'd bounce golf balls to Kelly's two-year old twins, even as she grew increasingly concerned about them and the brand new vehicles in the showroom. Granddad Butch smiled and calmly said, "There is no damage that can't be fixed."

For many years Moe dropped into Stedelbauer every summer morning at 7:00 to chat with Butch and enjoy a Diet Coke or Pepsi, one of about fifteen he consumed during his day. He started every summer day with breakfast at the Carlisle Golf Club in Hamilton. His final stop was at the Foxwood Course in Baden, managed by Gus Maue. Gus and his wife Audrey were Moe's closest friends.

When he'd get a bit disturbed with Butch, Moe said emphatically, "You know, I don't have to buy my Cadillacs from you!" But he did. When Butch went to his computer to add up the various costs to arrive at the total, Moe would say, "What are you doing that for?" He'd have already totaled up the cost mentally.

Most of his life, Moe lived in boarding houses. Kelly said, "At one point he had to move into a motel with a kitchenette, as his landlady had passed on. Dad, along with a few close friends who also shared a kinship with Moe, gathered blankets and dishes to help get Moe settled in. But even with all the assistance, Moe moved to another boarding house. Butch wasn't ruffled in the least with all the work that was done and then undone. He knew it was what Moe was comfortable with, and that was all that really mattered."

Butch impressed his daughter by his compassionate actions once again, something that has helped significantly in developing her own habit of showing compassion to others, regardless of how special or ordinary the recipients.

Moe won most of his tournaments and prize money in his younger years. There was no money to be made as a professional golfer in Canada, so he remained an amateur. He worked as a pin-setter in a bowling alley all winter, before automatic pin-setters arrived. He was so accomplished that he worked three lanes. The money he earned allowed him to play golf in the summer.

Moe went through a hard time in the 1980s and early 1990s. These were the times he slept in his car. But he went to a PGA Merchandise Show in Orlando, Florida and met Wally Uihlein, the CEO of Titleist Golf. Moe had used Titleist balls for over forty years. Uihlein asked Moe if anyone had ever done anything for him. Moe replied that no one had, nor had he ever asked. Uihlein shook Moe's hand and told him he'd be receiving five thousand dollars a month for the rest of his life. With that and some income from a golf teaching program, he opened his first bank account.

Butch's Elmira Polar Kings teammate, Neil Colborne, an accountant, helped Moe in the management of his finances.

Moe felt alienated from his immediate family. He hadn't attended a family function for fifty years. None came to see him golf. In 1999 he was reunited with his sister Doreen at a restaurant in Waterloo.

In 1988, the release of the movie Rainman won Oscars for Best Picture, Best Actor (Dustin Hoffman), and Best Screenwriter (Barry Morrow). Hoffman's role was that of Raymond, an autistic savant. Screenwriter Morrow wrote a letter to Moe containing these words, "It's been two years since I read about you in Golf Digest, and marveled at your journey as a person and golf legend. Since then I've thought about you many times. I am a screenwriter, and I believe your story would make a terrific motion picture. I also believe I'm the person to write it."

Morrow travelled from California to meet with Moe at Stedelbauer in Kitchener. Butch and Tom Schnurr were on duty at the time. Tom remembers Moe coming into his office when he became aware of Morrow's presence. When someone requested that he come out and speak to Morrow, Moe said, "I'm talking with my friend, Tom." Eventually Butch arrived and encouraged Moe to end the conversation and meet with Morrow.

Schnurr felt that Moe's antics, although appearing to be rude, were an example of his social awkwardness and insecurity.

As of 2014, no movie about Moe's story has been released. Morrow had suggested that Justin Timberlake might work well in playing the role of Moe.

Moe Norman died on September 4, 2004, of congestive heart failure. Over six hundred people attended his funeral at Saint Louis Roman Catholic Church in Waterloo.

Butch lost a dear and special friend.

GALT TERRIERS

Allan Cup Winners 1961 (*Canadian Senior Hockey Champions*)

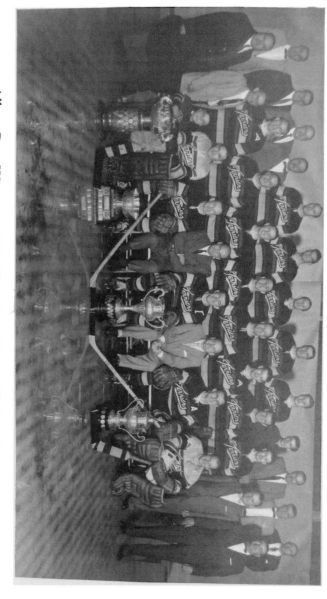

FRONT ROW (Left to Right) – DONNIE BROUSE (Mascot), HAROLD "Boat" HURLEY, BILL WYLIE, DR. K. H. BERKELEY, President; FLOYD "Butch" MARTIN, Captain; LEN GAUDETTE, General Manager; DARRYL SLY, JOHN REINHART.

MIDDLE ROW (Left to Right) – ARTHUR WHITE, Honorary President; JOE BARRADELL, Executive; TED MAKI, HARRY NEALE, PETER KOWALCHUK, GEORGE AITKEN, GAR VASEY, BOBBY MADER, ALEC KEELING, JOE HOGAN, HORACE BARDWELL, Treasurer; LLOYD ROUBELL, Coach.

TOP ROW (Left to Right) – BILL PATTERSON, Secretary; DON HIBBS, Assistant Manager; BUD FRASER, Executive; E. K. "Tony" LAST, Trainer; FREDDIE PLETSCH, FRANKIE CARROLL, BOB McKNIGHT, JOE MALO, ABNER MARTIN, KENT LILLIE, Trainer; MACK BROUSE, Executive; ANDREW MEMMOTT, Executive; T. J. "Dabby" DUVALL, Vice-President.

A Johnstown Jet - 1962.

KITCHENER RANGERS 1963 - 1964

FRONT ROW: JOHN VOSS, JOHN BEECHEY, PETER BRENNAN, TERRY BALL,
JACK McCREARY, GARY KURT.
MIDDLE ROW: BUTCH MARTIN, BRENT MADILL, BILLY HWAY, SANDY
FITZPATRICK, BOB JONES, KEN GRATTON, MIKE ROBITAILLE
WAYNE GOETZ, ANGELO NIGRO.
BACK ROW: BOB HOWARD, RANDY LEGGE, WAYNE McLEISH, TOM MILLER,
GORD KANNEGEISEER.

Back: PeeWee, Butch and their daughter, Kelly
Front: Grandchildren Kristie and Paul

Butch's 60th birthday part at Westmount Golf Club in Waterloo. The celebration also recognized his induction into the Oldtimers Hockey Hall of Fame. Those who nominated him for this honor were (from left) Bill Clemens, Gord Trapp and Carl Buschert.

Induction into the Waterloo Hall of Fame - 1990.

A BRIEF HISTORY OF AB
ABNER MARTIN

When young Abner wasn't selling peanuts at Elmira Polar King games, he was playing hockey.

As a minor hockey player in Elmira, beginning at age nine, Ab led teams to five Ontario Minor Hockey Association championships. In the OMHA quarter-final game, played in February of 1950 he scored seven goals in his team's 9-0 win. A month later, he scored six goals and assisted on three others to help his team win the Ontario championship. Elmira's newspaper, The Signet, carried these comments: "This was Abner's best display of his hockey career. He seemed to be everywhere and always in the right place. His back-checking was outstanding, and he was a tower of strength to his team."

When Ab got home that night, his dad Nelson gave him sixty-cents: five cents for each goal, and ten cents for each assist. That was the father-son "contract" throughout Ab's minor hockey years. He was two years younger than his teammates. Yet he was the team's leading scorer.

But Nelson's family, out of necessity, lived simply and frugally. Ab picked up broken hockey sticks at the arena, then patched them together to be game-worthy. There was no money to purchase shoulderpads or shinpads. His skates were hand-me-downs from his older brother Nelson.

Beginning as a ten-year-old, Ab started working on a farm for the summer months. The little money he earned was handed over to his father, when he returned home on Labor Day. Fortunately there were no fees for joining a minor team in Elmira. At the end of one championship season, his family scrounged so Ab could purchase a championship jacket.

The Martins were one of the first Mennonite families to move into Elmira from the farm. Ab was the youngest of three girls and three boys.

For a hockey enthusiast, the small, cozy home Nelson purchased on Arthur Street was perfectly situated. Ab could see the Elmira Memorial Arena when he looked out the front window. The first Elmira arena, the one in which he'd first played organized hockey, was a five-minute walk from his back door down King Street.

But his Mennonite friend Don Martin had an outdoor rink. It was a block away, a minute's sprint along Bauman Street. That's where Ab developed his skating and stickhandling abilities before he joined an organized team. With boards only six inches high, hoisting was forbidden.

The kid who lived across the street from the rink was a regular at their games of shinny. His name was Byrle Klinck. Decades later, Byrle was Butch's Dutchmen teammate at the 1956 Winter Olympic Games.

Don Martin became CEO of the very successful. Martin Feed Mills, expanding a business that his father Eli had begun. Don became a highly respected entrepreneur. He also gained a sterling reputation for his philanthropic actions, especially in his home community.

"Li'l Abner" had no dreams about becoming an NHL player. He just loved playing hockey on Don Martin's outdoor rink.

Merv Duke was the principal of Elmira Public School, the one Ab attended. He also was honored by the Ontario Minor Hockey League for his lengthy and outstanding service as a minor hockey coach in Elmira. Mr. Duke was a stern taskmaster, in the classroom and at the rink. His players understood that playing a hockey game on the same night you had a school assignment was no excuse for not having it completed in the morning.

Many of us former students continued to address him as "Mr. Duke" when we were mature adults. It was not something he expected or relished. Rather, it showed that the respect we had for him had not faded.

Mr. Duke asked Ab to join a bantam team and was his coach for all but one of his minor hockey years. Ab was always his team's leading point-getter. But the coach's philosophy about team play didn't leave room for what he deemed as selfish play. It was all about playing as a team—with one person in charge, one person giving directions.

The Elmira Memorial Arena had stairs at one end that led to a large space where fans could enjoy snacks and drink coffee. Occasionally Coach Duke would stand at the top of the stairs as his team was scrimmaging during practice. When instructions were called for, he gave them with the aid of a microphone, set up by the arena's manager, Jack Sumner. Ab was a center-man. So preparing to take a face-off, he stepped out of the face-off circle to strategically position his winger. The coach noticed and succinctly, pointedly and loudly; aided by the microphone, told his top point-getter to look after his own game and he'd do the coaching. After sixty years, Ab clearly remembered.

During one game, Ab started in his own end, stick-handled through the entire opposition, cleverly deked the goalie, and scored a beautiful goal. When he returned to the bench, Coach Duke told him to sit at the end, and he missed a few shifts. The coach reminded Ab that there were others on the team and if they were open, he should make sure to pass the puck to them.

In the spring of 1947 Ab's Bantam needed funds to travel to Sundridge to play the first of a two-game series. The winner would be Ontario Champions. Elmira's Recreation Council's funds were depleted. So Norval Leslie, the team's manager, knocked on doors and raised $216 to cover the costs. The result was another championship. On May 13, over two hundred Elmira residents paid $1.25 each to attend a banquet at the local high school to honor the boys. Their guest speaker was Ted "Teeder" Kennedy, then captain of the Toronto Maple Leafs.

Another year the Elmira Midget team played Midland for the all-Ontario championship. Ab was also a member of the team. The final game was in Elmira. With emotions running high, things got a little out of hand on the ice.

In the "feature" fight, Midland's biggest player, a defenseman, was pummeling a smaller Elmira player along the boards. The spectator closest to the action was Butch Martin. He instinctively reached over the boards and grabbed the big guy. Things quickly settled down. Ab's team went on to win another championship.

Having graduated from the midget division, the same Elmira team, now juveniles, defeated Parry Sound to take home another OMHA championship trophy. Ab was drafted by Hap Emms and the Barrie Flyers when he played juvenile. Emms wouldn't coach on Sundays, and he promised Ab he wouldn't have to play on Sundays. Ab's parents said a firm "No." He was happy that they did.

The draft situation at that time was that a Junior A team could only draft a minor hockey player for one year. The next year that player was open to draft by any junior team.

The juvenile team, sporting their championship powder blue cowboy hats, and celebrating another big win made their way to a Parry Sound hotel. They were booked for the night. About 2:00 a.m. the fire siren roused them from their sleep and they evacuated the building, blue hats in tow. They watched, unbelievably, as an entire downtown business-block burned down. It was Ab's first-ever stay in a hotel.

A Toronto Marlboro Junior A team scout took in the final juvenile game in Parry Sound. He called management in Toronto with his report. His boss, with an auspicious office at Maple Leaf Gardens, was Stafford Smythe, the Marlies' managing director. He was a growing and influential presence in professional hockey circles. His father Conn had built the Gardens in 1931.

The scout recommended that Smythe draft one of the Elmira players—Abner Martin. The scout's assessment was that the Elmira boy was a very fast skater, a talented stickhandler, and had a knack for scoring goals from in close. His shot needed some work. But he warned Smythe he might have to do a selling job. There were rumors that Martin refused to play hockey on Sundays. The Marlies invited Ab to training camp at the Gardens.

At age the age of eighteen, Ab took the train, by himself, from Elmira to Toronto's downtown Union Station. To this day he wonders why. The only hockey equipment with him was a pair of skates. He walked east on Front Street, then north on Jarvis to the Westminster Hotel, known for its long buffet table, the first in Canada. There he met his roommate, Bob Pulford, who would become an NHL legend. In 1991, Pulford was inducted into the Hockey Hall of Fame. His NHL record included fourteen years as a Leaf player, and thirty years as a coach and executive with the Chicago Black Hawks. This would be his first of two years with the Marlies.

Ab was in the company of some big names in the business of hockey. His first practice at the Gardens was run by Turk Broda, recently appointed as the Marlies coach. Turk was a five-time Stanley Cup winner with the Leafs. His eight-year NHL career as a goalie was spent entirely as a Maple Leaf. He was one of the most popular players of his era, often sought out for his sharp wit—"The Leafs pay me for work in practice. I throw in the games for free." His approach to the game was not lost on Ab.

In the first two exhibition games with the Marlies, Ab played on a line with Pulford and Bob Nevin. After his junior career, Nevin went on to play over one thousand NHL games. He was captain of the New York Rangers for six years, and won three Stanley Cups with the Leafs. In each game, one with Peterborough, the other with Guelph, Ab scored two goals. Coach Turk Broda was pleased with the line's performance.

Ab says he didn't think it was such a big deal. But after the Peterborough game, on October 18, he received a request to meet Smythe in his Garden's second floor office. Smythe was in a conciliatory mood, shook Ab's hand, and congratulated him. He would be a Marlie! A contract with a "No Sunday" clause lay on a massive desk and was signed by the first-ever Marlie from Elmira.

Stafford Smythe, with a reputation for being a little "crusty" much like his father Conn, loved being the man in charge. His business acumen and hockey connections would take him to the lofty heights as president of Maple Leaf Gardens and president of the Leafs Hockey Club. He bought control of the Leafs from his father in 1961 and was in that position during the Leaf's glory days of the 1960s. His name was engraved on the Stanley Cup on five occasions. At nine years of age, when he was the mascot of the Leafs, he was the youngest person to have his name appear on the Cup. The Stafford Smythe Memorial Trophy is presented annually to the junior player selected as MVP in the Memorial Cup finals.

In Ab, Smythe felt he'd signed a kid who could skate with anyone and looked good between Pulford and Nevin. But he'd have to sell him on playing Sunday games: Sunday games at the Gardens were a big deal. Marlies and St. Mikes played back-to-back home games on Sunday afternoons, and the gate was substantial.

As Ab was leaving the second floor office, Smythe said, "Ab, I'll see you at 2:00 on Sunday afternoon." Ab wasn't sure whether the words constituted a statement or a command.

Ab's body stiffened, his hands were clenched into fists. But his legs took him towards the large desk. He said, "Mr. Smythe, I've just signed a contract with you that guaranteed I wouldn't have to play on Sundays. And I'm sticking to that decision."

Smythe leaned back in his chair, and clasped his hands together above his head. He said, "Heck, when you skate onto the

Gardens ice in front of over twelve thousand fans, you'll change your mind."

Ab closed the heavy office door, and with shoulders slumped, slowly made his way past the giant photos of Syl Apps and "Teeder" Kennedy to the Garden's Carlton Street exit. What he'd heard from Smythe was totally unexpected. He turned right onto Church Street, past a homeless man curled up over a sidewalk heating grate. Pulford had told him that he should simply walk away rather than bending down to try to assist someone in that condition. It was risky.

The second thoughts that had tugged at Ab from his first day in Toronto were now more pronounced. The Westminster's splendid buffet was ready. Ab loaded his plate with prime rib, sautéed mushrooms, and three-tiered jellied salad. He didn't make it past the salad before he had made a decision.

On Friday, October 24, Ab asked Pulford to tell Smythe he wouldn't be back. Union Station was a fifteen-minute walk down Yonge Street to Front. Ronnie Hawkins was belting out "Bo Diddley" at Yonge Street's Le Coq d'Or tavern. Ab Martin was on his way back to Elmira.

The next day, Saturday, Hurricane Hazel struck with a vengeance. One day later, Nelson died. His youngest son had returned in time to say goodbye.

Ab never heard from Smythe again.

That year Broda's Marlies, led by Pulford and Nevin, won the Memorial Cup as Canada's Junior A champions.

Butch's stand on Sunday hockey had a strong influence on Ab's thought process. The path which Butch, some five years older, had taken made Ab's choice a little less stressful. Yet when starring in minor hockey, there were some Mennonite parents who didn't want their children playing with Ab because of his hockey activities. His Sunday School teacher reminded him that he wasn't setting a good example by playing hockey. He felt that in some youth social situations he was marginalized because of his participation.

When Ab Martin's minor hockey coach needed a goal, he sent Ab over the boards. But when Ab was a coach of one Elmira team, the young player he'd tap on the shoulder was Darryl Sittler, future captain of the Toronto Maple Leafs and member of the Hockey Hall of Fame.

Darryl spent twelve years as a Toronto Maple Leaf, and became the second youngest team captain in Leaf history. Growing up in St Jacobs, Darryl sometimes played shinny matches on the frozen Mill Pond that flowed from the dam to Snyder's Flour Mill. Sometimes, the hockey stick he used was a discard from the Mennonite Church League Thursday night games at the Elmira rink. Darryl and a St. Jacobs pal spent many Thursday evenings at the Elmira Arena collecting broken sticks.

Back home, at age 19, Ab joined Butch and the hometown Polar Kings for one season. He said, "Butch was a stand-out. But then, he was a stand-out on every team he played. He set high expectations for himself. And he expected others to do the same. At the right moment, Butch would let me know that he expected more from me. I needed that."

But Ab also met the coach he'd remember most fondly. He was Bill Becker, Elmira resident, former OHA Senior A player. Becker was knowledgeable, quiet spoken, respectful, and had the ability to mold a team into a winner. He'd been Butch's coach during the Polar Kings championship years.

But the OHA Junior A teams seemed relentless in their desire to have Ab join them. He was employed at Elmira's Dominion Bank, a job he'd started at age fifteen. The bank's staff was temporarily working out of the local Legion Hall while the bank building was being restored following a fire.

One morning, Ab had just settled in behind his teller's counter when Mr. Hugh Bowring, the bank's manager, told him a stranger wanted to talk to him on the phone—some guy named Sam. The stranger said, "Ab, Pollock here, I represent the Kitchener Canucks Junior A hockey club. Give me directions to where you work and I'll be right there." Ab had never heard of a man named Sam Pollock.

Pollock had done his homework. He told Ab he wouldn't have to play Sundays, and his pay would be forty dollars a week. The terms were part of a contract to play for the Canucks.

This was Mr. Sam Pollock! In the following decades he would amass an enviable and outstanding record in sports. In a fourteen-year association with the Montreal Canadiens, he had his name inscribed on the Stanley Cup twelve times, nine times as general manager. He would be responsible for signing the likes of Guy Lafleur, Ken Dryden, Serge Savard and Larry Robinson. He was well known for negotiating many clever trades that helped to strengthen the Habs. In 1978 he was inducted into the Hockey Hall of Fame as a Builder. From 1995-2000 he was CEO and President of the Toronto Blue Jays.

But on this day he was at smalltown Elmira's Legion, hoping to sign a young banker. The second year Junior A Canucks were looking to bolster their roster.

Ab was a young teller, but even then had a nose for business and finance that would eventually put him behind the manager's desk. Quickly leaving his post, he caught up to Pollock as he was closing the Legion building's front door. A little out of breath, Ab said, "Mr. Pollock, make it sixty dollars a week, or you can forget about it." Sam Pollock hesitated, adjusted his black Biltmore hat, then shook Ab's hand. They had a deal. Ab, to this day, doesn't know where he found the courage.

When Ab coddled his first pass from Kent Douglas, he had no idea that the Kitchener Canuck defenseman would go on to win the Calder Trophy with the Leafs as the NHL's top rookie. Neither did he know that Fredericton, New Brunswick native Willie

O'Ree, the speedy winger with the nice touch around the net, would eventually be deemed "The Jackie Robinson of Hockey."

But he was aware of the reputation of Canuck's coach, John Sherratt "Black Jack" Stewart. The coach had earned his reputation honestly as one of the NHL's hardest body-checkers. He played the game tough, but clean. Detroit Red Wing teammate and NHL tough guy Ted Lindsay said about Stewart, "When he had that smile, it was time for the opposition to look out." In a twelve-season NHL career, Stewart suffered a fractured skull and played an entire season with a broken hand. He was a five-time all-star. In 1964 he was inducted into the Hockey Hall of Fame.

But Douglas, O'Ree, Martin and the rest of the Canucks found him anything but a tough coach. He paid more attention to the motivation part of the game than the techniques.

The Canucks were in tough in the 1955-56 season. The St. Michael Majors team was led by almost-Dutchie Dave Keon, By the end of his illustrious NHL career, the former Maple Leaf captain was considered by many as the best Leaf ever. Stafford Smythe's Toronto Marlies had on board the marvelous skater and scorer Frank Mahovlich. Bobby Baun, another Leaf great, was a bruising defenseman with the Marlies.

But the most skillful, physical and highly touted group in the year Ab played for the Canucks was the St. Catharines TeePees. Their lineup boasted what would become for many years the heart and soul of the Chicago Black Hawks. Coach Rudy Pilous could send out Stan Mikita to take an important face-off. Bobby Hull would leap over the boards on a power play, positioned to unload his potent shot from the point. Big Elmer "Moose" Vasko could handily take care of clearing the front of the net. In a six-year period, the TeePees powerhouse would have five league-scoring champions and three Most Valuable Player Awards. Ab and the Canucks didn't like them much!

Midway during the season, a highly touted sixteen-year-old joined the Canucks. Bob Ertel grew up on Riverside Drive in

Elmira, attended public and high schools there and was a star on Elmira's minor hockey teams. He knew Ab and Butch well. At fifteen, he was counted on as a valuable member of the Waterloo Siskins Junior B team. Early on, he gained a reputation as a strong skater with a good shot. He relished and could handle well the physical part of the game. His Junior A career also included stops with Peterborough and Guelph.

In later years, Ertel and Butch were opponents when Butch played for Johnstown in the Eastern Professional League. Bob was a tough winger with the New Haven Blades. When he joined the Portland Buckaroos of the Western Professional Hockey League, his signing was called by management "the most significant one of the season." When he retired from a very successful hockey career, Bob became involved in the coaching and managerial side of the game. That included a stint as coach and later general manager of the Junior A Kitchener Rangers.

(My one and only claim to "fame" was that Bob and I were undefeated in the annual three-legged race during our years at Elmira Public School!)

Coach Stewart and Ab got along. But his refusal to play on Sundays seemed to put Ab in a tenuous position. It caused disruption in the lineup, and the position he held on the top line alongside top point-getter Stan Baluik eluded him. There were many variables at play, but Ab feels the "Sunday thing" was likely a contributing factor. No Canuck player ever brought up the subject with Ab. The Canucks were eliminated by Barrie in the first round of the 1955-56 playoffs.

Ab's recollections of all his hockey experiences are positive ones. If he had one wish, it was that he could have had the experience of being captain of a team.

In 1998, Ab and a few Elmira friends travelled the snow-covered Queen Elizabeth Way to Buffalo to see the Sabres play at the Memorial Auditorium. At intermission Ab noticed a man who looked familiar being interviewed. Security was tight but Ab explained that he knew the interviewee and would like to speak to him. When their eyes met, the man said, "You old Mennonite you. You were the only one on our team who didn't have a curfew." Ab and Willie O'Ree, his former Kitchener Canuck teammate embraced and shared memories of a single memorable season under the tutelage of Black Jack Stewart.

William Eldon "Willie" O'Ree is in the NHL's record books. He had a secret; not revealed until his retirement from hockey: no one was told or found out that he had sight in only one eye. Yet he played at the highest level. He'd severely injured his eye as Ab's teammate in a Canuck game in Guelph on November 22, 1955. But the more important, and record-making moment came on January 18, 1958. When O'Ree took to the ice in the Boston Garden as a member of the Bruins, he immediately ensured his place in hockey history as the first black man to play in the NHL— hence the reference to him as "The Jackie Robinson of Hockey."

Willie responded to that honor. "They've called me the Jackie Robinson of Hockey. And I'm aware of being the first, and the responsibilities. But I'm also aware that there have not been, and are not many black players able to play hockey. There has never been the discrimination in this game that there was in baseball. And I don't face any of the very real problems Robinson had to face."

On January 16, 1984, in Fredericton, a state-of-the-art recreational facility, Willie O'Ree Place, was officially opened. It has two NHL-size ice surfaces and a youth facility. The same year, O'Ree received the Lester Patrick Trophy, presented annually to one individual for service to hockey in the United States.

In 1958, Ab was transferred by the bank to their St. Catharines branch and caught on with the Welland-Thorold Combines of the OHA Senior B League. When his team entered the OHA playoffs, they met the Elmira Polar Kings in an early round. Ab was looking forward to playing against his former teammates. But the return was less auspicious than one single occurrence. The play was in the Polar Kings' end when Ab attempted to score on a close-in play. Inadvertently, the King's goalie, Ron Kilby, a friend of Ab's, brought his stick up and caught Ab in his mouth. It resulted in him losing four front teeth, but not his friendship with Kilby. The Kings went on to eliminate the Combines from further playoff action.

After a year in St. Catharines, Ab returned to Waterloo County. A call from Ernie Goman, manager of the Kitchener-Waterloo Dutchmen, resulted in him and Butch being reunited on the Senior A team before Butch was off to the Olympics at Squaw Valley.

Butch and Ab were in the same locker room again as members of the Galt Terriers. They were key contributors in the Terriers' trek to the Allan Cup in 1961. Due to an injury sustained in the series with Rouyn-Noranda, Ab was unable to play in the championship series against the Winnipeg Maroons.

Ab closed out his competitive hockey career in Milverton along with some Elmira buddies. He said, "I think I retired then came back at least three times." At age thirty-five he received a call from Butch with an invitation to join the Elmira Polar Kings Old Timers team.

A LEAGUE OF THEIR OWN

When they weren't playing hockey together, Butch and Ab were on the same diamond, and often on the same team, playing softball or fastball, lots of fastball.

In the 1950s and '60s, young Woolwich Township men who played hockey at a high level spent winters hundreds or occasionally thousands of miles away from their families and hometown buddies. They played for teams in the United States and Canada that garnered plenty of attention in sports sections of newspapers. Some linemates were on a track to the NHL. Their coach or manager may have played in the NHL. As they made their way from their home arena dressing rooms, thousands of fans would cheer. Ardent followers lined up for tickets, hoping to get a seat for a deciding playoff game. They played cards on long bus trips or on air flights to places they'd only read about. A few played on the national or international stage.

When their hockey season ended, they looked for another sport to play. In Woolwich, that was softball. But, as their pitcher warmed up and their first baseman threw grounders to the infielders before the start of a game, there were usually fewer than fifty people sitting on the bare wooden stands. Many of those were relatives and friends. If they were regulars, they knew to bring a few coins in their pockets, ready to plunk into a ball cap, when it was passed through the stands at the end of the seventh inning, a donation to help defray the expenses of the umpires, and the purchase of new balls.

When the home-plate umpire, who might have been the pitcher's neighbor, shouted, "Play ball' he might have frightened the crows in the cornfield that crowded left field. The bat-boy, probably the coach's son and wearing a uniform like his father's, had a job to do before the first inning ended: he was given the responsibility to find a source of water, often an outdoor hand pump situated on the front lawn of a friendly neighbor. Struggling to keep his balance to lessen the potential spill, he would lug a metal pail, filled with the cool, refreshing liquid to the players' bench, and float an empty metal container on the surface. On a humid, July evening, the young boy might spend most of the time on a trail from the water pump to the players' bench.

Elmira, whose population barely stretched beyond three thousand inhabitants, was the largest center in the North Waterloo Rural Softball League. The league's beginnings went back to the days when only the catcher and the first baseman wore ball gloves.

Road trips weren't onerous or time consuming. It seldom took more than twenty minutes to get from Elmira to Breslau, St. Jacobs, Conestoga, St. Clements or Bloomingdale. But if your day's work ended at 6:00 p.m. you had to hustle to make it downtown to the team's gathering place: Frankie McCormick's main street service station. The first batter had to be in the batter's box, home or away, by shortly after 7:00 p.m. Only the St. Clements field had floodlights. Most diamonds had outfields that weren't enclosed with an outfield fence.

The North Waterloo Rural Teams played softball, not fastball. The difference lay mainly in the manner in which the pitcher threw the ball. But softball wasn't slow-pitch; neither was it played with a softball. It was played with the same kind of ball that is used for fastball today. The style of pitching was called "orthodox." That meant that the pitcher delivered the ball in a completely underhand motion with little wind-up but with all his effort put into the pitch.

The NWRSL had a feature which is doubtful that any other softball league anywhere emulated. Like baseball, a base-runner could lead off from a base. But unlike baseball, a pitcher could, without penalty, abruptly stop his pitching motion to the plate with the intention of picking off the base-runner. In baseball terms, he could blatantly balk.

Many lineups of teams in the NWRSL had on them men who played hockey at a high competitive level. At one time, the Elmira team had Allan Cup winners at the catching and center field positions; 1956 Winter Olympic Medal winners at second and first base; a professional hockey player at short-stop, and, at least one other team member who played at the Junior A level. I was their pitcher: a decent player in the local Church Hockey League.

Ab was an outstanding outfielder. With no home-run fence, I knew that Ab could sprint a very long way back to make an over-the-shoulder catch. Likewise he could come in a long way in to pull off an acrobatic shoestring catch like the great professional baseball player Willie Mays.

Competitions among players and teams were robust. Their desire to win didn't suddenly disappear when they'd packed their hockey equipment away at the end of the season. But whoever was on their softball team was as important to them as the player they might have set up for a winning goal in a playoff hockey game. After all, these were hometown friends, some of whom they'd known through grade school.

The "Mennonite factor" was not a major factor at all on the Elmira team, or throughout the league. Our games were played on Tuesday and Thursday evenings so the question of playing on Sundays was not an issue. The St. Clements team had a manager whose contributions to the community were many. His popularity was ubiquitous. He was known for his competitiveness and enthusiasm when it came to games in which his team was involved.

Occasionally, when Ab came to bat for our Elmira team, the one-of-a kind manager yelled at his pitcher, "Throw it buggy-wheel high!" in reference to the Old Order Mennonite community who drove horse and buggies. There was no ill will intended by the remark. And the laughter that rippled through the crowd was shared by members of both teams, including Martin, the batter.

Personable and successful cattle buyer, Bob Mader, a member of the Breslau team in the NWRSL was as superb at playing softball as he was patrolling the wing on a Senior A hockey team. As an excellent pitcher and outstanding batter, he led his softball team to ten straight league championship seasons, and right into the Waterloo County Hall of Fame. Bob was named Most Valuable Player in the League on at least one occasion.

In the NHL 2014 entry draft, seventeen-year-old Sam Reinhart was expected to be taken high in the first round. His grandfather Wib was Mader's teammate on the excellent Breslau softball team.

It was in neighboring Wellesley and Mapleton Townships where Butch and Ab first met legendary fastball pitchers Brooker Thomas and Eddie Johnston. Moorefield and Linwood were small, quiet villages more than fifty years ago. In 2014, Moorefield still had a population of less than three hundred.

On a summer Friday night, by the time Thomas threw his first pitch, there were hundreds of fans spreading out from the bleachers and standing around the perimeter of the diamond in Linwood, a total number substantially larger than the population of both villages combined. Teenager Frank Martin lived on a farm a short distance from Linwood. If he could see the floodlights on at the ball diamond and a stream of cars going past the end of his lane, he knew how he'd spend the evening.

The games were billed as Moorefield vs Linwood. But the reason people drove for many miles, with kids in tow, was to see the featured stars. They were big, they were from Detroit; and unlike any of the local citizenry, they were black. Eddie Johnston, the black pitcher from Detroit, on the mound for tiny Moorefield, was an anomaly. Watching him strike out seemingly helpless batters with his blazing fastballs was like being at the show. All eyes were on him in the center of the ring.

But Eddie needed a catcher; someone who could hang on to his assortment of pitches. With Butch he'd found his man.

It took some courage for batters to dig in at home plate, hoping to get the bat on the ball when facing Eddie. But it took audacity and athleticism to be that pitcher's battery mate. Eddie's catcher game after game was Butch. Butch said, "Really, it was easy. I'd just put up my glove where I wanted the ball. I wouldn't have to move. Eddie's pitch would land right on target." Butch Martin is a modest man.

Eddie assured Butch that, regardless of the circumstances, he had things under control. During a game against Sebringville, the improbable happened. An opposing batter reached first base, and attempted to steal second. Butch instinctively tried to throw out the daring runner. But the speedster slid under the throw and was called safe by the umpire. At the end of the play the big left-hander slowly took a few long strides towards home plate and said, "No, no Butch! I got 'em. I got 'em!" Eddie got them with uncanny regularity.

Against flame-throwers like Eddie and Brooker, getting one runner on base was gold. He would often represent the only run scored in the game. A stolen base, or sacrifice bunt and a follow-up single brought him home. It also meant that on those occasions when the ball was put into play by the batter, a tight defense was essential.

Butch knew that Ab could do all of those things and urged him to join the team. So at age sixteen, Ab, a speedy center-fielder, joined Butch in Moorefield. It wasn't unusual for Ab to single, steal second, and then for Butch to single him home—for a 1-0

Moorefield win.

Butch's view was that while Ab was a really talented hockey player, he was exceptionally talented as a fastball outfielder.

There were times during his fastball career that Ab stole home, blazing in from third base. Few players could lay claim to that feat.

Butch and Ab were the icing on Eddie Johnston's cake.

There were very few times when either Ab or Butch got visibly upset about an umpire's call. The one memorable time when Ab humorously gave an umpire a "rough time," the encounter eventually resulted in him marrying that umpire's daughter, Anne. Ab, and Anne became parents of four wonderful children.

Elmira Hockey Team

Ab Martin - farthest right in the first row, Don Martin - farthest left in the back row
Beryl Klinck - second from right in back row, Coach Merv Duke - middle back

Ab Martin as a Kitchener Canuck - with centreman
Kenny Gribbons and winger Whitey Youngberg

GRUMPY OLD MEN
POLAR KING OLDTIMERS

So we come here, for just a few hours to feel special: to be with people who know our same feeling and are as interested in it as we are.

Ken Dryden
The Game

At age fifty-seven, Butch was playing about one hundred hockey games a season. He said, "I feel as good as ever." Under the guidance of his doctor, John Briggs, he was down fifteen pounds from his Dutchmen and Terrier playing days.

Butch was recognized as probably the best player for his age in Waterloo County and beyond. Like most old-timer athletes, he seemed far younger than his chronological age. He observed, "I'm sure I can't skate as fast as before, but I still think I can. I enjoy the game as much as I used to and enjoy the friendship more than ever."

The consistent theme among old timer hockey players was clearly the camaraderie, with exercise and the "odd" beer tied for second place. Their motivation wasn't financial nor improving their performance to get drafted or to be selected to move up to a more elite league. To be the best player as an old-timer was usually connected with being among the youngest. A hockey player could be eligible as an old-timer at thirty-five.

In 1974, John Govett left his job as a school principal to start up the Canadian Old Timers Hockey Association. He is considered one of the forefathers of old-timer hockey in Canada. During February of 1975, Govett organized and hosted the first National Old Timers Tournament in Peterborough. Fifty-six teams and one thousand players showed up.

By 1991 there were 2500 teams in Canada. In 2014 there were about 50,000 teams and a million players. There were thousands of other teams in fifty-five nations under the banner of the International Ice Hockey Federation.

Butch returned full circle when he joined the Elmira Polar Kings Old-Timers team. He'd been a Polar Kings' captain and leader during their glory years of the 1950s. At age twenty-three he had led them to their first championship. He was their most prominent and acclaimed player. That remained an accurate description of Butch as an old-timer Polar King. And he was once again their captain.

Butch was forty-seven in 1976, the initial season of the Elmira Polar Kings Old-Timers team. Most team members had played for previous Kings teams. Their home rink, like the original Polar Kings, was the Elmira Arena, the place where they'd won championships, experienced bitter defeats, played in front of sold-out crowds, and were recognized for individual accomplishments.

Among them were a lawyer, a bank manager, an accountant, a saw-mill owner, the proprietor of a butcher shop, tradesmen and business people. All were stalwart community men, contributing through service clubs, churches and minor sports organizations. There were bachelors, fathers, and grandfathers. All told tales that in some cases became more impressive the greater the time period from the actual occurrence. None had more stories to tell or accomplishments in hockey than Butch. But his stories, as one might expect, weren't about his accomplishments. Rather, they were about the wonderful and sometimes unusual people he had met, or the memorable moments he'd experienced in a life time of memorable moments.

The old timer Polar Kings played their home games on Sundays, immediately following public skating. Usually there was also one game a week away from home.

Old timers played without physical contact. It had been the part of Butch's game at the Senior A level that helped make him most effective. But those days had passed. Like all old timers, he relied on his well-honed hockey skills and smarts. He could have written an instructional book about them.

The "old" guys didn't have as much stamina as they had in their younger years. Butch said that he'd get out on the ice with the intention of taking it easy once the game started, that thought soon disappeared, about as quickly as some people's strange idea that if you were an old-timer you weren't in the game to compete hard and win.

On his sixtieth birthday, Butch's teammate Bill Clemens said, "I'd still rather win than lose. I think that when the time comes that I don't care about winning, then it is time to do something else."

But winning as an old timer was far removed from the idea winning at all costs. In every old-timer hockey team's list of rules and regulations was a statement that its members would remember that the game at this age should be mainly for enjoyment and physical exercise. There were also warnings of stiff penalties for those whose actions on the ice displayed poor sportsmanship or over-aggressive play. Too many infractions in one game, even though minor, resulted in extended suspension from further play.

There were many distant memories for the guys; such as a time when a goal might make the difference in winning a playoff series or even result in a championship; when a goalie's spectacular save inspired the team to victory; and, when a full house on your home rink stood and cheered in recognition of those actions. Times were different for the senior Polar Kings and their opponents as they now played in front of mainly family and friends.

But yet there were very special moments as an old-timer like a father seeing his young daughter smiling proudly and waving after he'd tapped his stick on the ice to get her attention. Or the times when a grandson yelled out "Good goal grandpa!" The "old guys" were enjoying themselves while setting good examples for exercise and good sportsmanship to the next generations.

In 1978 the Polar King Old-Timers, with their wives, and some fans, travelled to Copenhagen, Denmark for an international tournament. The team played games against teams from Sweden, Quebec and Ontario.

In his first shift of the second period of the first game, Ab Martin sustained an injury which resulted in him being hospitalized. Unfortunately, but in the best interest of his health, Ab and his wife Anne returned to their home in Elmira to allow him to recuperate.

In 1980, six weeks after the United Stated Olympic Hockey team's "Miracle on Ice" at the Winter Olympic Games, Butch and the Polar Kings played at the same location in Lake Placid, New York. They were part of an international tournament in which they lost only their final game.

The Kings also participated in the Canadian Championship tournament in Ottawa. Between games they attended a session of Parliament as spectators in the public gallery. Coach Carl Buschert arranged to chat with a Member of Parliament whom he had met previously. While speaking to the federal politician, Prime Minister Pierre Trudeau entered the room and joined the conversation. Buschert presented the Prime Minister with a Polar King button. It left the room on the lapel of Canada's most prestigious citizen.

While gaining substantially in popularity, some physicians and sports medicine researchers warned of the danger of heart attacks among middle-aged and older hockey players. They referred to the stress that sudden acceleration brings to one's heart. But none suggested that men in this age group stop playing hockey. The problem, they suggested, was to the individual who went out for hockey once a week and the remainder of the time lived a sedentary lifestyle. It was not so much a question of too much exercise as it was too little exercise done properly.

Throughout his life Butch was anything but sedentary. He was physically active while he was employed in the sawmill. From his days playing hockey on the dam through his journey to the old-timers, he'd been engaged in active sports at the hockey rink, the ball field and on the golf course.

Butch was approaching his sixtieth year when Kitchener sports writer Larry Anstett interviewed him. He told Anstett, "When you skate hard, things happen." He was on to something. His opinion, although expressed in more general terms, is shared in recent sports research literature. It suggests that aging athletes should be competing as intensely as they can instead of holding back out of fear because of their age. "Many senior athletes are reluctant to do so at first. But they soon realize that by asking their bodies to deal with controlled stress, they preserve and develop their strength much more effectively than playing it safe all the time."

Those who played on the Polar King Old-Timers team said that Butch was a dominant player and could control the pace of a game in his old-timer years. He played his hardest, reacted to the multitude of game situations effectively, and kept up with the speed of the game. He might have been the senior member of the Polar King team but his effect on the outcome of a game belied his age.

An old-timers teammate said, "I'm forty-five now and I never thought I'd have many years left. But after watching Butch, he gives you the inspiration to keep going forever."

Hockey players like Butch who've been in the heat of the battle will identify with the comments of Dr. Cal Botterill who teaches courses in Sport Psychology at the University of Winnipeg. Botterill was a member of Canada's men's national hockey team from 1967-69. His research results are a summary of the character strengths exhibited by highly regarded hockey players.

In The Journal of Sports Psychology he describes hockey as one of the most complex environments. From findings in his extensive research, he concluded that the game's fundamental elements are passion, toughness, and competitiveness. He found people with character in hockey are those who participate with humility, respect and a love for the game.

That seems like an appropriate description of the hockey career of Butch Martin, even as an old-timer.

Butch's excellence as an old-timer player was recognized on the occasion of his sixtieth birthday celebration at Westmount Golf and Country Club in Waterloo, and arranged by PeeWee and Kelly. Polar King teammates, Carl Buschert, Bill Clemens and Gord Trapp presented a very surprised Butch with a plaque and an Eskimo carving, that recognized his acceptance into the Hockey News Old-Timers Hockey Hall of Fame in Peterborough.

At the event, a Kitchener-Waterloo Record reporter asked Butch if he thought that a similar crowd might have been celebrating his induction into the NHL's Hall of Fame. Butch replied, "I'm probably better off this way. I'm happy with the way things went, and I have no regrets."

Dr. Howie Green was a professor of kinesiology at the University of Waterloo. He was also an avid old-timer hockey player. Butch was moving well into his senior years when Green suggested that he should have a physical examination to determine if he should really be playing the game. Butch asked, "What if they say I shouldn't be playing?" Green said that if such was the case, then he should stop. Butch replied, "Well, I'm going to keep playing, so I might as well not have the test."

Butch said, "I think I've slowed down a bit, don't kid yourself. But as long as I feel good, as long as I'm healthy, I'll be playing hockey."

When Neil Colborne played for the Senior A Stratford Indians, one of the opposing teams was the Kitchener-Waterloo Dutchmen. Butch was with the Dutchmen. Colborne played for other senior teams as well, after finishing a three-year Junior B career in St. Thomas. He later went to Europe to play in Bolzano, a city in northern Italy, about one hundred kilometers west of Cortina d'Ampezzo where Butch and the Dutchmen played in the 1956 Winter Games.

Butch was tough to play against in the Senior A league. Colborne said, "You couldn't get the puck away from him. He was strong and rugged. Butch would either keep it or pass it to an open teammate. He never gave the puck away. He took a European approach to offense, retreating in the offensive zone, if necessary, and then making an always accurate pass. He kept moving with the puck until an opening came."

It was as brilliant NHL star Bobby Orr said, "If you hold onto the puck and keep your head up, more often than not your opportunity will present itself. When my feet were moving and the puck was on my stick, most of the choices became mine, and I always liked being in that position."

Colborne and Butch played together on the Polar King Old-Timer team for eight years. Their coach, Carl Buschert, convinced them of the advantage of playing defense. It gave them more ice time and the team an advantage by their presence on the ice. Buschert said, "The two were a perfect combination, knowing where the other one was and finding him with an accurate pass."

Buschert was in a role that couldn't have been predicted. The young teenager who had been taken into their home by Butch and PeeWee was now the coach and manager of the team of which Butch was a member. Their friendship and mutual respect continued. Colborne said, "You could see that they liked and respected each other."

Colborne felt that Butch played the game intelligently. Cleverly working together, the two of them approached it like a chess game, being patient and finding the play that could be made at the right time and in the most effective manner. There were many players Colborne saw who were very skilled. They could skate really well but didn't have a plan as to what to do with the puck after they'd skated the length of the ice with it. That was never a description of he and Butch playing hockey together as old-timers.

But Colborne didn't leave Butch's reputation unscathed. In jest, he wondered why a former Olympian, even though he was now a senior, always looked for the parking spot closest to an arena's front door so he wouldn't have to carry his equipment so far.

Colborne purchased his new vehicles from Butch. On one occasion, he said that he was pleased with the car Butch showed him but wasn't fond of the color. Butch said, "It'll grow on you."

Butch retired from the Polar Kings in his seventieth year after spending about twenty-five years playing hockey with his hometown friends, something he'd chosen to do almost fifty years earlier.

In 1990 Butch was inducted into the Waterloo County Hall of Fame. In 2007 he was inducted into the Waterloo Wall of Fame.

SCENES FROM A MARRIAGE

Kelly says: I only came to realize the importance of my pregnancy to Dad during "Martin Night" in the Elmira Arena. The town was raising funds for a new arena roof. So this was a night of hockey, fun and fellowship, with all proceeds going to the roof project. I was about seven months pregnant and the size of a barn. During the presentations, an incredible painting of my father in his Polar Kings sweater was given to our family. My mom and I were brought to center ice and each presented with a gorgeous bouquet of roses. An oversized check was presented to Dad in honor of the funds collected. In a response, Dad said, "As I'm sure you can all see my daughter is gonna have twins soon and they tell me one is gonna be a boy. So the Martin hockey tradition will live on!"

And the tradition did live on. Dad taught Paul and Kristie to skate when they were about two and a half years old. Poppa was a fixture at every soccer, t-ball, or hockey game in which the kids were involved. He became the 'other parent' on the school roster when the kids weren't feeling well. He was the male role model in our family, as I was a single mom. I truly believe my kids have turned out so wonderful, due to the influence of my dad. I know my kids feel the same way.

Clearly, what became increasingly important to Butch as the years went on, were his family and his friendships. A pleased granddad was told that Paul skated in the same manner and with the same body posture as he did.

From time to time Butch's adoring grandchildren got caught up in the special emotions that came with seeing him and his Olympic teammates honored, not only by their community but also by their country. They burst with pride in hearing what he'd accomplished, even though they hadn't been there to see him in action. But no one was prouder than their granddad was of them.

Kelly says, Growing up I watched my dad play old-timers hockey. He jumped onto the ice, made plays and scored goals as if he was ageless. I heard about his glorious career. But one memory stands out for our family. Dad was invited to march on Parliament Hill for Canada Day. A red and white track suit for Dad and hotel bookings for the entire family arrived. When we got to Ottawa my father was greeted by a welcoming committee, and pictures were taken. My twelve-year-old children knew Poppa was important, but all this attention seemed overwhelming. Along with former teammates, we all shuffled up to the Hill—Dad with his Olympic medals displayed around his neck and wearing his red and white suit. The security guard recognized him and allowed him to enter. Paul and Kristie scooted in as well.

"Sorry, wee folks, you have to stay out here," said the guard. "Only very special people like your grandfather are allowed this close to the Prime Minister." The kids' eyes grew wide as the importance of his statement sank in. Mom, the kids and I were directed to an area for families where we watched the ceremony, After speeches, songs sung by choirs and an address by the Prime Minister, each of the players was introduced. The kids were jumping up and down and calling out to Poppa. And like always, he found us in the crowd and gave a big smile and wave. As I write this, a lump forms in my throat, just as it did that day. I looked to my mom, as tears flowed down her cheeks, proving after all these years that she was still his biggest fan.

In the December 31, 1999 edition of The Kitchener-Waterloo Record, an article entitled, "Waterloo County's Most Influential People of the Last Century—People Who Shaped Our Community" was published. Butch was on the list, along with Bobby Bauer and his Kraut Line teammates, renowned artist Peter Etril Snyder, and downhill skier Todd Brooker. Todd was the son of Charlie Brooker who was a Dutchmen teammate of Butch's at the 1956 Winter Olympic Games in Cortina d'Ampezzo.

On January 19, 2010, an "Olympics Dreams" dinner was held at the Edelweiss Banquet Hall in Kitchener. The evening of celebration honored past, current and future Olympians and Paralympians while raising funds for the Kitchener Sports Association's "Olympic Dreams" program. Butch and his 1956 Dutchmen teammate, Beryl Klinck were honored, as were broadcaster Don Cameron and Olympic wrestler Kurt Boese.

Kelly says, One Christmas I was off to the mall to buy a present for my dad. What do you get the guy who needs nothing? After hours of scouting I resigned myself to the bookstore. A book caught my attention "Canada's Olympic Hockey Teams: The Complete History 1920-1998." I looked at its cover and thought, 'Hold on, that's my dad!' There in full glory was Butch splitting two Russian defensemen! Tears began to fill my eyes. I had the perfect Christmas gift. The book contains stories and stats from both the '56 and '60 Olympics along with pictures to boot! Photographs of Dad playing hockey were hard to come by.Christmas arrived and the kids and I had saved the best gift for last. We all watched in silence as Butch opened his gift. "Hey PeeWe, look—it's me on the cover!" Mom hadn't known about the gift. As we ate breakfast, Butch had his nose in the book. That's funny, if you know the Martin family. Food was always at the center of our gatherings. Good heavens, we even had Donut Day to celebrate the maple syrup flowing. By the time my parents came back for dinner, Dad had relived those precious times again with Mom. That gift was the best surprise the entire Martin family ever had at Christmas.

Grandmas hold our tiny hands for just a little while, but our hearts forever.
-Anonymous

Ethleen "PeeWee" Gerber, the outgoing, attractive young woman Butch met at roller skating at the Waterloo Arena was his greatest supporter throughout his many seasons in hockey. She was his wife for almost sixty years. After a lengthy career as the voice of Uniroyal in

Elmira, she and her daughter Kelly opened Kelly's Classic Touch, not far from the Martin's home in Waterloo.

After a lengthy illness, Ethleen died, on January 12, 2010. She was seventy-seven years old. The funeral arrangements were entrusted to Robert Ruggle Funeral Home in Waterloo. Mr. Ruggle was the former owner of Ruggle's General Store, in Floradale. Pastor Catherine Hunsberger of Kitchener's First Mennonite Church, where Ethleen and Butch were married, was in charge of the memorial service.

A wife, mother, and grandmother is dearly missed.

Kelly says, After the passing of my mom, Dad reminded me that he'd never lived alone. While living in Floradale he was part of a large family. When he left home he married my mom. And when he was away playing hockey he always had a roommate. My son Paul was living on his own, so said he'd live with his poppa. We all joked at dinner that night that there would now be the boys house and the girls house. But the boys would have no one to cook. Dad laughed and said, "You girls can cook and we boys have Tupperware!" Four years later Paul moved out to start a wonderful life with his lady friend. Kristie stepped right up to the plate, along with her chef boyfriend by moving in and making sure the plates are never empty for Poppa.

This moment contains all moments.
C.S. Lewis

Kelly adds, 2014 brought the Winter Olympic Games in Sochi, Russia. CBC Radio in Kitchener was looking for members of the famous Kitchener Dutchmen team. I contacted Amanda Grant at CBC which resulted in Dad and I being invited to come in for an interview. When Dad became aware that the studio was in Kitchener, he said, "Well we'd have gone to Toronto if we had to." On the day of the interview, Dad showed up two hours early, so we went for lunch. We returned and the interview was held in the sound booth, with all the necessary equipment. Amanda skillfully led Butch and me as we gave stories of how it was to be an Olympian and what it was like to have an Olympian for a dad. The day the interview was aired, he arrived early at my house.

We gathered around, coffee and toast nearby and listened. It was a great success and became another treasured memory. Dad was also invited to speak to two kindergarten classes, with instructions to bring his medals along. He was amazed at the children. The teacher showed a picture of the 1956 Dutchmen on the overhead. Quickly, the children asked, "Why didn't you wear helmets?" Dad replied that in those days you just didn't. The children reminded him that whenever they played hockey, the first thing they put on was their helmet.

Those kids touched my dad's heart and I believe he touched theirs. We were sent copies of their journal entries and handmade thank you cards. We are all better people for having generations brought together by just one twenty-minute visit.

AFTERWORD

Many of the Elmira Donuts and Deli regulars called the bitterly cold winter of 2014 "old fashioned," bringing back delightful memories of their childhood escapades in snow piled as high as the hydro poles, and shinny games with frozen horse "buns" replacing pucks. But in the plummeting temperatures in the winter of '14, young students were kept inside for recesses. The weather channel warned of dangerous wind chill factors. Home heating costs escalated. Municipalities dipped into their reserve funds to cover the extra cost of snow removal. "Sun Vacations" gained in popularity.

On a sunny and frosty January Sunday afternoon of that memorable season of overworked snowblowers and snowed in farmers lanes, not a creature was seen or heard in the environs of Floradale dam. It was hauntingly quiet; other than the crackling of tiny pieces of ice falling from the dark, bare branches of trees standing like sculptures along the shore line. The "world" had gone to sleep.

Then, as if on cue, two human silhouettes came slowly into view: one wearing a black bonnet and the other a black, broad-brimmed hat. Milton and Susannah Weber, an elderly Old Order Mennonite couple were cautiously beginning their annual trek across the barren expanse of ice that was the Floradale dam. Its shiny smoothness was partially blanketed by a layer of stubborn, crusty snow.

Decades earlier they'd spent many winter Sunday afternoons skating at this now-abandoned, lonely place. They were amongst hundreds of mostly farm and rural village children and young people enjoying the freedom: breathing in the cold, invigorating air, and endlessly smiling. Bundled in thick scarves, grandma-made woolen mittens, and wearing hand-me-down, ill-fitting, wrinkled skates, the youngest children of large families held on to their older sisters' hands. Their brothers were playing shinny.

The action wound down as the darkness of the early afternoon began to envelop them. Now perspiring, they carried their heavy outer clothing as they trudged to the warmth of their homes where hot apple cider and buttered popcorn awaited them.

Milton and Susannah wished they could snap their fingers and be surrounded by children racing and twirling; shinny games breaking out; high-pitched laughter and shouting; and the special, special feelings that only a close community coming together at a gathering place like the dam could provoke.

But their tiny village and their beloved dam were as quiet as the tranquil sky above them.

Wayne Gretzky and Bobby Orr said the most enjoyable times of their hockey careers were playing hockey on frozen ponds, like the Floradale dam, just having fun.

The NHL outdoor classics were immensely popular in 2014. Hockey stars said they really enjoyed the experiences because they reminded them of the fun of their outdoor shinny matches as children.

By 2014, across Canada, pond hockey leagues had gained in popularity amongst males and females of all ages. Pond hockey tournaments increased in number. Even old-timers were once again getting in touch with the freedom they had had as children when they played hockey in the elements. They were revisiting some carefree and untroubled times.

In 2008 the documentary Pond Hockey was released and received with critical acclaim. ESPN called it the best sports movie ever produced. Among the cast were John Mayasich, Willard Ikola and Wendall Anderson who'd played for the American Olympic team against Butch and Canada. They and present NHL stars, including Sidney Crosby and Marian Gaborik, harkened back to their days of frozen ponds and rivers: the days of fun.

Young Floyd Martin had experienced the freedom of it all on the Floradale dam: playing a game with no off-sides, icings or penalties; no coaches, game plans or systems. A brief rest meant taking a turn in goal, protecting the space between two winter boots or jackets. It meant working on deceptive moves in stick-handling without concerns about the consequences of losing control of the puck. Equipment was skates and a hockey stick.

In those early days there were many Martins playing against other Martins on the Floradale dam. The tradition continued when Butch and his grandson Paul played in the Martin hockey game during the 2010 Woolwich Hockeyville Celebrations.

It would be great to re-congregate the Hockeyville Martins, this time at the Floradale dam, to play in the Butch Martin Winter Classic. Ab Martin would be among them.

Each "home team" player would have "Martin" on the back of his sweater, but the sweaters would differ as there would be a Waterloo Raiter Martin, a Guelph Biltmore Martin, a Kitchener-Waterloo Dutchmen Martin, an Elmira Polar King Martin, a Galt Terrier Martin, a Johnstown Jet Martin, a Guelph Regal Martin, and an Elmira Polar King Old-timer Martin. The "visiting team," made up of the remainder of the Martins, would each have the name of a country on the back of his sweater. Countries represented would be Germany, Czechoslovakia, USSR, Great Britain, Japan, Switzerland, Norway, Italy, Austria, Finland, Sweden and the United States. Butch had played against them all.

The game would no doubt attract a large crowd of fans with the Region of Waterloo well represented. Mike Forester from the

1952 Polar King team would be there.

As the players would line up for the opening face-off, Floyd "Butch" Martin, the Martins' captain, would skate slowly to the center face-off dot. The applause would be tremendous. Butch would be wearing the team sweater he'd chosen for this special occasion to honor him.

Only Butch knows which team's sweater he'd choose.

BIBLIOGRAPHY

INTERVIEWS

- Buehler, Zenas. Elmira, Ontario

- Buschert, Carl. Wellesley, Ontario

- Colborne, Neil. Waterloo, Ontario

- Klinck, Beryl. Kitchener, Ontario

- Mader, Bob. Breslau, Ontario

- Martin, Ab. Elmira, Ontario

- Martin Floyd "Butch". Waterloo, Ontario

- Schnurr, Tom. Waterloo, Ontario

FILES, AND MICROFICHE FILMS

- Bonnie Lou's Lunch. Floradale, Ontario

- Bowman, Terry. Elmira

- Mader, Bob

- Martin, Ab

- Martin, Kelly. Waterloo

- Conrad Grebel University Library. Waterloo

- Dana Porter Library. University of Waterloo

- Ellis LIttle Room. Waterloo Public Library

- Elmira Public Library: Elmira Signet publications

- Galt Public Library: Galt Reporter publications

- Guelph Museum Archives: Guelph Biltmores Program-1948

- Guelph Public Library: Guelph Mercury publications

- Kitchener Public Library: Kitchener-Waterloo Record publications

- Waterloo Region Museum

- Waterloo County Hall of Fame

WATERLOO HOCKEY WALL OF FAME
VARIOUS INTERNET SITES
COLLECTIONS

- Bowman, Terry
- Martin, Ab
- Martin, Kelly
- Mader, Bob

MOVIE

- Slap Shot. Written by Nancy Dodd. Directed by George Roy Hill: 1977

ARTICLES

- Botterill, Cal. Journal of Sports Psychology. - University of Winnipeg.

- Bowman, Hugh. And Away We Go: Guelph Mercury-1965

- Campbell, Ken. Swedish Hammer. The Hockey News 2011-2012 Yearbook.

- MacKinnon, Dan. Myth, Memory and the Kitchener-Waterloo Dutchmen in Canadian International Hockey.

- Miller, Chuck. From Atlantic City to Toronto: The Boardwalk Trophy and the Eastern Hockey League.

- Reder, Toby Charles. Olympic Games and the Cold War. The U. S. Government and the Propoganda Campaign Against Communist Sport: University of Western Ontario-2011.

- Soars, John. Cold War, Hot Ice: International Ice Hockey, 1947-1980. Department of History at the University of Notre Dame: 2007

- Schroeder, Anna L. Mennonites at Olympics; Canadian Mennonite Magazine; February 3, 1956.

- Szenberg and Podnieks. IIHF Top 100 Hockey Stories of All Time.

- Wharmsby, Tim. Where Are They Now? Toronto Globe and Mail: May 25, 2009

OTHER PUBLICATIONS

- Canada's Olympic Hockey Teams: The Complete History 1920-1998. Andrew Podnieks. Doubleday Canada Limited-1997

- Floradale Then and Now. Project of the Floradale Mennonite Church Newsletter Committee-2011

- Johnstown and Slap Shot. The Making of Slap Shot. Jonathan Jackson-2010

- Moe and Me: Encounters with Moe Norman, Golf's Mysterious Genius. Lorne Rubenstein. ECW Press-2012

- ORR My Story. Bobby Orr. Viking-2013

- Our Hockey-Our Game. A journey through the past fifty seasons of Kitchener Rangers Hockey. Roderick Cunningham. Kitchener Rangers Junior "A" Hockey Club - 2012

- The Game. 30th Anniversary Edition. Ken Dryden. Collins-2013